NIKITA

A Tale of the Ring and Redemption

To
Karen,
Love Jesus —

2 COR
5:10

Also from Crowbar Press

Inside Out
by Ole Anderson with Scott Teal
0-9745545-0-2

Wrestlers Are Like Seagulls
by James J. Dillon with Scott Teal and Philip Varriale
0-9745545-2-9

Assassin: The Man Behind the Mask
by Joe Hamilton with Scott Teal
0-9745545-3-7

"Is That Wrestling Fake?"
by Ivan Koloff with Scott Teal
978-0-9745545-4-9

Bruiser Brody
by Emerson Murray
978-0-9745545-5-6

Wrestling with the Truth
by Bruno Lauer
0-9745545-7-0

The Solie Chronicles
by Bob Allyn with Pamela S Allyn and Scott Teal
978-0-9745545-8-7

Wrestling in the Canadian West
by Vance Nevada
978-0-9745545-9-4

Long Days and Short Pays
by Hal West
978-0-9844090-0-6

Drawing Heat
by Jim Freedman
978-0-9844090-1-3

ATLAS: Too Much, Too Soon
by Tony Atlas with Scott Teal
978-0-9844090-2-0

The Last Laugh
by Bill De Mott with Scott Teal
978-0-9844090-3-7

HOOKER
by Lou Thesz with Kit Bauman
978-0-9844090-4-4

The Last Outlaw
by Stan Hansen with Scott Teal
978-0-9844090-5-1

NIKITA

A Tale of the Ring and Redemption

by
Nikita Koloff

as told to William Murdock

Edited by Scott Teal

CROWBAR
PRESS

Gallatin, Tennessee

NIKITA

A Tale of the Ring and Redemption

> This book is dedicated to all who will read it, in hopes
> it will inspire and impact their life in some positive way.

Published by Crowbar Press
106 Tattnal Court
Gallatin, Tennessee 37066.

http://www.crowbarpress.com

Book layout and cover design by Scott Teal

Library of Congress Cataloging-in-Publication Data

Koloff, Nikita
   NIKITA / by Nikita Koloff as told to William Murdock

1. Koloff, Nikita.   2. Sports—United States—Biography.   3. Wrestling—
United States—Biography.   I. Murdock, William.   II. Title.

Printed in the United States of America
ISBN 978-0-9844090-6-8

First Edition / February 2012

Table of Contents

Acknowledgements
by Nikita Koloff

First and foremost: my God, my Saviour, Jesus Christ. Who without Him, I wouldn't exist. I'd have no life story to tell. And no story for someone to read. I'd still be wandering in the wilderness.

My family: Dad, Mom,Teryn,Chad,Salem,Tawni,Kendra and Kolby. The true gems of my life. It's an honor to be your Grandpa, Poppi, Pops, Dad, Daddy and Son. I love you.

Bill Murdock: My dear friend. Words can not, will not express my gratitude for you. Your tireless hours of work and research on this project, though long in coming about, will be a blessing to many, I'm sure. As you are a true blessing to me. Thank you.

Lex Luger: Who would have ever thought in a million years we would become best friends and 3P's (another story). It is truly an honor to call you friend, but even more, a brother in Christ. Thank you for your input. The journey awaits us.

Ted DiBiase: My friend. Although our paths never crossed in the ring, it has been a real honor to get to know you and 'tag team' with you outside the squared circle. The school assemblies, wrestling outreaches and ministries we have teamed together on, have been far more rewarding than any match we might have been a part of inside the ring. In the ring, we might have entertained millions as partners or opponents (it would have been dynamic I'm sure) but to lead thousands and thousands to the Lord together, has been priceless. Thank you Ted. Your friendship is cherished.

Ivan Koloff and Don Kernodle: "Uncle" Ivan and "Pride of the USA." Can words even convey my gratitude? Answer, no. If not for you guys, Nikita Koloff would not even exist. Your hours upon hours of dedicated sacrifice is what led to my success. Wow, what a career, thanks to you. Forever friends.

Scott Teal: Scott, thank you for bringing this story into a reality. May you be blessed abundantly for your efforts in helping get this book distributed. As this book touches the hearts and lives of many, know that you had a major role in that happening.

To All My Fans: Wrestling fans are without a doubt the greatest fans in the world. If not for you, I'd be long forgotten. I hope to meet as many of you as I can. Thank you for keeping my name alive and inspiring me to achieve even greater things in life.

To everyone else, too many to name: As you have in some way made an impact on my life, I say, a heartfelt thank you. I really am a better man because of you.

Foreword

by Lex Luger

When I first met Nikita Koloff nearly 25 years ago, I have to admit I was not impressed. I know that may not sound like something someone would say in the foreword of a book about one of their closest friends, but it's true.

I arrived in the Charlotte territory in 1987 to wrestle for the Crocketts. I hadn't been in the business very long and I was eager to get into the ring in the hottest territory in the country. The roster for Jim Crockett Promotions read like the "Who's Who" of professional wrestling. Each night, the card boasted the top names in the sport: Ric Flair, Dusty Rhodes, Arn Anderson, Barry Windham, Ivan Koloff, the Road Warriors, and, of course, the "Russian Nightmare" — Nikita Koloff. I was stepping into the most prominent ring during one of the largest booms in wrestling history, and I would do so against Nikita, the reigning United States heavyweight champion.

As I said, the first time I saw Nikita in the dressing room, I was far from impressed. In fact, I remember thinking he may have had more than a few marbles loose. There had to be something wrong with the guy. In the world of professional wrestling, that was saying something. What I mean is that even in the dressing room with the boys [the wr*estlers*], Nikita was always Nikita Koloff. He kept to himself, and he always spoke, albeit rarely, in Russian. He was Nikita Koloff in and out of the ring. I just kept wondering, *"What is up with this guy?"*

But in our subsequent years, I would learn that that was just who Nikita was: not the Russian, but a man who commits himself to the nth degree in everything he does. No matter what Nik is involved in, he gives it his all. He did that during his days in the ring and he does that now in his speaking engagements, business ventures, and ministry.

My first major series of matches for World Championship Wrestling was against Nikita for his U.S. belt. He had held the title for almost a year after defeating Magnum T.A. in the classic "Best of Seven" series for the U.S. championship. I took the belt from Nikita on July 11, 1987 in Greensboro, North Carolina. I wish I could say we had a run of classic matches as well, but they were far from that. I do believe the fans enjoyed seeing us against each other, but I think I can speak for Nikita, as well as myself, that they were not the finest moments in the ring for either one of us.

The reason being was that there is no doubt that styles make matches, and our styles were so similar that they did not give way to timeless encounters as Jack Brisco and Dory Funk Jr. did a decade or so before us. We both had strong styles in that we were both powerful in the ring and were being promoted as practically invincible. The unstoppable force meets the immovable object.

There was no way I was going to take many bumps or fly around the ring for Nikita, and he certainly wasn't going to do that for me. It would have weakened one or the other of our characters. One of us would have to give.

That isn't to say Nikita and I didn't get along. I liked Nikita. We were just different back then. We didn't hang out together. He was a nice guy who didn't head out to the nightspots after the matches like so many of the rest of us did. In time, however, our lives would dramatically change and we would forge a lasting friendship.

I first attended an Athlete's International Ministry [AIM] conference in Phoenix, Arizona in the summer of 2006. AIC is a ministry that reaches out to athletes, coaches, and others involved in athletics to help them meet the unique challenges they face in the public eye and to use the platform that many athletes are often given to influence their communities.

It was through that conference that I realized Nikita and I had a bond that was immensely stronger than any power move either one of us had in our ring repertoire. It was our common faith that brought us together, and the fact that it was Nikita who not only shared his belief in Jesus Christ with me, but mentored, discipled, and prayed for me. Within a short time, I would learn that Nikita's faith went far beyond mere words.

In October 2007, during a flight from Atlanta to a personal appearance in San Francisco, I spent a great deal of the flight talking with the young lady beside me. There was nothing unusual about either the flight or our conversation, but the aftermath of that flight would take me down a path I am still traveling on and will be for some time to come.

When I tried to get out of bed on the following morning, I couldn't move. I was completely paralyzed. I was later told the paralysis came from the swelling of my spinal cord, which was caused by the cumulative injuries from the many years in the ring. Apparently, the position I had sat in for so long on the plane was just enough to cause this "spinal stroke" and render me a quadriplegic.

I was flown back to Atlanta to a rehabilitation hospital, where I underwent a long series of therapy and intravenous antibiotic treatments devised to help me regain the use of my arms and legs. During those dark times, my faith was not only strengthened by God's grace, but by the love, friendship, and commitment of my friend and brother, Nikita Koloff.

Each week, Nik would drive to Atlanta from his home near Charlotte to talk with me, pray with me, keep me company, and to feed me. And when I say feed me, I mean just that. Actually feed me. He would cut up my food and raise the fork or spoon to my mouth so I could eat. I can only imagine what that might have looked like to anyone who may have happened to be passing by my room. They would see two adversaries of the ring in the same room:

one showing the utmost kindness by driving nearly five hours to help the other do a simple task that so many of us take for granted: picking up a fork or spoon and eating. The "Russian Nightmare" helped the "Total Package" make it through one of the darkest periods of his life.

With no television cameras present, and no reporters or bloggers looking on, my friend came to reach out to me when few others did, and he continues to do so to this day. After six surgeries and countless hours of therapy, I am now able to stand on my own and walk with the aid of a walker and walking sticks. Through all of this, I have seen first-hand the power of God and the results of the prayers of so many, when most of my physicians had thrown in the towel and gave me little, if any, hope of me walking or using my arms again.

I also learned about the power of friendship and who the man most of the world knows as Nikita Koloff really is. I truly value his friendship and the time we spend together. No words exist that will ever be able to convey the love and respect I have for my friend who I met nearly twenty-five years ago in that dressing room in North Carolina.

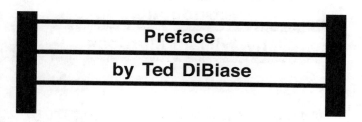

Preface
by Ted DiBiase

The world of professional wrestling is full of colorful and unusual characters. Through the many years I have spent as the "Million Dollar Man," I certainly have met them all. The cowboys, the Native Americans, the giants, the noblemen, the masked men, and the Russians, have all kept millions in front of their television sets week after week and brought them into arenas across the world. But even with all the stories the ring has produced, few are as compelling as Nikita Koloff's. From a hardscrabble beginning to main events around the globe, Nikita's story is one that stands out as a life that has touched so many fans and friends alike.

It has always seemed somewhat ironic to me that Nikita and I never met in the ring. Through the hundreds of thousands of miles we both traveled during our careers, our paths crossed briefly only once.

I remember meeting Nikita in Atlanta when I was working for World Championship Wrestling. He was there spending some time with his old college friend, Animal, of the Road Warriors. Our introduction was nothing more than a few words and a brief handshake. His look was far from the massive wrestling machine from the Soviet Union. He seemed to me a lot like so many other young athletes I encountered during that time. He was polite, quiet, and looked to be in tremendous shape. He also had a full head of blow-dried hair that looked a lot like John Travolta's in the movie *Saturday Night Fever*.

A few years later, I kept hearing about this giant "shooting" Russian that Jim Crockett had found and brought into the Mid-Atlantic territory. From the talk in the locker room, this wrestler we were hearing about was not only carving a large path through the Carolinas, but he could actually wrestle. Standing 6-foot-2 and weighing 285 pounds, the word among the boys was that he was unbeatable. Later, I learned that this Soviet wrestling machine who couldn't speak English was the "kid with the perfect hair" I had met in Atlanta a few years earlier. Only Nikita could have pulled it off in such a fashion.

That was just the beginning of Nikita's career and the story you hold in your hands. Each of us has a unique story to tell, but it would be difficult to find one any more interesting or enthralling as Nikita's. I am honored to count him as one of my closest friends ... and come to think of it, we would have made quite a tag team.

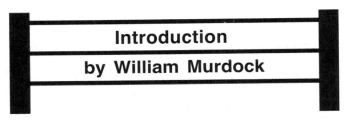

Introduction

by William Murdock

The writing of this book began and ended in an unusual place, neither of which one would necessarily find someone writing a story or someone relating one at any given time. But this is not your usual story.

This particular biography and volume of wrestling history began on a Friday morning with a conversation at the Krispy Kreme doughnut shop on Patton Avenue in Asheville, North Carolina. Nikita and I had worked out a time to get together to begin our project, but we couldn't find a particularly quiet place for him to begin to tell me his story. We left my office a few blocks away and thought, the time of day being what it was, the  doughnut shop was the place to go. With a little luck, there wouldn't be many people there. Not that there would be since the Krispy Kreme only had five tables and would only seat about 20 patrons. Nik and I ordered a couple of doughnuts and some milk and began to talk about the beginning of his career and the end of Jim Crockett promotions and Mid-Atlantic Wrestling.

For all practical purposes, the project ended in Newton, Iowa, at the Dan Gable International Wrestling Institute. Nikita was being inducted into the George Tragos/Lou Thesz Professional Wrestling Hall of Fame as he was receiving the Frank Gotch Award for his career and the recognition he brought to wrestling both in and out of the ring.

Finishing the book at the wrestling institute wasn't unusual, but the location inside the institute was. Nik was sitting comfortably in a purple, velvet easy chair that was the favorite place of repose of Frank Gotch, the first American to win the world heavyweight wrestling title. To make the final interview more memorable, I was scribbling my notes seated at Gotch's roll-top desk. I could only imagine the greatest wrestler of all time sitting where I was then, answering correspondence, or perhaps reviewing the George Hackenschmidt contract that would take him to the world championship. Not that it mattered what he was doing at his desk. I was pleased to have an opportunity to work at it, as well. I was hoping he didn't mind.

I first became interested in wrestling during the latter part of my sixth grade year when I moved to North Carolina from Bowling Green, Kentucky. I was fortunate to make friends with a group of kids who not only brought me into their number, but also introduced me to professional wrestling. By way of the Saturday afternoon Mid-Atlantic Championship Wrestling television program, which aired every week at one in the afternoon on Channel Four, Greg Gore, Randy Elingberg, John Creegan, David Norton, Kenny Rainwater, and Lee Harrell introduced me to George Scott, Mr. Wrestling, Skull Murphy, Rip Hawk, Swede Hanson, Abe Jacobs, and many other ring warriors. I have countless memories of watching our heroes on Saturday afternoons as they battled against the insidious heels, or times when we were lucky enough to persuade our parents and grandparents to take us to the live matches at the Asheville City Auditorium on Wednesday nights. This book never would have happened without them.

As the 1970s came to an end, the landscape of wrestling was changing quickly. The old fiefdoms of the regional territories were beginning to wane; cable television was making its way into more and more households every week. Even those who swore they would never pay for television when they could still get it for free were beginning to acquiesce and find the wonders of having more than three channels.

The 1980s gave way to a new era in professional wrestling. By the turn of the decade, many of the legends whose names were synonymous with the sport were finishing their careers in the ring: Lou Thesz, Buddy Rogers, Jack Brisco, Dory Funk Jr. and Verne Gagne had left or were in the process of leaving the battles between the ropes to pursue new battles in other pursuits. Some were still in the wrestling business, while others were totally willing to hang up their boots and enter a different way of life.

The wrestling industry, if nothing else, has always been able to not only survive, but to flourish as it has continually reinvented itself to keep up with the times. In many cases, entrepreneurs such as Vince McMahon, the CEO of the World Wrestling Entertainment corporation, changed the sport before the times themselves dictated change.

As with their network predecessors of the 1950s, cable companies made professional wrestling the centerpiece of their programming schedule. Replacing Mr. Moto, Gene Stanlee, Buddy Rogers, and world champion Lou Thesz was Roddy Piper, Hulk Hogan, Ric Flair ... and Nikita Koloff, the "Russian Nightmare"

It was hard not to notice Nikita Koloff the moment I first saw him on television. He was running through his opponents like so much chaff, but even so, all eyes in the Mid-Atlantic were on the "Nature Boy," Ric Flair. Ric was in his third reign as the NWA world heavyweight champion and he was defending the belt across the globe with frequent stops in his home territory of the Carolinas. Wrestling fans wondered what would happen when Flair met Koloff in the ring, but it looked like they were traveling on different paths.

The first time I remember Nikita making me stop and really take notice was one Friday evening when I was on my way home from working in the men's department at Byrd's Department Store. On the way home, I stopped at Ingle's Market. As always, I made my way to the back wall where the magazine stand was located to catch up on the news; wrestling and otherwise.

What caught my eye among the dozens of magazines was the August 1985 issue of *Sports Review Wrestling.* The cover featured Ric and Nikita standing side by side, with the headline proclaiming *"Why this could be the match of the century!"* I remember thinking, *"There is no way Flair can beat this guy."* They had me hooked, as they had so many others. I shelled out the $1.75 cover price and couldn't wait to get home to read about the most anticipated match in years. What I never could have imagined was that 20 years later, I would be sitting with Nikita two blocks down the road and beginning to write the book you now hold in your hands.

Nikita took the Mid-Atlantic territory by storm and, within an extremely short period of time, was catapulted to main event status and was headlining major cards throughout the world. Nik's unique place in history transcends what he accomplished in the ring. He had an exclusive viewpoint as the dying days of territories gave birth to the head-to-head combat between the World Wrestling Federation [WWF] and the National Wrestling Alliance [NWA]. The NWA represented the long-established system that had served the sport for decades.

His story exceeds the tale of an athlete and the stories of the road that have become part and parcel of wrestling lore. It is a journal of an incredible story, detailing Nik's rise from a hardscrabble beginning to celebrity and wealth. It is a journal of personal triumphs and tragedies. It is a journal of rising to the top in professional sports entertainment and falling to the depths of obscurity, only to find the way back again. It is the saga of a journey that travels through a "dark night of the soul" into the peace that only a profound faith can attain. His story brings the world of wrestling with all its glamour, pain, politics, laughter, and despair, into a light that can only be shone by one who was at the epicenter of wrestling history. It is a story only Nikita Koloff can tell.

In his 1993 book, *A Season is a Lifetime,* Duke basketball coach, Mike Krzyzewski, compared a basketball season to a lifetime. That is, a season has a life of its own; a beginning and an end, as well as being entwined with various people and places. And as a new season begins, so does a new life. The same seems true with writing a book. Each book spans a lifetime of its own, not just in the case of *Koloff* and the life it reflects upon, but in the time and paths it takes.

This book is dedicated to George Scott, the late Jack Brisco, and to the late Lou Thesz and his wife Charlie. It is through their many years of friendship and the marvelous stories and insight into wrestling history this book was able to be written. George, Jack, and Lou all showed me that sometimes, those who you admire in your youth for who you think they are, you can admire as an adult for who they really are.

My gratitude also goes to my favorite authors and historians: Mike Mooneyham, the late Jim Melby, Mike Chapman, and Scott Teal (who also was the editor for this book), whose writings have fascinated me for years and still do today.

Last, but far from least, my wife Robin, who has put up with me writing another book and for her love and encouragement. Also to our dog Bailey, who again has had to forgo many of our nightly Frisbee games and early Saturday morning rides. And to all I have the privilege to work with, and all who have touched my life through these many years, I will always be in your debt.

Chapter 1

The Truth

I suppose I should begin with the truth; I am not a Russian. My parents weren't Russian. My grandparents weren't Russian. In fact, I don't believe I ever met that many people who are Russian. It is ironic that nearly everything I have achieved in my adult life, and most of the recognition I have been fortunate enough to obtain, is due to the fact that most people believed I was just that … a Russian. Welcome to the world of professional wrestling.

I am proud to have been a professional athlete and particularly proud of being a professional wrestler. I have wrestled in 43 of our 50 states and in more than 20 countries, and I have wrestled some of the greatest names in the history of the sport in front of hundreds of thousands of people. I take great satisfaction in knowing I have had even a small part of entertaining the wonderful people we know as "wrestling fans." Hopefully, I have given them some exciting memories to share with their children and grandchildren.

In a way, I am also proud of the fact that so many, for so long, believed that Nikita Koloff was from the Soviet Union. My pride does not derive from the fact that I willfully fooled so many people for decades, but from the fact I was able to do my job so well.

I was no different from any other athlete, banker, attorney, doctor, mechanic, or businessperson, who performed at the peak of their abilities, taking pride in doing their best in their chosen field of endeavor. Mine may have been a little more visible than most, but it still is basically the same, and through all this, Nikita Koloff, wrestling's "Russian Nightmare," became one of the most famous, or infamous wrestlers, for more than a decade. Looking back, it is somewhat ironic that Nikita Koloff was known the world over, but few people in comparison has ever heard of the real man behind this perceived giant Russian.

My given name is Scott Simpson. Just as the Green Hornet is really Britt Reid, just as Superman is really Clark Kent, just as Cary Grant was really Archibald Leach, and John Wayne was really Marion Morrison, Nikita Koloff is really Scott Simpson. To pull another brick from the wall of legend, I am not just Scott Simpson, but Scott Simpson from Minneapolis, Minnesota. Sorry, not from Moscow or Kiev, not from the motherland, but from the Midwest.

The closest thing I can claim to my alter ego is that the winters in Minnesota on their worst days may be able to rival the best winter days in the Soviet Union. Ours may not last as long, but they can certainly make Minnesotans as hardy of a people as those from the Russian countryside. It is the great state of Minnesota — the home of June, July, and winter — that was the birthplace of the man who would become Nikita Koloff.

If you believed I was really from the Soviet Union, don't feel badly. Thousands upon thousands of people did, and if you are among that number, you have actually paid me the greatest compliment I could receive. If you believed I was Russian, then I did my job well. My job was not only to get in the ring, wrestle, and entertain the fans, but it was my job to lead the fans, and anyone else I came into contact with, that I was actually from the Soviet Union. I was supposed to convince everyone that I could not speak English and that my mission was to conquer the United States. At times, it was difficult to carry it off, but to the many people who saw me in the ring or met me on the street, all I can say is thanks. You helped make Nikita Koloff "The Russian Nightmare." And you have to admit, that has a much better ring to it than Scott Simpson, the Minnesota Nightmare.

I never thought of professional wrestling as a career. In fact, when I was growing up, I never was much of a fan of wrestling, so I guess I never really thought much about it at all. Wrestling was very popular in the Midwest during the time I was growing up thanks to the legendary Minnesotan Verne Gagne, and the likes of Dick the Bruiser, the Crusher, Mad Dog and Butcher Vachon, Larry "The Axe" Henning, Baron von Raschke, and Dr. X. I was somewhat familiar with professional wrestling; it was just as hard not to know of the AWA as it was not to know about the Minnesota Vikings. Verne saw to that. Minneapolis had been the headquarters of the American Wrestling Association [AWA] since the days of its inception in the late 1950s. I used to catch some of the matches on the weekend while I was channel surfing. All Star Wrestling, the TV wrestling program taped in Minneapolis, aired on channel nine on Sunday afternoon.

It's funny when I think of the few matches to which I did actually pay attention. What I remember is not Gagne defending his version of the world heavyweight championship, or the Vachons battling it out with the Crusher and the Bruiser for the tag belts, but it was of a journeyman named Kenny Benkowski, better known in the ring as "Sodbuster" Kenny Jay. Kenny's career was memorable to me due to the fact that I never saw him win a match. I would like to think he did somewhere down the line, but I never saw him win. Even so, he had a cult following, if for nothing else than the fact that he never, or very seldom, won a match. World Championship Wrestling had the same thing years later with what came to be known as "Mulkeymania." The Mulkey Brothers, a beleaguered brother tag-team that rarely won a match, still maintained a small, but somewhat fanatical, following.

In sitting down to write an autobiography, it seems difficult to decide where to begin the story. How far back does one go to make sure the important key elements of one's life aren't left by the wayside, and what details need to be left out in order to avoid boring the brave souls who venture into this book.

In the case at hand, I do believe that in order to see who the "Russian Nightmare" is and how he came to be, it's important to go back as far as possible to see how this boy from Minnesota became one of the most feared men to step through the ropes. As the late singer/songwriter Jim Croce wrote, "After all, it's what we've done that makes us what we are."

I came into the world on a frigid March day to Olive Mary Besse Simpson and

Paige Arrileas Simpson. My mom was almost 40 years old when I was born and my father was all but non-existent.

Mom was born in Cumberland City, England, near the Scottish border. She and my grandmother made the trek from the British Isles to America during the 1920s. For whatever reason she had, my grandmother chose not to raise my mother. That task fell to her sister, my mother's aunt. My mother has always had that stoic, stubborn, "keep your chin up," English pride. Always quite reserved, she never seemed to have much time for affection, but I know it never was her fault. She never had any example to draw from; certainly not from her mother. And having little to draw from, she had little to pass on to those she did love. The first time I heard her say "I love you" to me, she was 76 years old. I knew she loved me, as my brothers and sister knew she loved them, but love in our house came in the form of knowledge and the occasional smile, not in the form of hugs or words.

Nikita's grandmother and mother

My dad was a military man who served in the Army during World War II. In fact, it was the military that precipitated the meeting of my parents. My mother was working in a munitions factory during the war. One day, while on a bus trip out west, she ended up sitting next to my father. I don't know if it was love at first sight, but I do know that meeting was all it took. They were married soon after they met.

Upon leaving the military, my father went to work for the postal service and stayed there until his retirement. By the time I was three years old, my dad had his fill of family life and decided to look for greener pastures elsewhere. So, in 1962, his wander-lust got the better of him and he left us. He finally settled near Chicago. Even though Dad was gone, he came around occasionally to see us and to make sure we were okay.

Dad's parents were of Swedish descent and lived in Holdridge, Nebraska. My Grandfather and Grandmother Simpson had a farm and Grandpa Simpson was always hunting jack-rabbits. He always had a pocket full of rabbit feet that he would give away to people he met. He assumed it would bring them good luck. I reasoned that the luck the rabbit's foot contained might have worked for people, but not so much for rabbits. After all, rabbits had four of them ... and look what happened.

I know we made a few trips to visit my grandparents in the Cornhusker State, but I only recall one in particular. That was the one he and I made by ourselves. It was one of the only times I can remember the two of us spending any amount of time alone. Being only seven or so at the time, I don't recollect a lot about the trip, but I do remember dad's big car. He always was a Chrysler man and drove around in a big pea-soup-green sedan wearing his big cowboy hat.

My first dreams of playing football came from our trips to Nebraska. I envisioned playing for the mighty Cornhuskers from the University of Nebraska because my grandparents came from there. I knew my dad and my grandparents would be proud of me if I wore the red and white.

Other than the trips, I don't have a lot of memories of my father during those years, although I remember him constantly rattling the change in his pocket and twirling his thumbs to expend some of his nervous energy. One other memory stands out: I remember him practicing his barbering skills, albeit limited, on my older brothers. Being a military man, you can probably guess that a military crew-cut was the style he was apt to apply to my brother's youthful heads. I don't know if they minded their hair style, not that it would have mattered much, I suppose. Thankfully, my sister Lori and I were spared from my dad's barbering; her due to her gender and me because I didn't have much hair at the time. In retrospect, that may have been the beginning of the look that would help mark the "Russian Nightmare" in the years to come.

Nikita's parents

I am the youngest of four children. My brothers Stephen and Glenn were twelve and seven years my senior, respectively, and my sister Lori was five years older than me. The age difference made it a bit difficult growing up as far as being close to my siblings. It wasn't that we didn't love or care for one another, but they all were well into their childhoods by the time I joined them.

The home in which I grew up was far from that of the Cleaver family, and the town was far from Mayfield, the mythical town in which they lived. The only thing that was even reminiscent of Wally and the Beaver was there seemed to be a lot of Eddie Haskells around. My father leaving also added an additional obstacle in that he left us with no personal, reliable manner of transportation. We didn't have a car, but even if we did, it wouldn't have mattered much since my mother didn't know how to drive and never had a driver's license. But with four children to support on her own, she didn't have time to think about acquiring a driver's license when there were meals to cook, laundry to do, and homework to check.

Besides my immediate family, the two relatives I was most close to were my Grandma Besse (my mother's mother) and my Uncle Billy (my mother's brother). Like my mom, my Uncle Billy never learned to drive, but he worked extremely hard all his life. He worked for a vacuum cleaner manufacturer until he retired. Billy was a devoted sports fan who loved all sports, but to him, hockey was king, and he held season tickets for his beloved Minnesota North Stars hockey team for years.

Some of the happiest times of my life growing up were spent with Uncle Billy. We would take the bus and spend the weekend in South Minneapolis, and during the summer, we would stay a week or more. In many ways, Uncle Billy was the father I never had. No matter how tired he was at the end of his work day, he would always be up for a backyard game of catching and throwing baseballs or footballs with me. On summer nights, we would walk the four or five blocks to the softball fields and stay for hours, or all day on weekends. We would watch the games on the ten different softball fields, eat hotdogs, and have a great time. Billy always would include me when he took his vacation each summer, taking me and grandma to Duluth, or to Thunder Bay, Ontario. We always went on the Greyhound Bus, which just added all the more to our adventures.

To support us, my mother worked as a teacher's aide in the Minnesota school system and did so proudly for more than 41 years. We lived in what would become known in later years as the projects, but growing up, it was politely referred to as "low-income housing," if it was referred to at all.

Living in the projects really was no different than living in a lot of other neighborhoods as a child. Your life revolves around your home, family, school, and friends. If we were poor or less fortunate than others, I certainly didn't know it, and neither did my brothers or sister. Our mother made sure we were well fed and taken care of as we grew.

For those who never had the opportunity to grow up where the snow could reach up to two feet in a 24-hour period missed a version of heaven on earth for any child. I was so excited every time it snowed, and the deeper it was, the better. We didn't miss much school because of it, but we loved it just the same. I'm sure the adults didn't share in my wide-eyed wonder. After all, they were the ones who had to battle it for so many months of the year, but to those of us who were too young to shovel, the snow provided us with a world all our own.

Sledding, ice hockey, and building forts all brightened the gray-sky-filled days, but the most fun was playing football; no matter what the temperature was, no matter the time of day. I can't imagine a single boy (or girl for that matter) who ever played football in the snow with their hands and feet freezing and the snow stinging their face, not seeing themselves as Fran Tarkington, Kenny "The Snake" Stabler, Bart Starr, or Carl Eller making the big play at the decisive moment of the big game ... or until our mothers called us in for dinner.

If there ever was a more glorious feeling, place, or a time for growing up, I can't imagine what or where it would be.

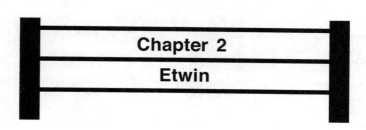

Chapter 2
Etwin

Where we lived was, I guess, what is now called a mixed neighborhood. It was a mixture of both black and white families, which may have been a bit unusual in the mid to early 1960s. It is ironic though, looking back, that I don't think it ever really dawned on us as children that we were different than our black neighbors and friends. We were all just kids. I'm sure that is at least one of the reasons why, during the turbulent 1960s, with all its racial strife, we never gave it a second thought. So many times, these days, I hear about cultural diversity, and how important it is, and how it should be accepted and embraced. I couldn't agree more, but growing up, we didn't talk about it or hold seminars to work on it. It was just a part of everyday life to which we gave no particular thought.

Our apartment had a kitchen and a small living room on the first floor. Upstairs, we had three tiny bedrooms and a bathroom. I shared a bedroom with my oldest brother, Stephen. Lori slept with my mom and Glenn got the third room all to himself. I know it seems a bit strange that Stephen, being the oldest, didn't get the bedroom to himself and I didn't bunk in with Glenn, but the answer was pretty simple. With my dad out of the picture, Stephen saw himself as sort of a surrogate father and believed it was up to him to keep his youngest brother on the straight and narrow. Since I didn't listen to Mom all that well, he was going to make sure I listened to him. Not surprisingly, I didn't listen to him much either. Not that it mattered. I was a lot faster than he was.

Two of my closest friends in our neighborhood were my next-door neighbors, Maynard and Myron Johnson. We were close in age and interests. They didn't have a father at home, either. I can't recall why, or maybe I didn't ask, but either way, this was one more thing that brought us closer together. They were the last Caucasian family to live in the projects. We moved out when I was ten, the second-to-last Caucasian family to leave. We had an opportunity to move out of public housing into a house a few miles away in Robbinsdale, a suburb on the outskirts of Minneapolis. Maynard, Myron, and I kept in touch throughout high school, but as it is with many friends, we lost touch after college.

The thing I remember the most about the three of us was the way we, with all our seven and eight-year-old bravado, would cross the four-lane Olsen Memorial Highway to reach our favorite destination; the local five-and-dime store that was part of the strip mall across from where we lived. There also was a small grocery store, as well as a number of other stores. We thought it was great that all of our basic needs—candy, comic books, football and baseball cards, and other treasures we couldn't live without—could be found so close to home..

We went there far more often than our parents knew and had more than a few close calls running in front of oncoming traffic. I'm sure the three of us added exponentially to the gray hair that our parents eventually had. Our parents didn't seem to hold the knowledge we held; that eight-year-old boys are invincible, or so we thought.

Even though Myron, Maynard, and I were close, my best friend and my hero was a boy named Edwin. Edwin, a black guy who was a couple of years older, had a reputation for being a pretty tough guy. For some reason, I could never pronounce his name correctly. I didn't have a speech impediment, but somehow, it always came out "Etwin." I don't know if it ever bothered him, but he was always "Etwin" to me.

Edwin was feared by every kid in our neighborhood, and for good reason. One day, when I was in the third grade at Bethune Cookman Elementary School, two members of our local rabble, Ira and Maurice, trapped me in the bathroom. They told me I was about to become their next victim; another notch on their desks as it were. They informed me they were going to pummel me after school. The funny thing about Ira and Maurice was they never did the actual fighting themselves. They farmed it out to their "minions" who would do their dirty work for them; not out of loyalty, but out of fear that if they didn't, Maurice and Ira would deal with them in worse fashion.

The rest of that day was anguish. All I could think about was the possibility of my life coming to an end or worse; the fact that I would live to tell about my beating. Now as far as I know, Maurice and Ira had no reason to want to beat me up, save for pure meanness, but nevertheless, it looked like it would be my turn.

Sometime during my anguish of thought, I concocted an escape route that I was certain, with any luck, would take me to the safety of my home. As soon as the final bell rang that afternoon, I hit the pavement and ran as hard and as fast as I could. I made it home without seeing either one of my two would-be assailants. They very well may have been the first tag team I had to face, and at the time, they seemed as menacing to me as the Road Warriors ever were.

When I got home, I found Edwin and told him what had happened to me at school that day. Edwin told me not to worry about it. He would "resolve" the problem for me the next day. It was kind of like the opening scene of the movie *The Godfather* where Don Corleone granted the favor to the undertaker who asked him to avenge his daughter. I have no idea what Edwin said or did to Ira and Maurice, but whatever it was, I never had any more difficulty with either of them. Thanks, Edwin, wherever you are.

I used to tease Edwin because I thought he had a rather large head compared to his body. He would tell me his mother told him a dresser had fallen on his head when he was a baby. Of course, I believed every word he said. In fact, we all believed *everything* Edwin said.

After my fourth-grade year, mom moved us out of the projects into a new neighborhood just outside of Robbinsdale about fifteen miles outside of Minneapolis.. I wasn't thrilled about moving away from my friends and where I felt comfortable, but the thought of living in an actual home trumped any fears

I may have had. We moved into an old farm house the week before school started. I couldn't believe we had a yard to play in and how much better I preferred grass to asphalt. Not only that, my oldest brother, Stephen, graduated from high school and headed off to business school. That meant I had captured the brass ring of any ten-year-old; my own room.

It wasn't exactly what you could call a room in more than an academic sense. It had four walls and a ceiling, but it was located between the back porch and the kitchen, so anyone who came in through the back door had to walk through my room to get into the house. I think the original thought was more of a laundry room. It was about eight feet by 12 feet and it had no door, which meant no privacy, but even so, it was my room.

What I disliked was the fact that I would have to start over with a new school and new friends. I remember being terrified walking those few steps to board the school bus that first day, but fortunately, I was able to make friends quickly and avoid guys like Ira and Maurice.

I never gave a lot of thought to school, I didn't like it all that much, but I didn't hate it, either. It was just something we had to do. Like most ten-year-old boys, I lived for recess and gym class. There was one thing I did try to avoid in school, however, and that was my name.

As you know, my given name is Scott Simpson, but what I didn't tell you is that my full name is Nelson Scott Simpson. Scott was alright with me, but I hated Nelson. I did everything I could while I was in school to make sure no one called me "Nelson." I would go to any length to make sure as few people as possible learned my first name. Each year when school started, I would make sure I was one of the first students to arrive on the first day of class. I would make a bee-line to the teacher to tell her I preferred to be called by my middle name, and not that "other name."

Much to my credit, I was pretty successful with my plan. That is, until I went to junior high, where I had more than one teacher. So on the first day, I did my utmost to be the first one in each class and inform the teacher that I was Scott, not Nelson. Try as I might, I wasn't able to reach each teacher before the roll was called, and when I heard the name "Nelson Simpson" called, I would put my head down on my desk, groan, timidly raise one finger in the air, and quietly answer "here." I still wince when I recall hearing that name in class.

But things began to look up during those years. During that time, I decided I needed to earn some spending money since extra money was scarce at my house. When I entered the sixth grade, I became a budding entrepreneur and took a paper route in my neighborhood for the *Minneapolis Star-Tribune*.

I not only delivered the daily news but I became aware very early that the more customers I had, the more money I could make. After all, I was passing all those houses, anyway, so why not have all of them as my customers? I went door to door and began signing up new customers. I'm not sure if it was sales ability or that people just felt sorry for me, but either through persistence or pity, I began to accumulate a lot of customers. The *Star-Tribune* provided additional motivation for my success by offering prizes and cash incentives for the top salesperson. It wasn't long until I became top dog.

One day, I was told I could make even more money if my house became the drop-off point for all the paper routes in my area. Hearing that, I immediately went to the man who was in charge of deliveries and told him I was willing to be a drop-off point. This meant quite a bit more work as I had to have all the other paper boys' papers counted and ready for them to pick up, as well as my own, before dawn. Sundays were exceptionally brutal because I had to be out of the house by three o'clock in the morning to insert the latest news and advertising flyers into the papers. It wasn't too bad in the summer, but in the middle of the Minnesota winters, the temperature could easily drop to 20 to 30 degrees below zero.

In addition to this new responsibility and my ever-growing list of clients, another route came open and I took that on as well, which both doubled my clients and my work load. All papers had to be delivered by seven o'clock in the morning. I would be lying if I said I never missed the mark, but by and large, I had the papers securely on my customer's front porch by the time they reached for their first cup of coffee.

I did pretty well with my first foray into the business world. Over the years, I used the money I earned to buy a seven-foot pool table, a mini-bike, and a ten-speed bike. When I was fifteen, I bought my first car from my brother Glenn. I also bought a lot of clothes and made it a point to dress up for school every day. In fact, I never wore a pair of jeans to school my entire freshman year. I probably did that to impress the girls I was too shy to ask out on a date. My success did have an adverse effect, which was to give me a reputation of being conceited, but the truth was, I was too bashful to approach girls to ask them for a date.

As well as I was doing in the business world, there was a larger voice calling me. My love for sports, especially football, became almost an obsession. I was excited when I was invited to play in our local youth football league, but it presented somewhat of a dilemma. I knew if I played football, I wouldn't be available to deliver the afternoon newspaper since football practice and paper delivery took place at the same time. As much as I wanted to play football, I didn't want to relinquish the income I had worked so hard to establish. Thus, the horns of my dilemma presented itself. The question remained: which horn to choose? When faced with a dilemma, a third option is often available; what is known as "escaping through the horns of the dilemma." And with the help of a friend named Richard, "escape through the horns" is exactly what I did.

I approached Richard with my idea. He would deliver my papers in the afternoon and I would collect the money, since I could do that after practice or on weekends. For his part, I would pay him a percentage each week. He didn't have to worry about the accounting and other details he had no interest in, while I didn't have to worry about getting the papers delivered on time or losing my income. It was the best of all possible worlds. For me, it was like getting paid to play football. Richard and I kept our partnership going for five years until I reached my junior year in high school. But with high school came other interests that began to forge the path that would take me to wrestling rings around the world.

Chapter 3

"Hockey is life ..."

The year I entered high school, there were three schools in what was known as district 81: Cooper, Armstrong, and Robbinsdale. The schools all vied for academic and sports supremacy in our town. I attended Robbinsdale, the oldest school in the district. I don't know exactly how old it was, but by the time I got there, it was really showing its age. Robbinsdale was a three-story brick building that looked more like a prison in an old George Raft movie than a high school. Not long after I graduated, the school board decided to consolidate and close one of the three high schools. It was no surprise that the venerable and historic edifice of Robbinsdale High School was the one to go. It was chosen, I am told, because it was the oldest of the three and not up to new codes of being handicap accessible. I am sure it was the correct decision, as sad as it was to see an era end.

With the dawn of high school, my interest in sports began to hit its zenith. Along with football, I began to take weight lifting seriously and I set my sights on the National Football League. My goal in athletics had always been to play professional football. Since those earliest memories playing in the snow with my friends, and at the "ripe old age" of ten, eleven, and twelve, I was running touchdowns, making key blocks, and running interceptions for the Minnesota Vikings. I was Fran Tarkington, Fred Biletnekoff, and Paul Horning rolled up into one. They were not just boyhood fantasies, mind you. They were what I was aspiring to; where I knew I'd be if I trained hard and kept focused. I had begun working out and lifting weights when I was twelve, but somehow, a new school and a new level of play inspired me to start laying the groundwork for my future. Now, more than ever, my entire world revolved around football. I knew it could easily be my ticket out of the projects and would allow me to secure a better life for myself.

I did try my hand at other sports; baseball, in particular. I didn't play baseball in high school, but I did play one year in the Babe Ruth League. I was kind of the utility guy, playing just about every position the team needed to fill at any one time. I learned how to switch hit because I hated the curve ball. That allowed me to hit left-handed against right-handed pitchers, and right-handed against left-handed pitchers. Ironically, I hit exactly the same number of singles, doubles, and triples, both right and left handed. But as good as I wanted to be, I never hit one over the fence. I came close a number of times, but as they say, no cigar. I played all three outfield positions, played infield a couple of times, and even pitched a little bit. I was chosen for a sort of All-Star team to play as a pitcher in the State tournament. Baseball was fun, but to me, football was everything, so after the state tournament, I left my glove on the field and looked ahead to the fall football season.

Even though I didn't see baseball as anything more than a pastime, there was one thing baseball did for me. It made me realize that I was developing into a pretty fair athlete. It was that awareness that bolstered my confidence and made me realize my NFL goals might not be just fantasies.

Playing football for the Robbinsdale Robins was what made life worth living for me. I know it sounds a bit strange to have a robin as our mascot, but that was it. All the teams in the city were named after birds. Cooper High School was the Hawks, Armstrong High School was the Falcons, and we proudly wore the blue and gold of the Robins. We weren't the "Fighting Robins," or the "Mighty Robins." We were just the Robins, proud birds as they are.

One thing Robbinsdale High School had that Cooper and Armstrong didn't was a football field, so we saw more action than most because all our home games, as well as all of theirs, were played on our field. When we faced them, if it was a designated home game for the Hawks or the Falcons, we wore our "away" jerseys. We didn't care; all we wanted to do was play and win.

We had quite a team during those years. I was a starting tight-end and my team mates included a who's who of future wrestling stars: Barry Darsow, who would later become Krusher Khrushchev (my future six-man tag team partner and later AX of WWF's Demolition), Curt Hennig (who would capture the AWA world heavyweight wrestling championship, the title which had been worn honorably for so many decades by another Robbinsdale alumni, the legendary Verne Gagne, and who later would become the WWF superstar, Mr. Perfect), Larry "The Axe" Hennig, Rick Rood (before he became Ravishing Rick Rude), "Z-man" Tom Zenk, John Nord (later known as Nord the Barbarian), and Brady Boone, who would wrestle for Jim Crockett. It is ironic that so many of us who grew up and were teammates in high school would all make our marks in the world of professional wrestling, a sport, at the time, in which we had little if no interest in at all. Of course we all knew who Curt's dad was: an excellent athlete and multi-titled world wrestling champion, Larry "The Axe" Hennig. If any of us had a healthy respect for any of our friend's parents, it was certainly him.

Robbinsdale High School had a reputation in our community, which I later learned extended throughout the Midwest, as a group of "muscleheads" who were trading the rigors of the scholarly life for a set of barbells and various weight machines. True enough, we took weight-lifting as seriously as others took to their books. We considered our training to be every bit as much of an art as our classmates regarded their passion for music or other academic pursuits. The main reason for that was our junior-high health teacher, Gerry McFarland.

Gerry, a champion bodybuilder in his own right, not only instructed us in the correct form of lifting, but built his own equipment. With us as his apprentices, he showed us how to weld and grind down the iron to create our own gear. Athletes from the four junior high schools and three high schools in District 281 all gravitated to Coach McFarland and his weight room. During high school, many of us used Jerry's weight room and his technique to train, including

Barry Darsow. Barry and Wayne Bloom trained there for the world two-man deadlift championship, which they won with a winning lift of 1,434¼ pounds, a world record at the time.

Just as we were known as "muscleheads," our biggest out-of-town rivals, Edina High School, were known to us as the "boys with the silver spoons." They were the polar opposites of who we were and they had as much disdain for us as we did for them. They were rich and we were not. They had every advantage that we only dreamed of. As F. Scott Fitzgerald wrote, *"Let me tell you about the very rich. They are different from you and me ... they think deep in their hearts that they are better than we are..."* And the guys from Edina certainly did. At least, that was the impression we all had at the time. They excelled in almost every sport, but where they left everyone behind was in hockey. Not only could they skate rings around the rest of us, but they looked good doing it. Their uniforms were immaculate, and they wore new ones every season. They had the finest equipment and endless opportunities.

Now, to understand Minnesota is to understand hockey. As popular as football, basketball, baseball, and wrestling were, they all paled in comparison when held up to the light of hockey. As the T-shirt reads "Hockey is Life ... the rest is just details."

One particular snowy night, we played Edina in a regular conference game. We played them in the arena in New Hope, a town "just down the road." Many of the teams played there because they had the best hockey facility around. Edina was at their best that night and we were not. Even if we had been on our game, I don't think it would have mattered much. They destroyed us for three periods, skating away with yet another win and one more step towards another state title. The game concluded about ten-thirty. As we were all making our way to leave, a number of Edina fans approached our team's bus and exchanged words with our team. Even with the temperature hovering below zero, things were heating up pretty fast.

The Robins Hockey Team retorted by yelling out the windows at the jubilant Edina fans and spilling out in the parking lot to defend their bruised honor. To add fuel to the fire, the Edina team came out to the parking lot and joined in the verbal assault.

Rick Rood, Barry Darsow, numerous "muscleheads," and I were watching the battle begin when Rick got into it with the Edina goalie, still in uniform. In fact, both teams were still in full gear as the schools were close by and it was much easier to shower back at our respective schools. Rick, who had quite a reputation as a boxer and street fighter, would give no quarter nor ask for any. His father, who had been a Golden Gloves boxer, was known to have been pretty rough on Rick, all of which added to his reputation and pugilistic skills.

I don't remember what prompted the fight between Rick and the goalie, but I do remember Rick taking him down and sitting on top of him, and then throwing round-house punches to a prone, albeit well-padded, adversary. The funniest thing about the scene was the goalie held onto his hockey stick and kept trying to hit Rick with it. His efforts to fend off Rick's punches were of little or no avail.

My first encounter with a "foreign object" came long before I ever stepped foot in a wrestling ring. I had been walking around and watching the action, which reminded me more of a Keystone Cops short film than the Battle of the Little Big Horn. I never found myself as an instigator in these situations, but more as a supporting cast member, making sure the fight was fair. And seeing the goalie with his stick, even though he was getting the worst of it, didn't seem

quite fair to me. I took the stick away from him just to make sure the fight would conclude on a fair note, not that the stick had anything to do with evening the playing field with the pre-Ravishing one. I do have to admit it was one of the funniest sights I have ever seen. Here was this big goalie in his full green-and-gold hockey regalia, looking like a turtle on his back, fending off Rick's looping roundhouse punches. In fact, he looked like one of the Teenage Mutant Ninja Turtles, but without the fighting ability.

I'm embarrassed to say that in the arrogance of my youth, I never fully understood the need for excelling in academics as I did in sports. I fully thought my athletic ability would get me not only through high school, but into any college of my choosing, and it did, to a certain degree. I wanted to go to a major college to play football, but because of my grades, I had to set my sights on a junior college and hope to make the leap to Division I by my junior year.

Recognizing my mistake in not hitting the books, I buckled down, gave my all to the glories of the academic world, and managed to get all Bs and one C. I wish I had begun earlier, at least in my sophomore or junior year, but even though I studied hard, it was too little, too late. I fell just short of the B honor roll, and with that fell short of playing for any major college. As a result, in the fall of 1977, I headed out to play for the Golden Valley Lutheran Royals.

Chapter 4

Clarence Darrow

Golden Valley Lutheran Junior College, located just outside of Minneapolis, had an enrollment of about 500 students. Located off Highway 55, the campus consisted of six buildings, much like many other small Bible colleges scattered across the Midwest.

Golden Valley didn't catch my attention because of its theological acumen, but because they had the top-ranked junior-college football team in the nation. There were two types of students at Golden Valley — the athletes and the "Bible-Bangers" — and without expending much thought, there was little doubt who was who. It was easy to tell by a glance that I belonged in the former group much more than the latter.

But as in high school, my freshman and sophomore years left me unscarred by the halls of academia and I did just enough to remain eligible to play ball. At least, that was my plan until the third game of the season.

I was again playing tight-end and enjoying the undefeated season that brought us to 2-0 and to Thief River Falls, six hours north of Minneapolis. Early in the first quarter, it looked like we were well on our way to another victory. It was towards the end of the first quarter when the game and my future, as I saw it, came to an abrupt halt. We ran the Oklahoma Wishbone offense, which meant we didn't pass all that much. I was running a simple pass play straight down the field when I heard the whistle blow. I turned my head towards the line of scrimmage while I was still in motion. The defensive back for Thief River, moving behind our split-end, was running a crossing pattern to cut off my angle to the goal line. I had him beaten until I slowed down for the whistle. When I turned my head back towards the line of scrimmage, our split-end pushed by their defensive back from behind and set him air borne, causing him to cross-body block me below my knee. The sound my knee made on impact was that of a dry twig that had snapped in two. He hit me with such force that we ended up laying on the field yards apart. Of course, very few of the fans saw that happen. They were watching the action going on towards the goal line.

The guy who hit me was one of the leaders of the Thief River team. Prior to the opening kick-off, we overheard him say from the adjoining dressing room that he was going to "get" those "goody-goody" boys from Golden Valley, and he taunted us as we took the field. I don't know if it was just wishful thinking on his part, but he did manage to "get" one of those "goody-goody" boys … me.

Lying on the field, I looked down at my leg, which seemed bent at a different angle than the shape in which it originally had been a few minutes before the collision. It seemed as if I had an extra joint between my knee and my ankle. My lower leg seemed to make a 90-degree turn in one direction with another 90-degree angle just above my ankle. The pain wasn't too bad, but my leg felt like it was on fire. As I would learn later, I broke both my tibia and fibula, just like Joe Theisman did years later in 1985 when he was hit by Lawrence Taylor on *Monday Night Football*.

My broken leg wasn't the only problem. Our trainer had never seen a break like that (or any other break as far as I know) and he had no idea about what he should do. We were six hours from home, it was early in the game, and the ambulance and medics hadn't yet arrived. The nearest hospital was across the state line in North Dakota and there was no visible way to get me there.

The trainer did do everything he could think of that might help relieve my pain. He took off my cleat and cut the tape from around my ankle. As soon as the tape was released, my ankle ballooned up to more than five times its normal size. My leg suddenly felt like a steak being thrown into a thousand-degree furnace. They tried to secure my leg with an air cast, but they couldn't figure out how to hold it above and below the break. My leg had swelled so much the cast wouldn't have fit, anyway. The game was held up for more than an hour while people from both sides of the field put their heads together and tried to figure out what to do.

I ended up being transported to the hospital in the back of a station wagon which belonged to the parents of one of the opposing players. The people in charge at the hospital did little more than the trainer did on the field and I just stayed there until the trainer came to get me after the game. He came into the room smiling, telling me we had won the game. Glad as I was to hear it, I had other things on my mind. They took a few x-rays, put on a temporary cast, and gave me some pain medication, which did absolutely nothing to ease my discomfort. He helped me into his van and we headed home. The six-hour drive home seemed more like sixty as I rode flat on my back in the rear of the van. The trainer called my mom and took me directly to North Memorial Hospital, arriving a little less than 12 hours after I first hit the field.

The doctors did everything they could to avoid putting me under the knife, so for the next 17 days, they tried everything to help my bones mend. But, try as they might, the bones wouldn't stay together and surgery became my only option. The surgeons put a stainless-steel plate in my tibia held in place by four screws. They thought the fibula would heal on its own. Fortunately for me, they were correct in their assumption. For the next 16 weeks, I remained in a cast. The first nine weeks were in a full cast and the last seven in a walking cast. Seventeen days on your back in the hospital gives you a lot of time to think and I spent much of it wondering about my future in pro football, but I was all the more determined to reach the goals I had set for myself. However, keeping a positive spirit was more difficult this time. There were times when I thought my football aspirations were over, but thanks to daily visits and calls by my coach and teammates, they made me see my situation as only a bump in the road. Had it not been for my best friend Tim Peltier, our quarterback, I really don't know where I would be today. I give many heartfelt thanks to Tim for all his visits and encouragement. I took his words to heart and decided that my problems were only temporary.

The next year, the composition of the team changed. We had all new coaches, along with some new players, and I was voted captain of the team. We were fortunate to secure Dave Skrien, who had played and coached for several years in the Canadian Football League. He had a spectacular career and won the Grey Cup, the CFL's equivalent of the Super Bowl, events which are chronicled in his book, *Countdown to the Grey Cup.* Dave had also coached Joe Kapp, who would become quarterback of the Vikings, and he was friends with Bud Grant, the Vikings coach. Coach Skrien hired Art Meadowcroft and George Adzick, who both played for the Vikings and around the NFL. I couldn't believe it. We had a professional coaching staff at our small junior college.

I made it through only one practice that year. I was hit in the shin with a helmet and the pain was so intense that I thought I had broken my leg again. After another trip to the hospital, I was relieved to learn I had only bruised the bone. I was left wondering if my leg would be in the shape necessary to play that year. I knew if I re-injured it, my plans for an NFL career would be out the window. I talked it over with my coaches and we all agreed it would be best for me to "red-shirt" and rehab my leg for another year.

If that wasn't enough, I made matters worse by getting expelled that year for slapping the son of the Dean of Students. The Dean's son had a reputation for being a "pothead," and the group of "jocks" I hung around with had little use, and even less patience, for drug users. I don't remember all the details of that evening, but I do remember him saying something smart to me. Before I knew it, reflexes got the better of me and I hit him with an open slap that sent his glasses flying and him reeling.

It didn't take long for news to travel throughout campus. By the time the last student got wind of my transgression, I was sitting in the dean's office and being told my days at Golden Valley Lutheran College were over. I was told I needed to find my way to the door and to do so quickly.

Fortunately for me, I had one last advocate to come to my rescue ... my football coach, Dave Skrien. He petitioned the academic board to reinstate me the following fall so I could play ball and earn my Associate degree in Liberal Arts. Clarence Darrow, on his best day, couldn't have surpassed the case Coach Skrien pleaded before the board. He convinced them that I was knee-deep in contrition and deserved a second chance.

The board unanimously agreed, but on one condition; that I sign an agreement which stated I couldn't enter any dorms, couldn't attend any social functions or anything else besides my classes, practice, and football games. If I screwed up again, it wouldn't be just my head. It would be Coach Skrien's head, as well. I was a marked man and I knew it. It was a hard lesson to learn, but there was no doubt I got what I deserved. I deserved to be kicked out of school, but thanks to the intercession and friendship of Coach Skrien, I was given something rare in life; a second chance. I wasn't about to blow it again, and I didn't.

During my convalescence, I knew that if I was to amount to anything on or off the field, I needed to be more responsible with hitting the books than I had been earlier. To do so, I took 22 to 23 credit hours for three of the four semesters when most of my classmates were taking 15 to 16 hours.

The team went on to have a banner year, holding the number-one spot in the nation for a majority of the year. We defeated most of our opponents by lopsided scores and, more times than not, racked up more than 300 yards per game.

We ran the wishbone offense, thanks to our quarterback, Tim Peltier. Tim graduated two years ahead of me, but he waited a year before entering college, which put him just one year ahead of me there. There was no doubt in anyone's mind that Tim was headed for a major college, but while he was out of bounds during one game, he was hit with a cheap shot that separated the shoulder on his throwing arm. Tim had Nebraska and Oklahoma looking at him, but they lost interest quickly after his injury.

Despite our injuries, he managed to lead us to one game short of the national championship game in Pasadena. It was dubbed the Junior Rose Bowl and we lost it to Normandale Community College. One interesting note about the

Dragon Athletics

Alex Nemzek Hall
218-236-2622

Moorhead State University   Moorhead, Minnesota 56560

Dear Squad Member:

Football season is fast approaching so this is the last letter you will get before reporting. I encourage you to work especially hard this last month on the conditioning program sent to you earlier so you will be in good physical shape when you arrive.

We want you to report to Ballard Hall between 8 and 12 AM on Thursday August 21st. The dorm will supply linen, blankets, and towels during the preschool practice but not during the regular school year. We have to pay for preschool dorms this year, therefore if you can live off campus do not check into the dorm. We will be issuing equipment from 10 AM to 2 PM. The first meal will be supper on the 21st.

Bring a swimsuit for recreation and tennis shoes in case we have to practice indoors. We will be giving physical exams at our health center.

We have a number of players that did not get into the dorms and do not have housing yet. If you have an apartment rented and need roommates indicate this on the enclosed form. If you need a room indicate this.

Enclosed is some information on our athletic insurance for you and your parents. Please return the enclosed insurance form right away.

Best of luck the rest of the summer.

"BEAT KEARNEY"

Sincerely,

Ross Fortier
HEAD FOOTBALL COACH
Moorhead State University

Moorhead State University football letter

game was that on the Normandale sideline, recovering from knee surgery, was another Robbinsdale High School graduate: the future world wrestling champion and WWF superstar, "Mr. Perfect" Curt Hennig.

Being "red-shirted" my sophomore year let me come back for a third year to my two-year school. With a good nucleus of returning players, an influx of some good new players, and our "pro-coaching" staff, we had another blockbuster year, setting conference records and finishing in the top ten nationally. And to top it off, in the fall of 1979, I finally graduated with my Associate of Arts degree.

My junior and senior year of college was a complete turnaround for me. I was recruited to play for the Dragons at Moorhead State by Coach Ross Fortier, who remembered me playing as a freshman. When he offered me a full ride, I jumped at the offer because of the reputation the team and coach had. A number of my high-school teammates were there, as well. I didn't start at tight end because of my absence the previous year. The tight-end position was already filled by Dean Johnson, who I played against when he was at Cooper High School. He went on to play with the Miami Dolphins under Don Shula. Instead, Coach Fortier put me at defensive end. I did manage to see a lot of action on the field when we used two tight ends. We didn't exactly set the football world on fire, but with a new coaching staff, new system, and new players, we held our own. By the end of the season, we started to gel as a team

My leg felt as strong as ever and never gave me a minute's trouble. We had a winning season behind our quarterback, Mark Reed, who went on to play with the New York Giants for four years as a back-up to Phil Simms. I was enjoying playing again and was even enjoying my classes.

I don't know what path I would have taken if it hadn't been for Coach Skrien's kindness towards me at Golden Valley, and the chance the academic review board took with me. I knew the board hadn't given me a second chance based on whatever attributes they saw in me. They gave me another opportunity based on what they saw in Coach Dave Skrien. Thank God for coaches like him. I hope every athlete, no matter what sport they are in, has a Coach Skrien somewhere in their lives.

But now I was in a new environment, at a new school, and on a new team, and I was more ready than ever to play my senior year and head for the pros. It finally looked like my past was far behind me both academically and as far as injuries were concerned. Going into the tenth game of the season, during which time we were undefeated and had spent the previous six or seven weeks as number one in our division in the country, we were scheduled to play Valley City, North Dakota at home on what was originally scheduled to be a bye week for us. The year before, as a team, we voted to skip our bye week and play as often as we could. Coach Fortier came to us as the schedule was being put together and asked what we wanted to do. He left it up to the seniors as it probably would be the last year of football for most of them. We voted unanimously to play, but in retrospect, I wished we hadn't.

With two minutes to play in the first half, we were leading 52-3 and had already been told by the coaches that the starting lineup would be sitting out the second half. So with all this in mind, we were entering the last 120 seconds of that fine autumn afternoon and looking forward to watching the rest of the game from the sidelines with the rest of the afternoon off to cheer on our teammates.

The play called for all the receivers to flood one side of the field, with me on the opposite side to false block and head across the field in the opposite direction, which would leave me wide open for the pass. The play worked as planned, and as I turned to run, I caught the shadow of the linebacker out of the corner of my eye. He barely caught my jersey and twisted me around as I was in full stride with all my weight on my left leg planted on the turf. As I spun around, I heard a familiar sound that I had hoped I would never hear again, but this time, from my left leg. As soon as I heard the sound, I knew I had broken the same two bones I had broken four years earlier in the same place as my right leg.

The force of the tackle sent me sailing into our sidelines, well off the field. This time, however, I knew what to do when I hit the ground. Almost as soon as I landed, I sat up and assessed the situation. When the trainer arrived, I told him I had broken my leg and not to cut the tape that surrounded my ankle. Being at home, we had more medical personnel and facilities nearby, so I headed to the hospital ... and surgery once again. Having been through it once before, my spirits were much higher this time and my determination to get past it was all the greater.

I returned to school within a few weeks, determined to graduate on time in spring 1982. My plan was to take a year to rehabilitate my leg and continue on to professional football. I graduate *cum laude*, was named an Academic All-American, and earned my Bachelor of Science degree in Physical Education with a minor in Health Education and Coaching.

After graduation, I planned to return to Moorhead State to rehabilitate and work as a graduate assistant coach while earning my masters degree in physical education. I would then play in the NFL for ten years before walking away to an illustrious career in coaching at the college level. I was set to go and thought my plan would come to fruition. That is, until Moorhead dropped its master program in physical education. So, once again, I had to reevaluate my plans. I decided to move back to Minneapolis while I tried to figure out what to do. Little did I know that a phone call I had made three years earlier would affect my life and put me on a path on which I had never dreamed of traveling.

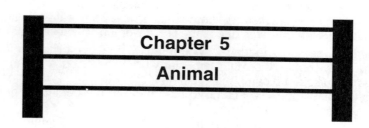

Chapter 5

Animal

If you ask any wrestling fan with even the most elementary knowledge of the sport from the early eighties on, one of the most feared and dominant tag teams would be the Road Warriors. The "Legion of Doom" made all their predecessors, no matter how tough they were or claimed to be, look like a Girl Scout troop. The Warriors were comprised of Animal and Hawk, along with their manager, Paul Ellering. They wreaked havoc around the globe as they "snacked on danger and dined on death," winning tag-team title s in every territory in which they appeared.

But long before the strains of Black Sabbath's *Iron Man* filled the arenas and brought fans to their feet as the face-painted, apocalyptic tag-team raced to the ring to annihilate their waiting opponents, Animal and Hawk were just two Minnesota boys by the name of Joe Laurinaitis and Michael Hegstrand.

It may surprise those who followed my feud with the Road Warriors in the ring throughout the 1980s that my first encounter with the Animal was over the phone in 1978 in the Golden Valley Lutheran Bible College's football office. I was trying to recruit him as an offensive guard for the Royals.

After breaking my leg the first time and being red-shirted my sophomore year, our team had a nearly complete overhaul. We lost a lot of our starting line up to graduation and all of our coaching staff moved on to bigger schools and bigger opportunities. To fill in the hole on our team, the athletic director asked me to help recruit players for the next season. I scoured the newspapers and high school football publications to find the right men to keep us on the winning side of the scoreboard during the upcoming season. I had seen Joe's name a number of times because he had made quite a reputation for himself on the high-school gridiron across the state. I called him and we hit it off right away. I invited him and his parents to visit and tour the campus and spent the greater part of the weekend with them.

From the moment we met, Joe and I became like family. We did everything together. We played football, worked out, and worked together making sandwiches in the Schlotski's Deli. We were like brothers. The same was true with his mom and dad. I don't know if they felt sorry for me coming from a broken home, or just what their reason was for them taking me in, but I have never met two more kind and loving people. We had a lot of fun together, and when Joe first began wrestling, I would go to their house on Saturday nights to watch him wrestle on television. Even today, with all those years between us,

I still think of them often.

Joe's mother, Lorna, was like a mother to me, as well. I spent many holidays with them. In fact, one Christmas, I had more presents under the tree than Joe or his two brothers, Johnny and Marc (who also found careers in wrestling). Even after I entered the ring, I stayed in contact with them and would visit them in Florida when I was on the road. Lorna passed away several years ago after battling Lupus. She truly was one of the finest women I have ever met.

That spring, Joe and I headed to Moorhead, Minnesota for spring football. Joe had actually enrolled there that semester, while I worked out an arrangement that was more like a pro camp than college football for me. I wasn't eager to return to the classroom, so I came to Moorhead at the beginning of spring practice and left at its conclusion.

As far as I was concerned, it was the best of all possible worlds. My days consisted of sleeping late, working out in the gym, more rest, and then heading out to practice at three in the afternoon. And even though I had yet to enroll, I won the starting guard position and became the starting tight end.

Summer came and went, which meant it was time for me to head back to school and fall training camp. Joe told me that he decided not to return to school. He and his girlfriend had decided to get married and join the work force. I tried every conceivable argument to change Joe's mind about school, but to no avail. He was getting married and getting a job and there was nothing that I, or anyone for that matter, could do to change his mind. Of course, I wasn't the only one who wasn't happy about Joe's decision. The coaches weren't happy to hear he wasn't coming back, either, but there was nothing they could do, so they began to make changes in the lineup for the upcoming season.

As camp progressed, a serious threat surfaced that would thwart my plans to play pro football. We were short an offensive lineman and the coaches were considering to move me to tackle. I was not happy with the idea. I pleaded my case and tried to convince the coaching staff that I was much stronger at tight end. In my opinion, I could do more for the team there than anywhere else. When I realized they were set in their decision, I did the only thing I knew to do that would help me keep my position; I called Joe.

When I phoned Joe, I literally begged him to come back to school and the team. I assured him that the coaches would welcome him with open arms, and that housing and other details could be worked out for him and his wife. Finally, after a long conversation, he agreed to come back. I was happy that my friend was coming back and that my tight end position was safe. In retrospect, I can't believe how selfish I was over the whole thing. The incident said much more about Joe's character than it did about mine. He showed loyalty to a friend; I showed that I was self-centered.

Joe didn't win back his starting position, but he did make the traveling squad for our opener in Kearney, Nebraska. The coaches didn't welcome Joe with open arms like I thought they would, and I don't believe they gave him the opportunity to show them what he had. What he did eventually have was a change of mind, and since he was not given the opportunity to show the coaches what he could do on the field, he headed back to Minneapolis.

Joe and I were nearly inseparable from the day we met. In fact, he was one of the reasons I went to Moorhead State. They had recruited Joe after he finished playing for Golden Valley. He played on both offense and defense as a guard and linebacker. That was rare for college football, but he was that good. He told the coaching staff at Moorhead about me and they recruited me, just as Golden Valley had recruited him.

Joe decided not to finish college at Moorhead and began looking for a career of his own. Since he had recently gotten married and had a child on the way, he needed to put school behind him. Joe's dad worked at Honeywell and got Joe a job with them while I was finishing college. We kept in touch and, after I graduated, we worked together as bouncers at the Libation Station, one of the roughest places in Minneapolis-St. Paul.

During our days at Golden Valley Lutheran College, Joe and I worked out at Jesse Ventura's Gym and were enthralled by the man who would one day become Minnesota's governor. We were fascinated by his gym, his look, and everything else about him. Joe and I both got our ears pierced, complete with the feathered earrings and bandanas, just like the "Body." Looking like we did, we didn't see too much trouble come our way.

But Joe wasn't satisfied with the night life or the money we were making at the bar. He wanted more for his family and began to seek out other options.

I'm not sure how Joe met Eddie Sharkey, but I would imagine it was at Jesse's gym. Eddie began his career as a carnival wrestler and had been an undercard guy in the 1960s for Verne Gagne's American Wrestling Association. When he left the ring as an active performer, he became a trainer for aspiring wrestlers. Based in Minneapolis, Eddie trained many of the stars of the 1980s, including Jesse Ventura, Bob Backlund, Road Warrior Hawk, Rick Rude, Barry Darsow, Rick and Scott Steiner, and several others. Joe and the rest of the boys worked well together, so Eddie had a whole crop of superstars on the horizon. I'm sure that must have driven Verne crazy. As the impresario of Midwestern wrestling, he thought he was the one who should choose and train the pros; not some retired mid-carder.

Joe became the "Road Warrior" when another Minnesota grappler-made-good, Ole Anderson, became inspired by the Mel Gibson film, *The Road Warrior*. As the booker for Jim Barnett and Georgia Championship Wrestling [GCW], Ole began to look for a wrestler to become his new creation. Having a long-standing relationship with Ole, Eddie invited him to visit his gym and look over his new and impressive-looking stable, Ole picked Joe for the role and they headed back to the Peach State.

In the ring, Joe looked unbeatable, but he was far too inexperienced to make much of an impact, so Joe quickly left Atlanta for Charlotte, where he would gain more experience and learn more about the business. While there, he dropped the Road Warrior gimmick and wrestled as Jim Laurin. Joe was discouraged by his character and the fact that he had to put over other wrestlers, which no one in their right mind would believe he would lose to even on his worst day.

One night, he was scheduled to wrestle Johnny Weaver, a long-time favorite in the south who was winding up his career. Joe was to lose to Johnny in one of the preliminary bouts that night in Fayetteville, North Carolina. Joe argued that there was no way that Weaver's signature sleeper hold would be effective on his massive neck. The fans wouldn't buy the fact that Weaver, who was on the verge of retirement, could put him out with the hold. Sgt. Slaughter and

Don Kernodle had to explain that it was part of the show. Yes, in competition, he never would be able to do it, but tonight was an exhibition, and in the minds of the fans, it was possible. Joe spent most of his time there as not much more than a jobber [a wrestler who regularly loses in order to make other wrestlers look good]. He eventually decided to go home and look for a new line of work.

Not long afterward, Ole returned to Minnesota to find a new tag team he could take back to Georgia and give a big push. Ole was still the booker for Georgia Championship Wrestling and the company was suffering some financial problems. He had a few headliners, but he needed to rebuild. With the creation of the National tag team title, he not only needed a team to hold the belts, but one that would leave the fans in awe and coming back week after week.

Once again, Ole's first stop was at Eddie Sharkey's, where he once again picked Joe, along with his friend, Michael Hegstrand. He gave them a manager named Paul Ellering, a former weightlifting champion from Melrose, Minnesota, and christened them the "Road Warriors." Their individual names were Animal [Joe] and Hawk [Michael]. When they entered the ring in June 1983, the world of wrestling would never be the same.

Road Warrior Animal, Paul Ellering, Road Warrior Hawk

And that is where my life took a turn that I never would have imagined, and it all began with me answering the phone. It was a phone call from Joe ... one that would change my life.

In what seemed at the time to be out of the blue, Joe invited me to stay with him for a while in Atlanta. He was beginning to do well and was having a great time learning the ropes as a professional wrestler. Now it was his turn to beg me to come join him, so on New Year's Eve 1983, after a number of calls, I finally agreed.

I wasn't doing a lot with my life or career at the time. I was still bouncing in clubs, but had reinjured my leg when I had been escorting a rather unfriendly, and quite drunken, patron to the door one evening. To thank me for my services, he leg-whipped me, causing a hairline fracture in my left tibia. Another surgery followed, only this time, the doctor inserted a steel rod in my tibia; no more fractures or broken legs. So with nothing better on the immediate horizon, I loaded up my car on New Year's Eve and, on January 1, 1984, I arrived in Stone Mountain, Georgia.

When I arrived, Joe was living with Jake Roberts, who later became "Jake the Snake" Roberts in the World Wrestling Federation. Talk about living the life of Riley. As soon as I got there, that is exactly what I did. I had nothing to do and all day to do it. My day consisted of sleeping until I wanted to get up, which was usually no earlier than noon, eating, laying around for a few more hours, going to the pool, and then heading to Bill Blanton's gym to work out. After working out, I would get something to eat, ride with Joe to whatever town he was wrestling in, and just hang out backstage with the boys. The next day, I would do it all over again.

It's funny that with the world of wrestling surrounding me, and so many of my friends heading in that direction, I never gave it much credence as far as making it a profession. I do remember one night in the Omni, as I was sitting in the VIP section (thanks to Joe) and watching the matches, I thought, "You know, I could do this," but it left my thoughts almost as quickly as it came. Besides, pro football was still my dream and I was having a great time just hanging out and taking it easy.

Georgia certainly was the hotbed of professional wrestling in the early 1980s. Nearly every major star was in the territory, or, at least, they were visiting from nearby territories like Charlotte and Florida.

One reason the territory was so hot was their appearance on WTBS, Channel 17, the Atlanta superstation. The fledgling cable network was showcasing the show and broadcasting it across the country. By doing this, wrestlers from other territories could get over [look good] and go back home a bigger star than when they left.

Another reason Georgia Championship Wrestling was doing so well was in large part due to their announcer, Gordon Solie, "The Dean of Wrestling Announcers." Gordon had more than earned the title "Dean" during the years he spent behind the microphone in Florida and Georgia. His unique interviewing skills, eloquent commentary, and imitable insight made the matches more colorful for the fans who tuned in. As the announcer on TBS, he drew a nationwide following of people to wrestling.

Gordon began his radio career in the 1950s after leaving the Air Force. He made a name for himself by being willing to announce lesser-known sports such as stock car racing and professional wrestling, and he did it very well. His entrée to the seat behind the mike at ringside began when he accepted a five-dollar-a-night job as a ring announcer for Cowboy Luttrall's wrestling promotion in Florida.

As with everything else he did, he took his job seriously and poured all of his heart, soul, and considerable talent into it. Little known to anyone, Gordon would revolutionize the way wrestling commentary was done and would set the standard for all who would follow. For more than 30 years, Gordon raised the bar for our sport and the vocabulary for wrestlers and fans alike.

Gordon's voice was silenced in November 1999 when he had his larynx removed to stop the spread of cancer that had invaded his throat. The most gifted announcer who had ever sat behind a microphone passed away from cancer a short time later, following his beloved wife "Smokey," who had succumbed to the same disease in 1997.

But in the decade before, when I had the pleasure of his company, Gordon's additional broadcasting responsibilities extended beyond the rings in Georgia and Florida to the Tampa Bay Bandits of the United States Football League. Gordon was always more than kind to me and I was fortunate to spend a lot of

time with him behind the scenes and told him of my aspirations of playing professional football.

Gordon had the connections that would help me get a tryout with the Bandits and he offered his assistance. Within a short time, he made good on his promise and secured a chance for me to try out for Coach Steve Spurrier.

The Tampa Bay Bandits were a part of the upstart United States Football League, which was founded in May 1982 by David Dixon, a New Orleans art and antique dealer. Somewhat like Vince McMahon's XFL, the USFL played its games in the spring and summer, giving football fans an additional season of excitement.

Gordon Solie

Teams like the Houston Gamblers, Memphis Showboats, Washington Federals, and the New Jersey Generals (led by Heisman Trophy winner, Herschel Walker), along with the Bandits, made up some of the twelve teams that ranged from Oakland to Orlando. Tampa was known for their reckless style of play, affectionately known as "Bandit Ball," and had winning seasons in all three years of their existence. It was the opportunity I was looking for and I wasn't about to squander it.

So, with the chance of a lifetime looming large in my immediate future, I decided it was time for me to get serious and head back home. I had been in Atlanta for three months, and even though I was having a good time, I never really felt comfortable there. It was time to stop playing and continue with the commitment I had made so many years earlier.

I was living an enviable lifestyle, but it didn't take a genius to see that it was getting me nowhere. More than that, it was taking me down a path that was nowhere near the one I wanted to be on ... one that would lead me to professional football. It was okay, but it just wasn't for me, so on March 9, my birthday, I packed up the Fleetwood and drove back to Minnesota. I was prepared to work out and focus on my aspirations in pro football until the Tampa Bay tryout was set up for me by Gordon. As far as I was concerned, it was time for me to get serious and to get back to work.

Chapter 6
Ivan Koloff's Nephew

When I arrived back in Minnesota, Brad Lyson, a buddy and workout partner, set me up working as a disc jockey in a small club that had a good business going. The club was divided into two parts; one half being a bar and the other a disco-dance floor. I worked two or three nights a week to give some relief to the other disc jockeys so they wouldn't have to work seven nights a week. The club would close at two in the morning and, with it being in St. Paul, it took me about twenty minutes to get back home. I would get home about three and didn't get to sleep until four or after. It gave me spending money and something to do besides working out as I was preparing for my tryout with the Bandits.

I had been working there for about a month and I was settling into my new routine when my phone rang one morning. In keeping with my regular, late-night routine, I hadn't been asleep very long, and I wasn't happy with whoever it was on the other end of the line. As I answered it, I was preparing to let them know, in no uncertain terms, how I felt about them calling so early. Ready to unload my sleep-deprived-induced wrath, I answer the phone in my most surly and not quite coherent voice. *"What?"*

I heard Joe's voice. *"What are you doing?"*

"I'm sleeping. What do you mean what am I doing?"

"Nah, I mean what are you doing? Are you working, going to school? What?"

"Not much really. I'm working out and trying to get my leg back in shape and make the Bandits."

"Well, if you aren't doing much, what do you think about wrestling?"

"I think what you guys are doing is great, why?"

"No, what I mean is, what do you think about you wrestling?"

"Like me getting in the ring and wrestling? Are you serious? I never thought about it. Give me a day or two to think about it. What exactly would I have to do?"

During that conversation, I was beginning to think, *"You know, if those guys can do it, I can, too. Besides, if it works out, great, and if it doesn't, I still have the tryout with the Bandits."*

Joe continued to tell me that he and Hawk were wrestling in the Carolinas for a promotion based out of Charlotte. The promotion was really catching on fire and they were looking for new talent to develop. When Joe told the promoter, Jim Crockett, about me, he told Joe to contact me.

Jim Crockett Promotions was founded by "Big" Jim Crockett in 1935 as Eastern States Championship Wrestling, a year before Lou Thesz won his first world heavyweight title from Everette Marshall in St. Louis. For nearly forty years, Jim ruled the rings of the Carolinas and Virginia and showcased stars such as George and Sandy Scott, Abe Jacobs, Tim "Mr. Wrestling" Woods, the Kentuckians, George Becker and Johnny Weaver, Brute Bernard and Skull Murphy, the Infernos, and Rip Hawk and Swede Hanson.

When Big Jim retired in 1973, his children took over the business with Jim Crockett Jr. taking the helm as the company president. Changing the name to Mid-Atlantic Championship Wrestling, Jim continued the successful road his father began and, by the early 1980s, the company became one of the most powerful promotions in the world. Jim reached a pinnacle of his profession when he was elected president of the National Wrestling Alliance [NWA] in 1980, which not only gave him the most influential position in the NWA, but also would give him control of the crown jewel of wrestling; the world heavyweight championship. But foremost, he was a promoter, and he had to make sure things were doing well in his core business at home. Like any wrestling promotion, Jim had to keep storylines fresh and new characters in development.

One day, a wrestler named Don Kernodle asked Animal if he knew of anyone who might be interested in wrestling in the Mid-Atlantic territory. He was looking for someone who could come in as Ivan Koloff's nephew and capitalize on the United States Olympic Games boycott. That person would be a new character in the ongoing United States versus the USSR storyline. Don and Sgt. Slaughter came up with the idea one evening while driving from Charleston, South Carolina to Savannah, Georgia. They were always bouncing ideas around and coming up with new angles and ways to keep the territory fresh and the fans excited about what was happening. They also cared deeply about the boys, as well. In fact, if it wasn't for them, there very well may not have been any Road Warriors. Joe had considered quitting a number of times, but it was always Sarge and Don who encouraged him to stick with it.

"I thought of you right away, Scott," Joe continued. *"What do you think? You have the size and the athletic ability. They can teach you the rest. What do you have to lose?"*

I remembered the night in the Omni when I had that fleeting thought of being able to do what Joe was doing. The more Animal tried to persuade me, the more the opportunity intrigued me.

My next question to Joe was, *"Do they know that I don't have any experience? I've never wrestled in my life. I've never been on a mat in high school or college and I certainly have never been in a ring before. Are you sure they wouldn't want someone who has experience?"*

"Don't worry about that, Scott. There is no problem with that. Come on down."

"Okay, Joe. I'll give it a try. What do I need to do?"

"Just call this number in Charlotte. Ask for Jim Crockett and he will tell you the rest."

"Okay, Joe. I'll call him right now. I'll let you know how it goes."

As soon as I hung up the phone, I dialed Jim Crockett Promotions in Charlotte. When Jim came onto the line at his end, I explained who I was. I felt compelled to tell him, *"I told Joe I had no experience in the ring. He said it wouldn't be a problem."*

"What?" Jim replied, *"I was told you had all kinds of experience. I thought you had wrestled for Gagne. Are you kidding me? I need someone who knows what he's doing. I can't believe you would call me and waste your time and mine."*

After ten seconds or so, which, to me, seemed like endless silence as I sat there with the phone pressed to my ear and feeling like a complete moron, Jim said *"Okay, okay. I'll tell you what. I need some new wrestlers down here, anyway. Come on down here and I'll see if I can use you. Can you be in my office on June fourth?"*

"Yes sir," I said, trying not to sound too eager and thinking what a mess it was turning out to be. I also entertained thoughts about how I was going to get even with Animal the next time I saw him. *"No problem. I can be there."*

"Oh! And one more thing, Mr. Simpson," Crockett added. *"Before you get here, have your head shaved."*

Shaving my head was not something I was interested in doing. This took place in May 1984 when I was sporting a kind of disco-feathered-pretty-boy haircut, like the one Shaun Cassidy had on *The Hardy Boys* television show. It looked pretty good (if I do say so myself), and trading my disco look for that reminiscent of Yul Brenner in *Anna and the King of Siam* was not something to which I was looking forward. However, I figured it would grow back if things didn't work out, so I decided to give it a try.

Getting to know Jim as I did in the subsequent years, I learned that our initial conversation regarding my experience (or lack of), was only part of his dry sense of humor coming out. He had been ribbing me, having been told by Animal that I was, indeed, a neophyte, and that I had no idea of what to do in the ring. But he was looking for new talent, and he knew that if I had any athletic ability at all, he could make me into a wrestler and use me in some capacity.

Leaving the club wouldn't be a problem. I was just filling in and they had plenty of time to replace me, but three weeks earlier, I had started another job driving a route for a courier service. I would pick up and deliver small packages and documents from physicians and businesses. The job was fairly easy and I learned my route in less than two days, when, as I had been told, it would normally take someone two weeks or more to commit their routes to memory.

When I walked in and told my boss I was quitting and going into wrestling, he told me he was sorry to hear that I was leaving, but he wished me well. He graciously added that if wrestling didn't work out, I would always have a job with him. I told him how much I appreciated that and I would try to keep in touch.

With those things settled, I figured it was a good time to shave my head and get used to it before I left for the Carolinas. Brad, my friend who got me the job at the night club, was actually the guy who shaved my head. I called him and told him of my plan to become a wrestler. I went over to his apartment and he shaved my head. Now, outside of Telly Savalas and Yul Brenner, there weren't many bald guys around at that time, except for someone's uncle or grandfather, so I suppose I did stand out a bit. I was still filling in at the club and everyone I knew would come up and ask what was going on with my hair, or lack of it. I must say I probably received as many quizzical looks with my answer about my becoming a wrestler as I got when they saw my new haircut.

With all my obligations taken care of, I decided to travel south once again and spend some time in Atlanta with Animal before I had to report in Charlotte. When I got there, Joe had some boots and trunks ready for me. It's funny, but I never gave much thought about getting into the ring or learning about what I was going to do. In retrospect, it probably would have been better to prepare more than I did, but at the time, I didn't know enough to know what I didn't know (if that makes sense). Joe was busy on the road, so I worked out and relaxed for a few weeks.

On the morning of June 5, 1984, I drove up I-85 into the Queen City. It took me a little longer to get there than I expected. As I drove into Charlotte, I saw the city sprawling out to the side of I-85 and began to think I had passed my exit. I pulled off the ramp on Sugarcreek Road and called the Crockett Promotions office. I have always been good at directions and had a feeling that I had driven too far. The receptionist told me to go back to Billy Graham Parkway and that would take me to where I wanted to go.

I was in the best shape of my life up to that time. I had been working out almost every day for 18 months and putting in close to eight hours daily. Due to my regimen for getting ready for the USFL, I had been focused on my weight routine, and due to that, I was in peak shape. I weighed 285 pounds with just eight percent body fat, stood 6-foot-2 with a 34-inch waist, and I had trapezium muscles that reached my ears.

I walked into the lobby, introduced myself to the receptionist, and was brought into Jim's office. He rose to introduce himself and, as he shook my hand, he looked at me almost in disbelief and shook his head back and forth. He took a second look, stepped back, and shook his head again. He kept walking backwards, looking at me, until he bumped against his desk.

"Would you mind taking off your shirt?" he asked.

"No sir," I said, and after I took it off, Crockett looked at me and said rather haltingly, *"Uh ... wait right here."*

Jim hurried out of the office and came back in a few minutes with two of his top stars, Ivan Koloff and Don Kernodle, who held the Mid-Atlantic version of the world tag team championship, and were the top heels, or villains, in the sport at the time. *"Gentlemen,"* Jim announced, *"meet your new partner."*

Don and Ivan looked at me, looked at each other, and seemed to be thinking, *"New partner? Who is this guy?"*

And that was pretty much it. I had the job.

The name Nikita Koloff came about that morning outside Jim's office, as well. I apparently had the look and the job, but somehow, the name Scott Simpson just didn't bode well for the newest immigrant from mother Russia. Jim said *"Okay, we have to think of a name and I think I've got it. Scott will be Ivan's nephew, Nikita. How does that sound?"* They had thought of another name, so I was given the choice between the two. I can't remember what the other name was, but it doesn't matter. Nikita was the one that stuck. *"I like the sound of*

Don Kernodle and Ivan Koloff

that," I said. And with that, Nikita Koloff was born. Not in Russia, but in Charlotte, North Carolina on June 5, 1984.

The reason Jim wanted me to report to Charlotte on June 5 was that it was the day the promotion was cutting promos for the upcoming matches in the territory. The interviews were usually taped in one afternoon and sent to the various towns to be aired on the syndicated wrestling shows. The same matches might be held in Charlotte, Fayetteville, Roanoke, or Spartanburg, but the wrestlers would have to plug the matches, mention the town, their opponents, and the degree of mayhem they were planning to disseminate on those who would dare step into the ring with them.

The taping usually took up an entire afternoon, but it was all done in-house, which was an effective way to save time and money. It was explained to me that the interviews were a central part in any wrestling story, and the better they were, the better we would do. Interviews are the lifeblood of the wrestling industry and are every bit as important as the work in the ring. They bring our characters to life and set the stage for the matches in whatever town we may be appearing on a particular day. The more intense the interview, the more interest there will be in the match, and that, hopefully, will result in a large crowd at the arena.

I don't know any other sport that has a relationship with the fans as wrestling does. The fans love or hate for a wrestler is more personal because they believe they know us. There is nothing between the wrestlers and the fans but a TV camera or a few feet of chairs and some ring ropes.

I was led to the back of the building into a room that was little more than a big warehouse or garage. Jim told me not to say a word; *"All I want you to do is to walk out behind Ivan and Don as they go out on camera, stand behind them, cross your arms, and look as menacing as you possibly can."* Jim asked Ivan to give me the chain he wore around his neck and instructed me, *"Just stare straight ahead and look mean. That's all I want you to do."*

I thought, *"This is great. This I can do."* So far, wrestling wasn't so bad.

We began about ten o'clock and cut interviews for the next five hours. I'm not sure how Vince does interviews now, but Crockett would cut a week or so worth of interviews on Tuesdays in the Jim Crockett Promotions office. Ivan, Don and I didn't do interviews non-stop. We would do one and then one of the other boys would do one. That would take some time since all the boys were there and would have to promote the upcoming towns. Gene Anderson would run the show and would call whoever was up to do their spot. He would tell them the name of the town and what type of match it was. He might call out, *"Blanchard, Philadelphia Civic Center, U.S. title defense, two-out-of-three falls,"* and Tully would get up and do his interview. Gene would then call, *"Don, Ivan, Fayetteville against the Rock 'n' Roll Express, falls count anywhere,"* and we would go up and tout the city and match.

One of the strange things about cutting interviews was the fact that what we were talking about was to air on the upcoming weekend on one of Jim's syndicated shows. Keep in mind that television taping would take place on Wednesday, and so many times, we would be talking about an incident that hadn't yet happened.

We may be setting up a feud with the Four Horsemen that was scheduled to begin on TV during a singles match that would end up in a schmoz. A schmoz is where the match gets out of hand and all the wrestlers run into the ring to aid their teammate or ally. Now, this would happen on Wednesday, but we had to talk about it on Tuesday, the day before it happened, as if it had just happened. The fans tuning in on the weekend could hear the retaliation promo and the revenge that would exacted in whatever town they were in for the upcoming matches. If it sounds a bit confusing; it was, but you would get used to it, and within a week or so, it was a natural as breathing.

Another thing about taping interviews is that nobody got paid for their time, and not only were we expected to be there, but we had no choice. It was a part of the business. We also had to make the interviews work in one take. We were more conscious of the time than Jackie Crockett (the man behind the camera) or Gene were. Interviews were not the only thing going on Tuesdays. We had to wrestle that night, as well, so we had to be on the road by three o'clock; five at the very latest.

After we finished the last spot, Jim walked over to me and said, *"Great job. Oh, by the way, you wrestle tomorrow night in Raleigh. I want you to get there a couple of hours early and work out with Ivan and Don so they can show you a few things."* I agreed and found a small hotel near the airport where a lot of the boys stayed. If you look up "fleabag" in the dictionary, I am sure you would find a picture of the place. I think it was something like $25 a night, which was extremely overpriced considering the accommodations.

I went to sleep thinking of the day's events, both excited and nervous about Raleigh, and wondering if all professional wrestlers were living in such luxury. Tomorrow would come soon enough … and I had no idea of the world that was about to open its doors to me.

Chapter 7

Jesse the Body

As I said earlier, Don Kernodle and Sgt. Slaughter get the credit for coming up with the idea for the Nikita Koloff character. In order to hold the interest of the fans so they continue to line up at the box office to buy tickets, wrestling needs fresh ideas on a regular basis, much like a soap opera.

The idea was this: Don Kernodle, who was wrestling as part of Slaughter's "army," would turn on the "All-American" sergeant and team with the "Russian Bear" [Ivan Koloff]. He would become, in effect, an American turncoat. That would raise the ire of the fans and continue the excitement in the Mid-Atlantic territory. Ivan and Don would then win the world tag team title and bring in Ivan's "nephew" from the Soviet Union. A side story was that the nephew had missed his opportunity to wrestle in the Olympics due to the 1980 boycott. Eventually, this new and solid "Russian" team would then turn on Don, sending him back to Slaughter's army to uphold his honor and that of his country with renewed patriotic spirit. Ivan and his nephew would then take the world tag team title and feud with the American team.

The only thing missing was the nephew.

When they spelled out their scenario to Crockett, he liked the idea and put the wheels into motion. That was the beginning of the story for me, but unfortunately, somewhat of the end of the story for Don.

Slaughter was promised the book by Crockett when I came into the area, but he got a better offer from the WWF and left for New York. His plan was to stay awhile, and after Ivan and I attacked Don and I was established, he would return to save the day and we would all battle for the belts, our respective country's flags, and a dozen of other match ideas. Everything began to go as planned. I was introduced, we built up my character, and we turned on Don. The problem was that

.Don Kernodle and Sgt. Slaughter

Sarge never came back from New York, so there was no part for Don to play in the program. So, instead of being involved in a major program, Don wound up somewhere in mid-card status teaming with his brother, Rocky. I always felt bad about how that happened, but it was just a part of the business. Much to his credit, Don took it in stride, but I still think it was unfortunate the way it all happened.

My first significant view of what wrestling really was all about came from Jesse Ventura. Of course, Jesse needs no introduction to wrestling fans, or the world at large, for that matter. As "The Body," this former Navy Seal gained fame in rings throughout the world and later became one the premier and most knowledgeable broadcasters in the wrestling industry. Since he had been a wrestling fan as a kid, he knew the history of the sport, and that enabled him to compare moves and ring strategies of the 1980s and 1990s to the stars and champions of the past, such as Edouard Carpentier, Omar Atlas, and Butcher and Mad Dog Vachon. He kept the fans interest during his commentating, much as he did in the ring when he was an active competitor.

Jesse Ventura

Ventura's story is the stuff of lore and legend. In case you have been asleep for the past ten years, Jesse became active in local politics and defeated a 25-year incumbent to become mayor of Brooklyn Park, Minnesota. He then shocked the political world by defeating two successful career politicians to become Minnesota's 38th governor. To the electorate, the "Body" became the "Mind," but to those of us who had known him, he had been the "Mind" all along, and those who took him lightly did so at their own peril.

During his active ring days, Jesse ran Ventura's Gym in North Minneapolis, which was a pretty rough part of town. Jesse's gym was no modern spa. It was hard core. It was a sweat box that welcomed only the most serious athletes, and that's where we wanted to be. I can still see Jesse sitting in his chair behind a rickety, old desk when I came in the door. Joe and I were just college kids, but Jesse would talk to us about upcoming matches he was having. He would tell us who he would be wrestling and we would give him things to say about his opponent for his interviews. It wasn't that Jesse needed any help on the microphone. He was one of the best talkers in the wrestling business, but he was always friendly and I think he got a kick out of letting us think we were helping. We would then watch Gagne's show and listen to Jesse's interview to see if he used any of our ideas. From time to time he would, and we would go crazy when we heard him using one of them.

I would work out there two to three times a week. Jesse would stop by from time to time when he returned from the road and he would talk to some of us as we worked out. As we got to know him, he would talk about wrestling. As fascinated as I was, I never gave a passing thought to wrestling as a career until much later.

Now, several years later, when I was about to enter the almost cloistered world of professional wrestling, I began to realize how much of an influence Jesse had been on me, and I never knew it.

Raleigh, North Carolina had always been a great town for wrestling. Throughout the years, fans in the Raleigh-Durham area saw some of the finest wrestlers ever to grace the ring in the Dorton Arena. Dorton Arena, located on the grounds of the North Carolina State Fair, was used to host everything from rodeos to car shows, and, of course, professional wrestling. Dorton was a strange place. It was built in the shape of a horseshoe and was all glass, which meant it had two basic temperatures; Sahara heat and Arctic cold. Matthew Nowicki, of the North Carolina State University, Department of Architecture, designed the building. He must have been crazy. The building may have looked good, but it was terrible to work in no matter what the weather. The dressing rooms were the only thing worse than the temperature. To access them, we had to walk down dark staircases into what looked like a pit. I don't think anyone looked forward to Wednesdays in Raleigh.

Don came by to pick me up and arrived an hour or so late. On the way, Kernodle filled my head with stories of the road and advice on how to handle myself in the ring that night. However, with Don being late, we arrived too late to work out much in the ring. Crockett was furious. When we arrived at the arena, we wound our way through the back door into the dressing room. We hurriedly changed into our wrestling gear and got into the ring. Less than five minutes or so later, someone came out and said, *"Okay, everybody out. We've got to let the people in now."* Don and Ivan had only had time to show me a move or two and how to hit the ropes. I knew just enough to be dangerous to myself and to whomever I was facing in the ring that night.

The dressing room was a "who's who" of wrestling: Harley Race, Ric Flair, Stan Hansen, Michael Hayes, Terry Gordy, Buddy Roberts, Ricky Steamboat, Wahoo McDaniel, Tully Blanchard, King Kong Bundy, and the Road Warriors, among others. They were all sitting around like it was just another day at the office. To them, I'm sure it was, but to me, it was as if I was entering a parallel universe. I wasn't so much in awe because I recognized only a few of the names, but never having really being a fan, I was more impressed with their looks and size than with their reputations.

I began to question my decision about my new profession. I had the size, but I lacked the confidence and the look that seemed to fill the room from every wrestler, from the guys in the opening match (known to the boys as the curtain-jerkers) to the main-event stars. Just the way they carried themselves, laced up their boots, and taped their wrists, reflected the fact that those men were professionals and were serious about why they were in Dorton Arena that night.

It wasn't a normal house show that usually would have six to eight matches with a main event, usually for a title of some sort, but my first entrée' into the ring came on the night of the weekly television taping. Television is the lifeblood of professional wrestling. Without it, the crowds would dwindle to a number that would make it difficult to draw enough money to rent the building, let alone pay the boys.

Wrestling has always been tailor-made for television. In the early days of television in the 1940s and 1950s, networks were always on the lookout for inexpensive programming that would fit the small screen, and professional wrestling fit the bill. Local stations would give the wrestling promoters free television time in trade for the rights to sell the advertising time. The Mid-Atlantic territory had stations reporting a wait list of five years or more to purchase ad time on the local wrestling broadcasts.

Wrestling was also one of the first sports to be broadcast to a national audience. The Dumont Network, as well as others, would broadcast live and taped programs featuring heroes and villains like Lou Thesz, "Nature Boy" Buddy Rogers, Mr. Moto, Antonino Rocca, Verne Gagne, Fritz von Goering, and others. Chicago's Marigold Arena, St. Louis' Chase Hotel, and the Cow Palace in San Francisco, all proudly broadcasted top-name grapplers from coast to coast.

Forty years later, on the night I entered the ring for the first time, things were no different. For more than a decade, the Crocketts taped their television show at the old WRAL, Channel 5 studios in Raleigh on Wednesday mornings. He then sent the various shows to local stations around the Carolinas and Virginia, trading the ad spots for the chance to reach their fans, establish their stars, and draw the faithful to the arenas around the territory.

There was no admission charge and the studio would hold only fifty or so fans in the makeshift bleachers. The ring would take up most of the studio, leaving little room for the fans and the small interview desk. The fans would all be crowded on one side of the ring so when the enormous cameras of the day pulled back to show the crowd, the studio would appear full. The tighter the quarters, the better the effect, and with the cheers and boos echoing throughout the studio, the entire show seemed larger than life.

Somewhere along the way, someone in the Crockett organization realized that with the growing request for free tickets to the tapings, a move to a larger venue and a charge for tickets could prove lucrative. The tapings were moved to Dorton Arena on Wednesday nights, expanded in length, and the registers began to ring at the door.

On the nights of the TV taping, the fans would sit through four to five hours of matches. At times, we found ourselves wrestling two to three times a night, depending on where we were in the pecking order and what program [series of matches with a storyline] we were working in at the time. The matches would then be packaged into hour-long shows with commentary and sent off to various television markets to build interest for our upcoming house shows.

The matches were nothing like the house shows, where each match would be a top star against another. The TV matches would usually be a top star against a lower-tier guy to showcase the star's ability and make him look good. Every now and then, they would put on a match like Jack and Jerry Brisco against Ricky Steamboat and Mark Youngblood to set up a program, but as a rule, each match was a squash.

We would get paid $40 for the TV taping, except for the guys in the "dark match." The "dark match" was a main-event-status match that would take place at the end of the TV taping. It wouldn't be shown on TV and it was a way of thanking the fans for sitting through the hours of misery. The fans would be treated to matches they would have to pay top dollar to see elsewhere. Matches like Ric Flair against Magnum T.A., Ivan and me against the Rock 'n' Roll Express [Ricky Morton and Robert Gibson], and other main event matches of that caliber. If we were picked for the "dark match," we would be paid a lot better, usually a percentage of the gate. But on June 6, 1984, I was a long way from being considered for a "dark match."

Chapter 8

On-the-Job Training

Our five minutes of practice in the ring did nothing more than infuriate Jim all the more. He certainly had a reason to be livid. He was taking a huge chance with me and had already spent most of the previous day establishing my image and building me up to the fans. Now he was faced with the possibility of me completely blowing it in a matter of seconds after I entered the ring.

"That's it," Jim shouted. *"He's out. He doesn't wrestle tonight."* Ivan went to Jim and did his best to calm him and to try to change his mind, but Jim was adamant about his decision. There was no way he was going to let me in the ring, only to see me fall flat on my face, embarrassing not only myself, but Jim Crockett Promotions in the process. To this day, I have no idea what Ivan said to Jim, but whatever he said, it eventually worked. That is just another of the countless things for which I have to thank "Uncle" Ivan.

After meeting with Jim, Ivan came back to the dressing room and said, *"Nikita, it's okay. We're all set, so get ready to go. Just one more thing; be careful getting into the ring. Crockett said if you trip over the ropes getting into the ring, you're finished."*

Great, as if I wasn't worried enough about what I was going to do when I got into the ring, now all I could think about was *how* I was going to get into the ring.

Everything was set, but no one told me when I was scheduled to go to the ring. I sat in the dressing room as the first hour went by, with not much else going on as far as I was concerned. When the second hour of taping began, I walked out with Ivan and Don and stood behind them while they did an interview. On the way back to the dressing room, they informed me that I would be wrestling in the third hour. *"Go out there and pulverize him,"* Ivan told me. *"Do it as fast as you can and finish him with the inverted back-breaker."*

"Oh, yeah," he added. *"Be sure not to trip."* And he grinned.

Every wrestler has, or at least needs to have, a signature hold or move to use as a finisher. A finisher is the move the fans can identify with you, and when they see it applied, they know the match is as good as over. Most of the main-event wrestlers have two or three finishing moves, and many of the great champions of the past, such as Lou Thesz, Buddy Rogers, Gene Kiniski, Dory Funk Jr., and Jack Brisco, had a number of finishing holds they used to win their matches.

The finishers are almost as famous as the men who used them: Verne Gagne had the sleeper hold; Buddy Rogers, Jack Brisco, and Ric Flair used the figure-four leg lock; The Funks had their spinning toehold; Abe Jacobs had the kiwi leg roll; and Rick Rude had the Rude Awakening. Finishers always played on their users strengths; whether it be speed or power. Being billed as this "Russian Nightmare," my signature moves would feature my strength, so I was given the bearhug, the inverted back-breaker, and later, the Russian Sickle. The power moves that were to be my signature in the ring were by no means unique to me. They were used by great champions before me, such as Bruno Sammartino, Ivan Koloff, "Superstar" Billy Graham, Jesse "The Body" Ventura, and the Road Warriors.

So there it was. I knew how to enter the ring, how to hit the ropes, I knew a move or two, and I had a finisher. Not a lot of training for a guy who hardly knew what professional wrestling was just a few days before, but I was ready to go. I set off to enter the ring and what was, unbeknownst to me at the time, a transformation that would become one of the turning points of my life. To my credit (and relief), I did make it into the ring without tripping and falling flat on my face.

Prior to entering the ring, I was told exactly what to expect. I was being "put over" that night. In other words, I was going to win, and in doing so, I was going to be made to look not only credible, but also invincible. My opponent for my inaugural match was a journeyman who wrestled under the name of Barry Hart, and who wrestled occasionally as Brett Hart. Not Bret "The Hitman" Hart, the multi-time world heavyweight champion, but a guy named Barry Horowitz, who actually had quite a career as a jobber. Every now and then, Barry would win a match, but most of the time, his job was to make guys like me look good.

It takes just as much courage and many times as much skill to make someone else look good. You really had to have a love for the sport to accept that particular role in the wrestling business, but without guys like Barry, there would not be a lot of upper tier guys finding their way to the main event.

Barry had an unusual talent in that he was able to reach back behind his head and pat himself on the back. Every time he would make a great move or escape getting pinned, he would pat himself on the back, usually to the mixed cheers and jeers of the crowd. On this particular night, Barry didn't have much time to congratulate himself for much of anything. I did as I was instructed to do. I rushed him at the bell, bent him over facing me, locked my arms around his waist, and lifted him onto my shoulder for the back breaker. Barry succumbed in eleven seconds, a record time for a television victory. Or, at least, that's what I was told. The announcers put me over to the fans in a remarkable fashion: *"Who is this guy? He doesn't talk. He just walks to the ring and destroys Hart. Unbelievable!"*

In retrospect, it's a good thing that my match was a "squash" and that it didn't last longer than eleven seconds. If the match had gone any longer than that, I would have been completely lost. To the fans, I looked like an unbeatable Soviet wrestling machine that had been released onto unsuspecting American wrestler at the height of the cold war, but to me, the eleven-second duration not only launched my wrestling career, it let me get through my first match without screwing it up and completely blowing my gimmick.

My second match lasted a little longer, but I won again in less than a minute. It wasn't a TV taping as the night before. It was a house show, where matches are not videotaped for television, but are held in various towns on a regular (usually weekly) basis. Ticket prices are higher than those for the TV shows, but to the fans, the matches are of a more competitive nature. They usually had two or three preliminary matches, one or two semi-finals, and one or two main events. There were no interviews; just wrestling. That was where the storylines continued to play out and build interest so the fans would return the following week (and buy another ticket) or whenever we appeared again. Prior to the days of pay-per-view, the house shows had always been the bread and butter of the wrestling industry.

From that day on, my training was "on the job." Between working out and traveling from town to town, there was not a lot of time to hone my ring skills. The gimmick of me being indestructible in the ring would work for a period of time, but sooner or later, I would have to join the ranks of the boys doing hour-long broadways [matches that go to a time-limit draw]. So, to increase my wrestling knowledge and to make me feel more comfortable in the ring, Ivan, Don and I would arrive in the towns early and get into the ring for an hour or so.

For the first six weeks, I wrestled early on the cards in matches that would last less than a minute, while Ivan and Don would defend the world tag team championship in the main event. I regularly faced wrestlers like Vinnie Valentino, Paul Kelly, Gary Royal, Mark Fleming, Pinky Larson, and Mike Jackson. Ivan would second me during my match by sitting in the corner, while I, in turn, would sit in Ivan and Don's corner during their match. To the fans, it was a show of solidarity, but it had a much more practical purpose. Ivan watched my match, albeit briefly, to later critique me on what I did well and what I didn't. I sat in their corner to take mental notes and learn the business in the ring from my post on the floor. The solidarity wasn't just a part of the show. I had a lot to learn, and as Yogi Berra once said, *"You can observe a lot just by watching."*

To protect my "invincible" gimmick, Jim Crockett told all my opponents that if they knocked me off of my feet at any time during the match, they would be fired. I wasn't made aware of this until sometime later when I ran into Gene Ligon after he retired from the ring. He told me about Crockett's directive as he recalled our first match, which took place in Columbia, South Carolina, on June 17. He had worked me into a corner of the ring and used a Beell Throw to send me flying across the ring. *"Oh, no,"* Gene thought, as he watched me sail through the air. *"I'm fired."* Gene kept his job, though, and we had a good laugh about it years later.

The Beell Throw is about as basic a move as a headlock. To do it, with both you and your opponent facing the same direction, your opponent hooks his arm underneath yours and behind your back, with his hand resting on the back of your shoulder. He then steps forward and uses his hip as leverage to send you flying. As with many of the fundamental moves, the hip toss finds its origins in the hallowed history of the sport. In this case, the move is attributed to Fred Beell, who wrestled during the turn of the 20th century. What made Fred so amazing was that he was one of the very few wrestlers who ever took a fall from the celebrated Frank Gotch, let alone defeat him in a match.

That is the substance of legends. Beell defeated Gotch on December, 1, 1906 in New Orleans. When Gotch entered the ring to face Beell that night, he was riding high after regaining the American heavyweight title from Tom Jenkins. Beell weighed 169 pounds, while the champion tipped the scales at 202 pounds. Having won all but seven of his previous 84 matches, there was no doubt that Gotch was the heavy favorite.

It was apparent early in the match that Frank had taken Fred somewhat lightly and played around with him before taking the first fall in 31 minutes, 22 seconds. During the second fall, Beell caught the champion napping and used his signature move to hurl the champion across the ring. Gotch landed off the mat in the process and hit his head, making him easy prey for the pin a short time later.

In the third fall, Gotch was "easy pickings" for the challenger. Beell, the Iowa farm boy, pinned Gotch with a half-nelson in five minutes, taking the coveted American championship (which later would be unified with the world title after Gotch won the belt from George Hackenschmidt) and enough money from side bets to make him independently wealthy. Sixteen days later, Gotch got his revenge in Kansas City, Missouri, by defeating the Wisconsin woodchopper decisively. A headline that shook the world in 1906 became nothing more than a footnote in wrestling history in the 1980s, but what a great story.

It wasn't long before the fans were clamoring for me to show my wrestling skills against more adept competition. The Mid-Atlantic territory was full of great wrestlers, but my invincibility in the ring had to be protected as they built towards me challenging Ric Flair for the NWA world title. My first appearance in a main event was in Conway, South Carolina, teaming with Don Kernodle to face the Renegade [JayYoungblood] and Mark Youngblood. I knew I was in good hands in the ring with Ivan, Jay and Mark, but I was still nervous going into the main event.

Nikita and Ivan Koloff

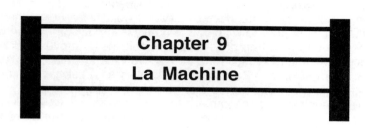

Chapter 9
La Machine

Ivan and Don were the world tag team champions when I arrived in the Carolinas. They won the belts from the popular team of Wahoo McDaniel and Mark Youngblood in Richmond, Virginia on May 8, 1984. There were, of course, other titles in the Mid-Atlantic territory.

As hard as it may be to conceive, there were a number of versions of "world" tag team titles, and since cable television, the Internet, and national coverage of professional wrestling was yet to be instituted, only fans who read the magazines were the wiser, and even then, they seemed not to care very much, if at all.

The world tag team title is the apex of any tag team's career, no matter what promotion they may have been working for at the time. Back in the day when the National Wrestling Alliance had more than 30 territories, many territories had a version of the title. They all ascribed to one NWA world heavyweight champion and had use of his time in their territories so many days a year, but to draw local fans to the arenas each week, regional titles were created, along with various versions of the United States heavyweight and world tag team titles.

The earliest version of the world tag team title I am aware of was the San Francisco version won by Ray Eckert and Hard Boiled Haggerty in April 1950. Not to be outdone by the west coast, Chicago instituted their own version by billing Lord Athol Layton and Lord James Blears as champions upon their arrival in the area. This was done frequently in order to save time with a tournament. Other promotions would report a fictitious tournament held in some far-off city to establish not only the title, but the credibility, as well.

The Chicago version was well known as matches from its famous Marigold Arena were broadcast throughout the country. As wrestling in the south grew, they needed to establish their own version of the title, so Art Neilson and Reggie Lisowski (later known as the "Crusher," the wrestler who made Milwaukee famous) made trips to Atlanta in 1954 and 1955 and eventually dropped the belts to Fred and Bill Blassie. They also lost "their title" a short time later in Moline, Illinois to future NWA world heavyweight champion Pat O'Connor and Roy McClarity, thus establishing new champions below the Mason-Dixon line and keeping the lineage of the Chicago title intact.

With the world tag team title doing great business in Georgia, promoter Nick Gulas was not to be outdone. In February 1957, he crowned Corsica Joe and

Corsica Jean as his champions and had them defend their belts in Tennessee, Kentucky, and Alabama.

That must have been the year for crowning new world tag team champions. In addition to Tennessee and Alabama, Verne Gagne and Wilbur Snyder were announced as the Texas version of the world tag team champions in July 1957. The Texas version probably has the most individual world heavyweight champions holding the tag belts prior to winning the heavyweight title, including Gagne and Snyder, Bill Longson, Fritz and Kerry von Erich, the Destroyer [Dick Beyer], Nick Bockwinkel, and Dory and Terry Funk. A few months later, Los Angeles saw the German duo of Hans Schmidt and Hans Herman wreak havoc throughout the Los Angeles area. It seemed that nearly every major promotion in the country had world tag team champions to draw in fans, except for New York. Early in 1957, the world tag champions from Tennessee, Jackie and Don Fargo, traveled to New York to face the United States tag team champions, Antonino Rocca and Miguel Perez. The Fargos "lost" the title to the fan favorites in the "Big Apple" on March 30. Of course, they returned to Nashville with the belts still in hand as if nothing had ever happened.

Other world tag team champions would follow as well. Ernie and Emil Dusek held the Central States version of the title in 1958, and in 1959, the team known as "Murder Incorporated," Tiny Mills and Stan Kowalski, reportedly won the first American Wrestling Association's world tag team title while on a tour of Japan. Florida promoted the German team of Kurt and Karl von Brauner as their world tag team champions in 1961, while Detroit followed suit with Chris and John Tolos in 1964. I'm sure there were others, but it gives a good idea of how the world tag team championship was established and the importance of the title wherever it was established.

Ironically, the title Ivan and Don were defending, and the one I would eventually win, didn't come into being until 1975. However, it would eventually become the one recognized as the true title.

The Crockett version of the title grew out of the territories' major tag-team title, the Atlantic Coast tag team championship, later to be renamed the Mid-Atlantic tag team title.

The roots of the Mid-Atlantic tag team title go back to 1954 when Jack and George Curtis were declared the NWA Southern tag team champions. During the next fifteen years, the title traded hands 33 times until Rip Hawk and Swede Hanson arrived in 1969 with their "newly-won" Atlantic Coast tag team championship. After Johnny Weaver and George Becker took the belts from Hawk and Hanson on May 1, 1969, the Southern title quietly disappeared from sight and the Atlantic Coast title became the main tag-team title in the Carolinas.

In January 1975, Ole and Gene Anderson announced they had won a tournament for the vacated world tag team title in California and then defeated Paul Jones and Tiger Conway Jr. in Greensboro for the Mid-Atlantic tag team title, thus unifying the belts and making the world tag team championship the main title in the Charlotte territory. That was the first major title to be defended regularly in the Carolinas. There is no doubt that "world tag team title" sounded much better than Mid-Atlantic or Southern tag team title, and even though it was just a regional title, the importance it carried in the fans' minds was second only to Flair's belt. In the '50s, fans in the Carolinas had seen occasional defenses of the Chicago version of the world tag title, but now they had a world title of their own. It would serve to be the springboard to all the major NWA titles within a few short years.

When I arrived in the Mid-Atlantic territory in 1984, other titles beside the world tag team title were the United States heavyweight title, the NWA television title [renamed the NWA world television title in 1985], the Mid-Atlantic heavyweight title, and a few other minor regional titles.

"Nature Boy" Ric Flair was in his fourth reign as world champion and, being the world champion, he was required to defend his belt in rings in territories across the country and around the world. Since the formation of the National Wrestling Alliance in 1948, various promoters throughout the world paid an annual membership fee and, in return, were allowed to operate under the NWA banner and have the use of the world heavyweight champion a certain number of days a year. Due to the contractual obligations of the NWA, the champion had to leave his home territory and defend his laurels against local contenders wherever the NWA logo was on display.

Championship matches have always been the pinnacle of the sport of wrestling. From the days of Frank Gotch and George Hackenschmidt to the modern era of Triple H, Kurt Angle, and the Rock, the supremacy in the ring transcends the sport itself. Whether it be in boxing or wrestling, the man who carries the belt is emblematic of the world champion, and the champion of the world can attract attention and draw interest like no other athlete.

In fact the world heavyweight wrestling championship has been so popular in the past that on one particular night in the 1930s, eight different matches were held in eight different cities across the country for the title.

Early promoters knew the value of the world title. The name value alone would draw far more money at the gate than that on any card without the world title on the line. The conventional thought of the day was, why promote just one world title when you could promote a number of different world heavyweight titles? The press of the day didn't carry much on wrestling and there was no national cable or internet, so each regional world title could thrive and the fans would be unaware of the subterfuge. If you think that sounds strange, take a look at the number of world heavyweight boxing champions there are today.

Wrestling remained in a state of disarray until the incomparable Lou Thesz went on tour in the early 1950s with a quest to unify the heavyweight title. At the time, there were a number of promotions that laid claim to the title. Lou unified two of them by defeating Gorgeous George and Baron Michele Leone. Lou remained the champion for most of the next two decades.

Lou's singular reign as world heavyweight champion didn't last long, however. In 1957, the championship puzzle began to unravel when Lou lost a controversial decision on a disqualification to Edouard Carpentier in Chicago. Lou was doing a favor for an old friend, Fred Kohler, by putting Carpentier over to help build Fred's territory with a world champion of his own. Carpentier, claiming the title, toured the country and lost his belt to Killer Kowalski in Boston, Verne Gagne in Omaha, and the Destroyer in Los Angeles. In the mean time, the National Wrestling Alliance returned the title to Lou, citing the title could not change hands on a disqualification. In a matter of months, the title went from one claimant to four.

While the other world champions were busy defending their titles, which were actually no more than regional titles, Lou was defending the title of lineage, finally dropping the belt in Toronto to three-time NCAA champion from Oklahoma A&M, Dick Hutton. It had been twenty years since Lou had first won the belt and he was ready for his tenure as champion to come to an end. The consummate champion, he won the title for the first time when he defeated Everette Marshall in St. Louis on December 27, 1936 at the age of 21. St. Louis was also the site of his sixth and last reign as champion when he lost the title to Gene Kiniski on January 7, 1966.

As great a wrestler as Dick was, he had a less-than-spectacular run with the title and kept it for fourteen months before dropping it to New Zealand's Pat O'Connor on January 9, 1959.

Meanwhile, Verne Gagne, who had defeated Carpentier in Nebraska, had been defending his title in the Omaha territory and had been issuing challenges to the reigning NWA champions, Thesz, Hutton, and O'Connor, respectively. But Gagne's challenges fell on deaf ears. Thesz had defeated Gagne a number of times when Verne was the NWA world junior heavyweight champion, and as hard as Verne tried, he could not secure a title match with Hutton or O'Connor.

Interestingly enough, Hutton and Gagne had met twice before on NCAA mats. Hutton won the first match, while Verne shocked the amateur wrestling world by winning a close decision to take the collegiate crown the following year, denying Dick the honor of being the first man to win the NCAA title four times.

Gagne issued a challenge to then champion Pat O'Connor to meet him within 90 days from the receipt of the challenge or forfeit the title to the Minnesota athlete. Of course, the NWA had no intention of meeting the demands of a rogue promotion and risking the chance of being double crossed for the belt in one of Verne's Midwest venues. When the time period elapsed, the AWA pulled its recognition from O'Connor, Gagne claimed the world title by default, and created the American Wrestling Association in August 1960. It's a shame the match never was made, world title or not. Politics of the day denied the fans of what could have been one of the greatest matchups of all time.

Once again, the wrestling world had two world heavyweight champions, both claiming the title in major territories. There were other claimants, as well, but their claim on the lineage of the title was as weak as their respective territories. That is, of course, until the WWWF created its own champion with "Nature Boy" Buddy Rogers as their first champion in 1963.

The American Wrestling Association world heavyweight title traded hands rapidly, citing 17 title changes within its first five years, and titleholders reads like a Who's Who, including future NWA world heavyweight champion Gene Kiniski, Dr. Bill Miller (who wrestled under a mask as Mr. M), the Crusher, Fritz von Erich, Mad Dog Vachon, and Dr. X (amateur star Dick Beyer, who had a tremendous career as the Intelligent, Sensational Destroyer). Mat greats such as Dick the Bruiser, Nick Bockwinkel, Jumbo Tsuruta, Rick Martel, Stan Hansen, my old friend Curt Hennig, Jerry Lawler, Larry Zbyszko, and Mr. Saito also brought honor and prestige to the belt. Even German promoter and European champion Otto Wanz held Verne's belt, even though it was for a little more than a month. He was probably the first world heavyweight champion to wear lederhosen. Verne, of course, always regained his belt, and controlled the promotion successfully for thirty years, holding the title ten times and retiring as champion in 1981.

When Vince McMahon began putting together his national promotion, he made raids on rival promotions. Verne had quite a stable of wrestlers at that time, and it was from the AWA where Vince got some of his best talent, convincing Jesse Ventura, Hulk Hogan, and Curt Hennig, among others, to leave Verne and join the World Wrestling Federation.

The third major claimant to the world heavyweight title was Bruno Sammartino, the Italian powerhouse who held onto the WWWF version of the world heavyweight title for more than eight years. That version of the title had changed hands eleven times by the time I first entered the ring.

With three champions defending their particular version of the world title, business was doing well. That system worked well for decades, but times were beginning to change. We were focused in on what we were doing with Crockett, rather than what Verne or Vince were doing elsewhere. We thought we were indestructible and the others were "also-rans." I guess we should have been paying more attention as events in the future would show. Little did we know that we were sitting ringside to the complete upheaval and transformation of the wrestling industry ... but more on that later.

During the years 1985 to 1987, Jim Crockett bought out several other NWA territories. Since he was the elected president of the NWA, he believed it would be as easy to control other parts of the country as it was to control the world title. So, with his world champion on the road, it was all the more important that other titles be created, won, and defended. There is something about the allure of a title, whether it be a world, regional, state, or neighborhood belt, that draws the fans interest far more than a match featuring two wrestlers with nothing but pride at stake. It makes the match all the more interesting and draws bigger crowds because, no matter who the fans are rooting for, they all hope they might be at ringside to witness a title belt changing hands.

Since Crockett's top draw was the world heavyweight champion, the other titles all were raised up a notch in importance. They were promoted and drew in the crowds throughout the Carolinas and Virginia.

But again, I was still a long way off from winning a belt — any belt — so I knew that if I was to make a go of wrestling and reach any kind of main event status, I needed to learn quickly. I was fortunate that all this was transpiring when I began wrestling because, not only did it give me a window of opportunity in the ring, but the access to the knowledge and experience that Ivan and Don had accumulated throughout the years. I couldn't have asked for better tutors or friends.

As I stated before, most of my training was on the job with Ivan and Don. In the car after the matches, the three of us would talk and they would critique my matches and offer suggestions. In turn, I would question them about why they did certain things during their matches. They would explain to me not only why they did what they did in the ring, but the psychology behind it and how it fit into the story they were telling.

Unbeknownst to me, I was receiving an accelerated tutorial of the wrestling business that was second to none, one which would prove invaluable to me for the rest of my career. My wrestling training may have been unorthodox, but it couldn't have been better.

In retrospect, I wouldn't have traded all my hours in the car with Ivan and Don for ten times the number of hours in the WCW Power Plant or any other more traditional training facilities. Many great athletes who went through their programs have done well and have gone on to outstanding careers in the ring, but I had the advantage of having the sole attention of two of the finest wrestlers of my time.

Don Kernodle came to the sport by way of the amateur ranks in high school and Elon College, where he excelled on the mat and as an arm wrestler. He had dreamed of being a wrestler since he was a boy, and as soon as he had the chance, he joined the Mid-Atlantic roster and was trained by the "Minnesota Wrecking Crew," Ole and Gene Anderson.

His first match, which took place in 1973, is one that is still talked about today. The story goes that he faced amateur and professional champion Bob Roop. Bob was accomplished; not only on the mat in world competition, but he had been on the pro circuit for years and more than knew his way around the ring. Gene Anderson would set up a lot of the boys' first matches and, if they were matched with Bob, Gene would tell Bob to stretch them a bit. By this, I mean Bob was supposed to work them over and apply legitimate pressure to holds to make them squirm. I'm not sure if it was to see if the new guy could take it, or just a joke Gene enjoyed having, but more than one of the novice grapplers leaped into the ring and limped out at the

Don Kernodle [1972]

end of the match. But, as the tale is told, Don hung in there with Bob and lasted longer than most in their first match. In doing so, he gained the respect of Bob and all the boys in the dressing room. In fact, years later, Bob told Don that if he had lasted another thirty seconds, Don might have pinned him.

Don was instrumental in my career, as well, and I owe him a tremendous debt of gratitude. Without him, there never would have been a Nikita Koloff.

In the world of professional wrestling, Ivan was portrayed as my uncle. Since then, one of the most frequently asked questions has been, *"Is Ivan Koloff really your uncle?"* I would always answer, *"No,"* but I would quickly add, *"but he should have been."* I am proud and honored to say without any reservation that Ivan was, and is, as much of an uncle to me as anyone ever had. I cannot imagine, even in my wildest dreams, having a better friend, mentor, or confidant than Ivan Koloff. He was, without a doubt, the man who taught me the business and how to be a success.

My "Uncle" Ivan, the "Russian Bear" is actually from Quebec, where he was born of Russian decent. He began his wrestling career under the name of Jim Parris and later Red McNulty (due to his red hair). Interestingly, Ivan tells of his first match being against Bruno Sammartino, the man he would defeat for the WWWF world heavyweight title years later. Becoming Ivan Koloff in 1967, he wrestled out of Canada, headlining main events in Toronto's Maple Leaf Gardens in 1968 and challenging then NWA world heavyweight champion, Dory Funk Jr. Experiencing success everywhere he wrestled, Ivan moved on to the World Wide Wrestling Federation [WWWF]. Ivan was the ultimate heel and fit into the scenario for promoter Vince McMahon Sr. He sent shock waves throughout the wrestling world when he defeated the "unbeatable" champion, Bruno

Sammartino, in Madison Square Garden on Monday night, January 18, 1971, ending Bruno's eight-year reign as WWWF heavyweight champion and stopping the number of successful title defenses at 110.

One of the most interesting things about Ivan's defeat of Sammartino was that it came cleanly in the middle of the ring. There was no interference, illegal tactics, or any kind of skullduggery involved. Ivan positioned Bruno on the mat, climbed the turnbuckle, landed a knee-drop across the Italian's neck, and pinned him at the 14:55 minute mark.

Ivan Koloff [1968]

According to Ivan, after the referee, Dick Kroll, slapped the mat for the third time, the crowd became deathly silent. They could not believe what they had just witnessed. Bruno tells the tale that after Kroll counted him out, and the crowd sat in solemn disbelief, he thought he had gone deaf. Not hearing the crowd's boisterous reaction at the Garden as he was used to, he thought Ivan's knee-drop had rendered him unable to hear. After a few minutes, Sammartino's manager, Arnold Skaaland, entered the ring and called out to Bruno to see if he was all right. Bruno heard Arnold's voice, but nothing else. It was only then that he realized he hadn't lost his hearing. He had just left the fans in the packed Garden speechless.

The silence didn't last long, however. As Ivan was announced as the new champion and his hand was raised, the fans began to riot and Ivan had to be escorted back to the dressing room by "New York's Finest," where he was awarded the title and the belt.

Ivan didn't keep the belt, long, however. Twenty-one days later, he lost the title to popular Puerto Rican star, Pedro Morales, in front of a record-breaking crowd in the Garden. Ivan later moved on to challenge Verne Gagne for his AWA "world" title and traveled throughout the world, drawing tremendous crowds and winning more than 30 titles during his career.

Ivan also holds an honor that I am not sure he is aware of even today. He is one of the only, perhaps the only wrestler, I have never heard a bad word about by anyone in the business. He was kind to everyone and treated everyone with respect — from the guys who set up the ring to the most established stars. He was, and is, a true gentleman.

He was known to the boys as La Machine. He could just go and go and hardly break a sweat. He would be in the dressing room before a match doing sit-ups, squats, and push-ups, and then after the match, he would do them all again. There were times I would look at him and say, *"Ivan, please stop. You're wearing me out just watching you."*

One night in Indiana, we were staying on the seventh floor of some hotel and we had arrived too late to get to a gym. I remember it was freezing outside and we had nowhere to work out. I thought I would take some time off and relax in my room. I went to find Ivan to tell him and knocked on his door, but there was no answer. I was thinking, *"Where the heck is Ivan?"* As I stepped out into the stairwell, there was Ivan ... running up and down seven flights of stairs.

"What are you doing?" I asked

"Just trying to keep in shape," he said, as he headed down the stairs for another round.

He was the consummate professional both in and out of the ring. More than that, "Uncle" Ivan will always be the champion to me. He was my uncle in every sense of the word. Wrestling fans worldwide remember him as a heel, or villain, in the ring, and selling his character as the "Russian Bear" was as important as the mayhem he caused within the confines of the ropes. In reality, nothing could have been further from the truth. Ivan is the kindest, most generous, and most gentle soul I have ever had the pleasure to meet. I could never give his kindness its due. To help you better understand, take Ivan's character in the ring and turn it inside out … and you have the real Ivan Koloff.

"Uncle Ivan wants you!"

Chapter 10
The Language Barrier

Heels, or "bad guys," in wrestling are every bit as important as the heroes, or "babyfaces," and the titles for which they battle. Wrestling is a sort of muscle morality play. It is a continuous story portrayed in a ring, rather than on a stage or movie screen. Watching wrestling is not that much different than watching Henry V, King Lear, or Hamlet. All the same elements are there: heroes, villains, intrigue, hope, expectations, and triumph.

Throughout history, the same thing that brought people to plays and movies brought legions of fans to local auditoriums, areas, gyms, and athletic clubs to watch the stories played out in the ring. This does not in any way diminish the athleticism or physicality of the sport. It just goes to underscore the success of the phenomena of professional wrestling. Promoters have known this since the first person bought the first ticket to witness a match. Joe Stecher knew it, "Strangler" Lewis knew it, and so did Sam Muchnick and Jim Crockett. Most of all Vince McMahon Sr. knew it, and his son, Vince McMahon Jr., knows it most of all.

Without heels, the brutal ballet in the ring would be one-sided. Long gone are the days when two babyfaces meet each other in the ring for grappling superiority. From time to time, there is the exception when two scientific wrestlers face each other with a thirty to 60-minute time-limit broadway [draw].

From the early days of the sport, fans would delight to see Thesz, Rogers, Funk, Brisco, Race, Flair, or any number of their local favorites, go an hour or so defending a title or trying to capture one. But it always seemed to capture more attention and draw larger crowds if there was more of a morality play at stake. Good versus evil. That's why, most of the time, a heel champion keeps the title longer than a babyface. The fans sympathize more with a hero trying to capture a belt from a heel than a heel trying to take the strap from their hero. There are some exceptions, like Bruno Sammartino and Hulk Hogan's runs, but they serve as the exception, rather than the rule.

I was hired to be a heel. Not just any heel, but the invulnerable Soviet wrestling machine that not only was going to win the world title, but take it home to "Mother Russia" … never to return. But I had a lot to learn and a long row to hoe to get the fans to believe the "Russian Nightmare" was real.

One's wrestling persona or character may come from a number of places. In most cases, the promoters come up with the name and the character as Don, Ivan, and Jim Crockett did with me. In some cases, the boys hit on an idea that goes over and the promotion agrees to go with it, as with "Stone Cold" Steve Austin. But no matter where it comes from, it is up to the wrestler to internalize it and make sure it gets over with the fans.

Nikita Koloff, at the time, was pretty much an extension of who I was. As my story went, I was portrayed as a Russian athlete just off the plane from Moscow where I have been training my entire life to take the Olympic Gold Medal in freestyle wrestling in the 1980 games, as well as weight lifting and track and field. But due to the political climate, and as the cold war raged on, the Soviet Union boycotted the Olympic Games that year, leaving me to wait another four years to complete my goal.

Undaunted by world events, but impatient at the political process, I turned my sights to a different gold medal; the most coveted prize in all of sports, the heavyweight title of the world and the belt that accompanied it. As soon as I won the title, I would return to the Fatherland, never to grace American soil or their rings again. Eventually, after I won the world tag team title and the world six-man tag team title, the world heavyweight title would be all I lacked. Ivan would say something along the lines of, *"The streets of Moscow will be paved with gold. The Kremlin will be well pleased."*

To continue the build-up of my apparent invincibility, along with my "squash" matches and my menacing glare, Crockett promotions set up five-minute vignettes of me working out in a Spartan workout room, dubbed the "dungeon," that would air on all his syndicated shows. The Dungeon, patterned after Mickey Goldmill's gym in the original *Rocky* film, was always announced that it was located in an undisclosed location, but it was actually in the corner of the interview room in the rear of Jim Crockett Promotions office.

We painted the walls black, brought in some old red lockers and set them in the corner, and hung the flag of the Soviet Union on the wall. There was a single, naked light bulb hanging down on a frayed cord, giving the only light and casting eerie and sinister shadows. The equipment was old and worn, as well. Free weights, an old bench-press bench, and an old heavy-bag with a picture of the "Nature Boy" taped on the center.

Jim aired weekly segments for the six weeks prior to my first meeting with Flair at the Great American Bash in Charlotte on July 6, 1985. Each week, Ivan walked up to David Crockett during someone's interview and interrupted, saying he wanted to show the latest film of his "nephew" Nikita working out, preparing to meet the world champion. David adamantly stated there was no way the tape would be shown. Of course, they would run the tape and Crockett would be aghast that the film was being shown.

Each week, the Dungeon segment would show me working out in one particular routine or another. One week, I would be doing bench-presses, the next week, working on my neck, and the following week, I'd be doing curls. The next would show me "sharpening" my Russian Sickle — my clothesline finishing move — by hitting the heavy bag across Flair's picture. At the end of each segment, I would look menacingly at the camera and growl in my best broken English, *"Ric Flair ... I going destroy you,"* as the picture faded to black.

David would sputter, saying he didn't see how we were able to show that spot, and how we must have paid someone off to run the segment. He would then speculate that we could be facing the worst scenario in the history of mankind. Nikita Koloff was one-half of the world tag-team champions and held

Ivan and Nikita in the Dungeon

one-third of the world six-man tag-team title, and if he was successful at the Great American Bash, he will have all the gold. And if that happens, it will bring his plan to fruition; He will return to Moscow with three world titles, never to return.

Kayfabe is an old carnival term that means to keep secret. Whatever is considered kayfabe is inside information and is not to be shared with those outside the business. In fact, a lot of wrestling jargon is derived from "carny" talk, and rightfully so. Much of the sport we have come to know as professional wrestling has evolved from the old carnival athletic or "AT shows" from the 1920s and 1930s which were held in the confines of the musty tents pitched at the outskirts of towns scattered across America.

In keeping with the tradition of kayfabe, and to make sure my character "got over" with the fans, I all but eradicated Scott Simpson and became, for all practical purposes, Nikita Koloff. To accomplish this, I didn't speak English anywhere. Well, almost anywhere. I did speak English in the car with Ivan and Don as they continued my education, but not anywhere else. Not in a restaurant after a match, not in the gym, and not even in the dressing room prior to matches.

I decided that if I was going to become Nikita Koloff, then I had to be Nikita Koloff constantly. In fact, the best testament of my commitment to my new identity came shortly after I moved to Charlotte. As I was setting up housekeeping, Ivan drove me around town, "translating" for me as I signed the lease to my apartment, signed my contract with Duke Power, BellSouth, and anything else I needed. He would co-sign all of my contracts and would assist with the language barrier, albeit imaginary as it was.

The crown jewel of my transformation occurred when I took out my initial membership at Gold's Gym in Charlotte. A lot of the boys worked out there and the staff was friendly and knowledgeable. We could work out there without any distractions or having people bother us while we were lifting weights.

When I decided to join, Ivan went with me to co-sign for my membership and "interpret for me." In his own rather broken English, Ivan explained to Roger, the manager, that I was new to the country. Having just arrived from Moscow, I didn't speak English as of yet. The manager said that wouldn't present any problem as far as he could see and that he would keep an eye out for me in case I needed any help. I just stood there, acting like I was trying to understand a word here or there, and looking around the gym with a critical eye, nodding occasionally and muttering my approval. From time to time, I would interrupt Ivan and ask him a question in "Russian," to which he would respond in kind. Or I would make a comment and he would respond and we would both laugh. Kind of the Soviet version of Rowan and Martin, I suppose.

I was already in the gym working out when the owner walked in, took a look at me, and remarked *"Man, I'm going to have to double the price of your membership. You're too big to work out in this gym."* I, of course, just glared at him with the same stare I honed from the first day on camera. I just let out a guttural *"ughh"* and walked away, shaking my head. The message was clear; I was not a man in which to be trifled.

The owner must have gotten ticked off because as soon as I walked away, he went directly to the manager and asked, *"What is this guy, some kind of jerk?"* The manager quickly explained that I was new to America and that I couldn't speak English. I guess the owner must have felt sorry for me because he calmed down and never said another word.

As I recall, I paid $25 for the first month's membership, but being on the road as much as I was, I inadvertently let more than a few months slip by without paying my dues. Strange as it seems, no one ever approached me for the money I owed, no matter how often I worked out in the gym. In retrospect, I think that part of the management's apprehension in approaching me came from how effectively I put over my character. I believe that everyone was a bit afraid to come up and talk to me.

The people who watched wrestling would see me, week after week, destroying every opponent who dared to enter the ring with me. They saw footage of me training alone in the dungeon and then walking into Gold's for more. If that wasn't enough to hold them at bay, they would see me strangle my opponent as I hung them over the top rope with my chain around their neck. I guess they figured I wasn't the kind of man you should readily ask for money. And so it went.

Eventually, Roger mustered enough courage to approach me and said, *"Nik-i-ta."* He stopped and scratched his head as if he was thinking, *"How do I say this,"* and continued: *"We need mon-ey. Mon-ey, mem-ber-ship."* As he was speaking, he kept rubbing his thumb over the tips of his four fingers, like it was some international sign for money.

That would happen to me frequently when people tried to communicate with me. I never understood why people think that if they spoke slowly, and broke up the English words into as many syllables as possible, that those they were speaking to could somehow understand the foreign language that they couldn't comprehend before. What a brilliant breakthrough. If only Berlitz had thought of this when he opened his first language school in 1878.

All through Roger's effort of trying to bridge the language gap, I just kept giving him a quizzical look. I would tilt my head from side to side, like a puppy trying to understand its' master's instructions. I would carry on this charade for a long as I could without a smile creeping across my face, which was about ten minutes or so. I would then walk away, stifling my laughter as I left Roger wading knee deep in frustration.

The next time I was there, the owner was waiting for me, deciding that he might be able to succeed where Roger had failed. He came up to me and repeated almost word for word what Roger had said only days before, complete with the hand gestures. *"Nik-i-ta, we need mon-ey for mem-ber-ship, mon-ey."* Again, I responded with my quizzical look and shook my head, indicating my total lack of understanding.

Peter then tried a new tact. *"Nik-i-ta, can you bring in I-van to-mor-row. Bring in your unc-le I-van to-mor-row."*

"I-van," I repeated. *"Da-da, I-van,"* meaning *"Yes, yes. Ivan."* I was showing him that I finally understood something from all his efforts. *"Yes, Uncle Ivan,"* he said. He was smiling as he believed he had broken the language barrier. I don't believe Peter could have been happier if he had negotiated Détente and won the Nobel Peace Prize. I walked off repeating, *"Da, da, Ivan,"* while Roger walked away with new-found bilingual skills and confident that he would soon see some money. I did come back the next day with Ivan and paid what I owed.

I knew that "Da" meant "yes" in Russian and I also knew that if I was to be convincing as a Russian, I would have to learn as many words in Russian as possible. The faux-Russian I was speaking would only get me so far. Sooner or later, a fan with even the most rudimentary knowledge of the Russian language would know I was speaking gibberish, and that being the case, chances were good that I wasn't Russian. So I bought an English-Russian workbook and began to teach myself Russian vocabulary. I knew I was safe with the vocabulary as I figured I, more than likely, wouldn't have to converse in Russian any time soon.

I transformed myself into Nikita Koloff so well that an old buddy of mine from Minnesota, Barry Darsow, was completely taken in by it.

Barry and I met in high school and became fast friends. Barry entered the wrestling business a few years before I did and was wrestling for Bill Watts in the Louisiana territory during the time I made my debut in the Carolinas. Barry had taken on a Russian partner named Nikolai Volkoff [Josip Nikolai Peruzovic] and was an American turncoat, much like Don Kernodle was in the Carolinas. Barry would later become Krusher Khrushchev when we brought him into Crockett's territory to be our tag team partner.

Barry had heard via the dressing room grapevine that Jim Crockett had actually gone to the Soviet Union and brought back a "shooting" Russian to challenge Flair for the world title. A shoot in wrestling vernacular means an actual contest. A "shooter," or "pistol man," is a professional wrestler who can actually wrestle. The term shooter brings up images of Jack Brisco, Lou Thesz, Verne Gagne,

Bob Backlund, Tim Woods, and Danny Hodge, as well as modern-day wrestlers like Kurt Angle, Brock Lesnar, Steve Williams, Mike Rotundo, Dan Severn, and Ken Shamrock. That isn't to say a lot of the other boys who didn't have a "shooting" background aren't tough. The ring has seen some of the greatest athletes that ever lived, even those who didn't have an amateur wrestling background. Just ask anyone who has wrestled Dory Funk Jr., Harley Race, "Superstar" Billy Graham, or Triple H.

But a "shooter" is in a different class, and beyond them in the pecking order are the "hookers." A "hooker" is a man like Thesz, Joe Stecher, Frank Gotch, or Billy Robinson (who learned his craft at the legendary and infamous Snakepit in Wigan, England). The boys hold "shooters" in high regard, so any word that a "shooter" has entered the business always gives one pause, and most certainly catches their attention.

Apparently, the word was spreading about a Russian "shooter" in the Carolinas. The speculation, rumors, and apprehension was of great interest to those who had plans to travel to Crockett's promotion at that time. When Barry and I finally crossed paths and he realized it was me that everyone was talking about, he just laughed and shook his head. Knowing that I always threw myself totally into everything I did, he said, *"I should have known it was you."*

I have been asked, many times, what I thought was the one thing that put me over so quickly in the business and help propel me to the main event as quickly as I did. In retrospect, I would have to say it was the fact that I became Nikita Koloff both in and out of the ring. I would settle for nothing less than a total transformation. I never lost sight of who I really was, but as far as the fans knew, I was only Nikita Koloff.

When you become someone else and take on a new identity, it's interesting to realize how it can consume you. I became Nikita in everything I did, but even when you spend as short a time in the business as I did, it's easy to become a mark yourself and actually believe your own publicity. When your own flight of the imagination begins to blur the lines of reality, trouble is not far behind.

We want the fans and other observers to buy into our character, but when we do, it is like traveling on the on-ramp to the apocalypse. Unfortunately, I have seen that play itself out with the tragic deaths of Kerry von Erich and several others. If it wasn't so tragic, it would be comical, like Uncle Teddy Brewster, who thought he was President Theodore Roosevelt in the film *Arsenic and Old Lace.* Every time he would ascend the stairs to his room, he would draw his sword, yell "charge," and run up the stairs as if it were San Juan Hill. But to make the fans believe it, you also had to believe it … at least to some extent.

One of the greatest examples of this was the incomparable Chief Jay Strongbow. The chief had a great run in the WWF in the 1970s and 1980s after a great deal of success in the late 1960s and early 1970s in the NWA's Georgia and Florida territories wrestling under his real name of Joe Scarpa. His new character of the Chief went over so well that it initiated a comment from Larry "The Axe" Hennig (of AWA fame and father of the late Mr. Perfect, Curt Hennig): *"Joe was the only Italian-Indian I have ever met."* But Joe became the Chief and the fans believed it because Joe believed it. To this day, we all call Joe, "Chief." We all believed it, and in professional wrestling, believability is the coin of the realm.

Chapter 11
Rocky Balboa

Staying true to my character took me in a different and totally unexpected direction a year or so into my wrestling career when I received a call from Don Kernodle, who had received a call from an old friend, Terry Funk.

Terry was a former NWA world heavyweight champion and the younger brother of another world champ, Dory Funk Jr. Terry intermingled his ring career with one on the silver screen. It was the acting side of Terry's calling that brought him to the attention of Sylvester Stallone. Terry appeared in the movies *Paradise Alley* and *Over the Top* with the "Italian Stallion" and they became friends.

Terry called Don, who had just been hired by Crockett as a booker, to ask if he had any wrestlers on the roster who could portray a Russian. Stallone was casting for his fourth installment of his Rocky series and needed a Russian character to be the foil to Rocky Balboa's champion in the upcoming *Rocky IV*. Don told Terry about me and suggested Sly give me a look and a screen test. After a few phone calls back and forth, he asked me to fly to Hollywood to read with him. I jumped at the chance when Don encouraged me to go and try to capture the part of Ivan Drago. Jim Crockett, however, wasn't as enthusiastic as Don. *"What if he gets the part?"* he asked. *"I've put a lot of time and money into Niki, and besides, he is the key to our main event programs. If he gets the part, we will lose him."*

Don saw the value in the possibility of me getting the part. He reasoned with Jim that if I did get the part, it would be great for business as it was when Hogan played "Thunder Lips" in *Rocky III*. When Hulk finished the part and returned to the ring, business went through the roof. Fans were not only seeing their wrestling hero, but they were seeing a movie star, as well. Jim was finally convinced and I was off to Hollywood.

Sylvester Stallone is an icon of our American culture. His story is as legendary as any of the characters he created or portrayed on the screen. Living in Hollywood, trying to break into the movie industry, he and his wife were "so broke that his dog was eating its own fleas." One evening, Sly attended the Muhammad Ali-Chuck Wepner fight. No one took the fight seriously as Wepner, known as the "Bayonne Bleeder," took on "The Greatest" for the ultimate prize of all sports — the heavyweight title of the world. The sports pundits predicted Chuck would be lucky if he lasted three rounds, but he went the 15-round distance with the champion, shocking not only the sports world, but the world at large.

Inspired by the events he witnessed, Stallone went home and immediately began working on Rocky Balboa, a walking cliché of sorts that embodied Sly's own story as much as that of Wepner's. He was offered $75,000 for the script with the caveat that Ryan O'Neal, Burt Reynolds, Paul Newman, Al Pacino, or any other major star of the time to take the role of the contender from Philadelphia. Sly knew this was his chance, and perhaps his only chance, to reach his goal. He refused their offer and kept on doing so, even when the offer reached more than a quarter of a million dollars. With only $106 in the bank, he remained true to his convictions and saw his courage and tenacity pay off as he kept the lead role and agreed to do it for scale. The rest, of course, is one of the things that makes Hollywood the place it is: the lore of people like Stallone and the stories they embody.

When I arrived in California, I learned that I was one of three being considered for the part of the Russian world amateur boxing champion. The other two up for the part were Dolph Lundgren and Kerry von Erich, the "Modern Day Warrior." I had heard a lot about von Erich, including his brief title reign as the NWA world heavyweight champion, defeating Flair in Texas Stadium. I was also aware of his erratic behavior both in and out of the ring.

When I arrived in Los Angeles, a limousine was waiting at the airport to take me to the hotel. When I arrived, I ran into Kerry, who seemed more than a little bit unprepared for the screen test. *"Do we have any lines or something we're supposed to do?"* he asked.

"Yeah," I said. *"They sent them to us some time ago. Didn't you memorize them?"*

"No, I guess not," Kerry said, and he walked away.

I have to say that everything Stallone did was first class: the flight, the hotel, the food, everything. He was kind and treated everyone there with the greatest courtesy and respect. I appreciated all he did, which made me more determined to win the part.

The first time I saw Stallone was when he pulled up in a red Corvette to meet me and do a reading. When he got out of his car, I had to take a second look. I was probably in the best shape of my life: 6-foot-2, 285 pounds, and less than ten percent body fat. Sly weighed about 165 pounds and stood 5-foot-6 or so. He was in fantastic shape, but a whole lot shorter than I expected. He had with him his girlfriend, Brigitte Nielsen, who was also starring in the film as Ivan Drago's wife.

I was required to do three readings for the screen test; two alone and one with Sly reading with me. It seems funny to me now, but I was so green back then that I didn't break character. I spoke to everyone in my best broken English, including Stallone.

Sly asked me if I knew how to pull a punch. I thought, *"If he only knew,"* and told him, *"I'll do whatever you want me to do, Mr. Stallone."* He looked at me and kind of shook his head, a lot like Jim Crockett did the first day we met in his office in Charlotte. *"Okay,"* he said, *"let's read."*

I was halfway through my lines when Sly asked me to turn towards him. I did, and we stood sort of nose-to-nose while I finished my lines. Stallone yelled, *"Cut."* He turned to the director and asked how it looked. The director said it was great up to the time I turned towards him and he lost Sly in my shadow. It was a combination of the difference in our size and the way the studio lighting was fixed. When I turned towards him, I literally overshadowed him.

When I heard the director's words, I knew it couldn't be good, so I left California without knowing if I was to become the next idol of the silver screen or not. A few weeks later, I received a call from the director, who told me the part went to the only non-wrestler of the bunch: Dolph Lundgren. The director diplomatically explained to me that, although I did well reading the lines, the size difference between Sly and me would be too much of a stretch for the audience to believe that an aging champion, Rocky Balboa, could defeat a younger, bigger champion. Audiences can suspend their disbelief. After all, that is part of the fun of going to the movies. But the screen makes everything so much bigger than in real life, and no one would believe that even Rocky could come back and win over such a ... I believe the director used the word "behemoth." He was also forthright in saying that there were some politics involved in the decision. I had heard that Dolph's girlfriend's mother had invested quite a bit of money in the film and that probably had something to do with their decision, but I'm sure he was probably the best of the lot.

I'm not sure that I would have done well in Hollywood, but it was a wonderful opportunity that I will always remember. I have nothing but the greatest respect for all those involved in the film industry. There is certainly a lot more to it than I ever realized. There is a tremendous amount of effort involved in every aspect of the movie business and it can be grueling at times. My hat is off to them. It was great to be a part of it, even if it was only for a couple of days.

Transforming myself from Scott Simpson into Nikita Koloff also had an effect on my family, especially in the beginning. I don't think they thought much about it at all. As I said before, my father left home when I was three years old and left my mom to fend for herself and our family. I'm not sure what she really thought, but when I walked into the kitchen on that particular day and announced, *"Mom, I'm going into professional wrestling,"* she just kind of looked at me and said, *"Uh, okay,"* sort of like her motherly, *"Oh, that's nice, dear,"* as she continued making dinner.

My sister didn't give it much thought either, I guess, but her two boys, Justin and Nicholas, thought it was great. They would go around telling their friends that their uncle was Nikita Koloff, the wrestler. Of course, at the time, they didn't believe them. They responded to their claim of kinship by saying, *"No way! He's from Moscow, so he can't be your uncle. He's Russian and you're not."* I regret that I couldn't have been more help to them in convincing their friends that what they were saying was true, but kayfabe is kayfabe.

Whenever I entered an arena, or any other place where I would run into fans, I would take great care not to speak to anyone. I would just pass by them and stare, or growl if I paid them any attention at all. I had to make sure that, to them, I was an unbeatable Russian wrestling machine on a quest to win the heavyweight title of the world.

To the fans, if there was a more focused athlete anywhere on the planet than me, he or she would be awfully hard to find. Fans would approach me when they would find the courage and hand me Russian-English dictionaries. They wanted me to learn English so badly that they would take their own lives in their hands (or so they thought).

I'm not sure what their thoughts were, but I always suspected they thought that if I could speak English, I might have a change of heart and adhere more closely to the rules in the ring. More importantly, if I did win the world heavyweight title, I would keep the title in the States, rather than taking it back to Moscow.

Not all the fans were as kind, however. There were as many, if not more, that wished I would return to Mother Russia, or better yet, disappear from the face of the earth altogether. And there were more than enough of them wanting to help do the job.

Chapter 12

Death Threats

One day, Jim Crockett received an anonymous phone call from a fan stating that the next time Ivan and I were scheduled to wrestle in Charleston, South Carolina, they would make sure we didn't leave the town alive.

Since 1670, Charleston has been one of America's most prominent cities (in fact, it was North America's fifth largest city until 1800). It is etched in history as where the American Civil War began as the state pulled out of the Union after the election of Abraham Lincoln. It stood for States rights, and on the night Ivan and I were arriving to wrestle, the fans flew their American flags high. They weren't going to tolerate two athletes from the Soviet Union coming to wrest the world tag title away from the American champions.

Of course, Crockett wasn't going to let a little thing like death threats keep two of his top heels from showing up for a match. *"Don't worry about it,"* Jim told us. *"They probably don't mean it."*

"Probably don't mean it" didn't make me feel a lot better, or Ivan either, I suppose. But, of course, Jim didn't have anything to worry about. By the time Ivan and I entered the ring that night, he would be sitting comfortably at home. To Jim's credit, he did hire additional security to escort us in and out of town. What a wonderful gesture on his part.

When we arrived, we had to have a police escort from the parking lot into the building. Police officers guarded our dressing room door so no patriotic fan would come into the dressing room and do their part to personally diminish the Cold War by two. The officers stayed close by, and when we got the signal to enter the ring, they escorted us out and remained until after the match when we were safely on our way out of town.

Being still green to the business, I was a little more than concerned during our drive to Charleston, but Ivan really wasn't bothered at all. To the contrary, I think he loved it. Uncle Ivan always had a way to bring out the "best" in the fans.

While doing the promos for the upcoming matches in Charleston, Ivan fueled the fire by saying in his broken-English-Russian accent, *"I want all you American soldier boys in Charleston to be in front row and to show up in your little yellow dresses."* We always drew a lot of heat in Charleston. The Charleston area is home to a number of military bases, including Shaw Air Force Base, Parris Island, and Fort Jackson. No wonder they wanted to kill us. We were not only viewed as an unbeatable Russian team, we were adding insult to injury by denigrating the elite of the American fighting forces.

One reason there was so much interest and emotion in our match was that Ivan and I were challenging the reigning world tag-team champions, Dusty Rhodes and the "Raging Bull" Manny Fernandez. Outside of Ivan and Don, Dusty probably had the most profound influence on my career than anyone else. He also still remains, to this day, one of the most controversial men ever to enter the ring or the booking office, but he always was kind to me and did his best to guide me in my career. For that I will be forever grateful. But I'm getting a bit ahead of myself here.

Manny was another story altogether. He was a veteran of the Vietnam War and had played football at West Texas State. Along with Nick Buoniconti and Jake Scott, he was a key player with Don Shula's 1972 Miami Dolphin's "No-Name Defense." Number "75" helped his team to the NFL's only undefeated season by going 17-0 and winning Super Bowl VII by defeating the Washington Redskins 14-7.

Manny began his wrestling career in 1978 and held more than his share of regional titles before settling in the Carolinas and winning the world tag team title by defeating Ivan and Don in Greensboro on October 20, 1984. They defended the belts successfully until Ivan and I met them in Fayetteville the following March and showed the fans and the soldiers stationed at Fort Bragg the superiority of "Russian" athletes.

As well as Dusty and I got along, Manny and I didn't. It wasn't that I had anything personal against him and I'm not sure what caused it. We just had a personality clash. It's possible that, like a number of the boys, he was a bit jealous of my success. But no matter our personal difficulties, when I stepped into the ring with him, as with all my opponents, I gave it my all.

Winning the belts from Dusty and Manny was great, but it wasn't my first title, or world title for that matter, but it did hold the most prestige. Ivan, Don, and I had been awarded the NWA world six-man tag team title in December 1984, just a few months after I began wrestling. Even though it was a world title, it didn't have the prestige of the world tag team title or the gold belt around Ric Flair's waist, but as far as the promotion went, it was another title to defend and to seek after, all of which meant more money at the box office. I think they awarded the belts to us for a number of reasons. Don and Ivan drew well and they had dropped the world tag team title to Dusty and Manny a few months earlier. The program of the "Russians" and the turncoat also was working well, and I suppose they wanted to see how I would do with a title.

A funny thing about the world six-man tag team title is that they let us change partners for the extra man, depending on where any one of us were booked. Krusher Khrushchev and Baron von Raschke were the other two who traded spots with Ivan, Don, and me. We held the title until May, 17, 1986 when Ivan, the Baron, and I lost to Dusty and the Road Warriors in Baltimore. The title would be kept on the back burner and would trade hands only three more times before it was abandoned in 1989. Crockett would also do the same with our newly-won world tag team title.

Tag team wrestling has been a staple of professional wrestling since the early part of the 20th century. According to some historians, the first tag-team match was held in San Francisco in 1901 to bring a little more action to the cards and

Ivan Koloff, Nikita Koloff and Krusher Khrushchev · September 1985

bring life to a somewhat struggling territory. Other schools of thought accredit Joe Stecher, three-time world heavyweight champion from Fort Dodge, Nebraska, in the late 1920s or early 1930s, along with his brother Tony, but no solid proof is available for either theory. The first authenticated tag team match was held on October 2, 1936 in Houston between Tiger Daula and Fazul Mohammad against Whiskers Savage and Milo Steinborn.

For years, tag team wrestling was viewed as little more than a novelty act. It grew in popularity through the '30s and '40s, but never gained the popularity that single matches did until the 1950s. Big Jim Crockett's Mid-Atlantic territory, for the greater part of the '60s, was known primarily as a tag-team territory. Teams like the "Flying" Scott Brothers, J.C. Dykes and the Infernos, Brute Bernard and Skull Murphy, George Becker and Johnny Weaver, the Masked Bolos, the Anderson Brothers, Rip Hawk and Swede Hanson, and the Kentuckians, all graced the rings for the fans in the Carolinas. It pretty much remained that way until George Scott took over the booking and rebuilt the territory around single matches, bringing in names like Johnny Valentine and Wahoo McDaniel.

The history of tag teams in our sport is fascinating in its own right and there is nowhere near enough space here to do it justice. But to look into this aspect of professional wrestling, the book *The Pro Wrestling Hall of Fame: The Tag Teams* [ECW Press, 2005] by Greg Oliver and Steven Johnson is an excellent source.

I talked earlier about the various versions of the NWA world tag team title, but as the territorial promotions began closing their doors, the Mid-Atlantic version was the only one that remained in the National Wrestling Alliance.

One of the things I learned about tag-team wrestling is that your opponent is every bit as important as your partner, and the contrast between the two teams make the program succeed or fail. Professional wrestling ebbs and flows, much like any other sector of the sports or entertainment industries. As with other sectors as well, anytime you can tap into the youth market, your ratings will increase and your coffers will begin to swell.

To tap into this ever desirable market and bring in the younger crowd, in July 1985, Jim brought in one of the most popular teams in the history of the Charlotte territory. our new foes in the quest for the world tag team title was the duo of Ricky Morton and Robert Gibson, the Rock 'n' Roll Express. They seemed to come out of nowhere and took the wrestling industry by storm. Actually, they did pretty much come out of nowhere, or pretty close anyway. They got their start in the small town circuit in Tennessee. Their energetic work in the ring and their appeal to the young girls quickly brought them to the attention of Jim Crockett and the rings of the Mid-Atlantic. It was amazing to watch them get over with the fans. They would come to the ring with their then-fashionable "mullet" haircuts, torn tee-shirts, and bandanas tied around their arms and legs. The kids went crazy whenever and wherever they appeared. They were pro wrestling's version of the Beatles craze that had hit the United States in the early 1960s.

The first time Ivan and I met them in the ring, I started the match against Ricky Morton. When Ricky and I locked up, instead of putting my head *beside* his, I locked up with my head down and centered. We cracked heads and Ricky fell back to his corner, holding his head in a daze. *"My, gosh,"* Ricky said to Robert. *"What's he doing out there? He'll kill me if he keeps doing things like that. Watch this ..."*

In wrestling, when someone nails his opponent for real, purposely or not, it is referred to as a potato. When you give too many potatoes, your opponent feels obligated to issue a receipt — in other words, throw a potato of their own — and that's just what Ricky did.

As I stepped into Ricky with my head down again, he threw out his elbow and the point of it caught me on the bridge of my nose. Now it was my turn to release the hold and head to my corner, all the while seeing little white bugs swirling around my head. It doesn't take long after a shot like that to learn to keep your head up. The third time we locked up, I not only kept my head up, but I kept it as far away as possible. In fact, I held my head so far back I could barely reach Ricky to tie up. The fans might have thought it looked a bit strange, but I'm sure they also had to be wondering about all the laughter that was coming from our partners at the corners of the ring.

There was quite a contrast between the Rock 'n' Roll Express and the Russians. But to make the contrast more vivid, not only were they young, good-looking kids, but they were a lot smaller than we were. That made the angle all the more interesting as the two young American wrestlers tried to achieve what so many before them had failed to do ... defeat Ivan and me and win the world tag team title that we won from Dusty and Manny Fernandez in Fayetteville, North Carolina, on March 18, 1985. To make the matches believable, Ivan and I had to rely on our power moves and attempt to win the matches quickly and decisively. Ricky and Robert would rely on their size, which allowed them to do things big men couldn't do. They would pick up the pace of the matches with dropkicks and other flying moves. That would take us off our game. Our size and strength became a disadvantage to us, rather than an asset. Ricky and Robert convinced the crowd that what they lacked in size, they more than made up for in courage. Every night, they would enter the ring to face us, not only to take the world title, but to uphold American pride and the hopes of a new generation of wrestling fans.

Morton and Gibson had been in the business a few years before coming to wrestle for the Crocketts and actually had more experience than me at the time. Being the professionals they were, they helped me perform to the level the fans expected every night. They were a pleasure to work with and would not hesitate to do anything we asked them to do in the ring that would make our match more exciting than the last. The fans loved to cheer on their heroes, and to them, our series of matches became "us" (Rock 'n' Roll Express) vs. "them" (The Russians). That was really good for business because the Rock 'n' Roll Express made the fans feel as if they were a part of the "us," while Ivan and I stood alone as "them."

Ivan and I had been wearing the world tag team title belts for four months when we entered into the program with Ricky and Robert and we drew well everywhere we went. On July 9, 1985, in an attempt to push the feud between us on the upcoming *Starrcade* scheduled for November 28, we dropped the belts to them in the little town of Shelby, North Carolina. Actually, I never lost the world tag team title to Ricky and Robert. Ivan and Krusher did. Since Jim was building me up for a run with Flair for the title, and was using me against different opponents in singles matches, the powers that be approved a sort of "corporate tag team," allowing any two of the three of us to defend the world title.

Ricky and Robert actually did something no one else has ever done (at least, to my knowledge) in the Mid-Atlantic territory. The match in which they won the belts was their very *first* match in the territory. Normally, promoters bring in new wrestlers and give them wins over underneath talent in order to build their reputation before giving them a title. Jim Crockett must have seen something special in the Rock 'n' Roll Express to forgo that preparation.

Three months later, on October 13, I rejoined Uncle Ivan in Charlotte and we took the world tag title back for the Motherland, setting the stage for one of the most memorable matches in the history of *Starrcade* and in my career.

In the '80s, *Starrcade* was the flagship event of the NWA. The first show, held in Greensboro on Thanksgiving night 1983, was broadcasted by way of closed-circuit television to venues across the country. It took place before *WrestleMania* and the *Survivor Series* pay-per-views. *Starrcade* was the event that started it all and made the supercard a mainstay in our sport.

Ivan and I culminated our feud with Morton and Gibson in a cage match at the third *Starrcade* in Greensboro on November 28 in front of a sold out crowd and again put them over to give them their second run with the title.

Funny thing … years later, an undercard wrestler came up and told me that he and his girlfriend were in the crowd that night. At the height of the match, while Ricky and I were battling while standing on the top rope, I threw Ricky over the top of the cage. He took quite a bump far below on the concrete floor. As he laid there bleeding, the guy left his seat, ran to the ring, vaulted over the barrier, knelt down on the floor next to Ricky, and pleaded with him to get up and get back into the ring, where Ivan and I were destroying his partner, Robert. The kid wasn't in the business at the time and he admitted that he was a total "mark." A mark is someone who isn't "smart" to the business. In other words, they believe that most of what goes on in the ring is true competition. I can't recall ever laughing so hard in my life as I did when he told that story to me. It was another tribute to the believability of our characters.

That was the type of reaction we were always looking for from the fans when we wrestled, albeit jumping over barricades is more than a little dangerous. That wasn't as much a tribute to what I was doing in the ring as it was to Ricky's prowess and the bumps he was willing to take. More importantly, I know very few people who could sell our moves as well as Ricky. Years later, when I sit down and watch the tapes, it's difficult for me to tell what was real and what wasn't. Those were great matches for the fans and Ivan and I had a great time working with the Rock 'n' Roll Express.

I also have to give credit to the fans because we derived a huge amount of energy from their enthusiasm. If there is anything as important as your partner and your opponent in the ring, it's the fans that surround it night after night. They are the life's blood of our sport. Without them, we would be nothing. They spend the money they worked hard for, and often drive hundreds of miles in all kinds of weather to cheer us on or root for our defeat. They also do something more for us. As much as we are there to entertain them, we receive as much from them as they do from us. Just as they feed off of what we do in the ring, we feed off of their reaction. It is their reaction that pumps us up and encourages us to bring the match to a new level. The fans are the true champions. I don't think I could say that enough. Without them, we are nothing.

Titles are vital to the wrestling industry, but not as important as a strong character, opponents, and programs. Look at the "Rowdy One," Rowdy Roddy Piper. He had captured a number of titles, including the United States heavyweight title and the WWF Intercontinental title, but he was as big of a star, if not bigger, when he didn't hold a strap. It was his personality and ring skills that put him over. He didn't necessarily need a belt. I had hoped the same would be true with me. Belt or no belt, I was not going to do anything but give my best in any match in which I was participating.

I had worked hard, especially during those initial thirteen months, to establish my character and get over with the fans. In fact, it was all of us at Crockett Promotions that made sure I was believable as the Soviet challenger. Along with that came what we were looking for — the hatred of the fans. Wrestling fans will flock to an arena for two main reasons; one to cheer on their heroes, the other to jeer the heels and see them get their reckoning for their evil deeds. Of course, some aren't satisfied with doing it from their seats. They want to get their "pound" of flesh personally and will go to great costs to get to any one of us to extract their revenge on behalf of their heroes. Every town, arena, gym, or other venue has them. The wrestlers are usually safe thanks to local police and sheriff's deputies, but there are times when even the Secret Service would have difficulty keeping some of them from finishing their quests.

One of the earliest fans made a name for herself in the 1950s as "Hatpin Mary," a little, elderly lady who would sit at ringside and stab the heels with a long hat pin as they came to and from the ring. I'm sure the wrestlers hated it as much as the fans loved it, but actions like that opened the door for more dangerous encounters along the way.

All of us who wrestled as heels have dozens of stories of fans interference, from the parking lot to the dressing room, and even into the ring. One of the worst I heard about took place one night in Greenville, South Carolina.

Ole Anderson [Alan Rogowski] knew the business well. Trained by Verne Gagne in Minnesota, he began his career using the name Rock Rogowski. Rock wrestled for Gagne's AWA Omaha promotion and took its version of the heavyweight title from Bob Orton in 1968. Moving to Charlotte in 1970, Rock changed his name to Ole Anderson and joined his "brother" Gene as the "Minnesota Wrecking Crew." They won every tag-team title available, including the Atlantic Coast tag team title on five different occasions and the world tag team title four times. The Minnesota Wrecking Crew redefined tag team wrestling and raised it, and the fans' ire, to a new echelon.

On Monday, May 24, 1976, after losing a match to defending world tag team champions Mr. Wrestling [Tim Woods] and Dino Bravo in the Greenville Memorial Auditorium, Ole was walking back to the dressing room when a 79-year-old man stabbed him with a hawk-billed knife. If it wasn't for the quick intercession of Tim and a few of the others in the dressing room, Ole would have died on the concrete floor from the loss of blood. His assailant didn't fare much better as Ole punched him in the face, which resulted in a trip to the hospital for the old man. Word has it that Ole was back in the ring two days later. Knowing Ole, I wonder what took him so long.

My encounters with the fans never reached that extreme, but security was a lot stronger by the time I began wrestling. We all learned early on, from the stories we heard, to always be vigilant for any unbalanced fans in the crowd. In fact, the most bizarre situations we encountered had to do with some of the more enthusiastic fans. I'm not talking about the fans who would cheer or boo us in the arenas, but the fans who took the sport much too seriously. We were all glad that the fans got into what we were doing in the ring and on television, but when it crossed the line beyond that, it could get a little dangerous.

When you are wrestling heel, you are always conscious of what fans may do to help extract a measure of revenge for what we did to their heroes in the ring. Death threats were not unusual and we didn't take them all that seriously, but we didn't entirely ignore them, either. We were all just careful, especially around the arenas. I don't think I was ever threatened in the grocery store or the gym. Most altercations usually happened right after a match. On occasion, though, we would have problems if we went to a club and a fan had his buddies with him, or if he had drank too much "liquid courage" and was looking to even the score for their vanquished favorite. Others were out to prove they knew wrestling was "fake," or to prove to their friends or girlfriends that they were just as tough as we were.

I must have had four or five incidents where fans rolled into the ring while I was wrestling. It isn't funny when that happens because you never know what someone, who is crazy enough to get in the ring with a professional wrestler, is capable of doing. The only humorous part is that one second when the guy has a moment of clarity. When he realizes what he's done, a look comes over his face that says, *"Oh, my gosh. What am I doing?"*

That is when you have to react. That one second is all you have to handle the guy before he continues on with whatever plan he had when he was stupid enough to get into the ring to join the fight. In those days, if somebody who wasn't with the program came through the ropes, they were considered fair game. That knowledge alone probably kept more fans in their seats than the local constabulary. As litigious as our society has become today, a wrestler being attacked in the ring would probably be sued by the fan for inciting him to act the way he did, but until the 1980s, we could do just about anything we needed to defend ourselves. We could boot them in the head, throw a forearm or an elbow, and the police wouldn't do anything but cart them out of the ring.

One of the first incidents I had in the ring was the first time I wrestled Ric Flair for the world heavyweight title. It was at the Great American Bash in Charlotte. We had been going at it hard for about forty minutes and, to everyone at ringside, it appeared that I was only moments away from accomplishing what I came to America to do: defeat Flair and capture the world title.

I had taken Flair down and he was lying on the mat. I heard something behind me and, as I turned my head to see what it was, someone grabbed me from behind in a waist lock. I thought it was Flair, but when I turned back around, I saw he was still prone on the mat. Then I thought it might be Ivan, who was my second for the match, but he was standing on the floor in my corner. His eyes were wide open and there was an expression of shock on his face. I then thought it might be the "special referee," David Crockett, but when I looked around, I saw David in another section of the ring.

Then it hit me … it had to be a fan. I turned quickly and a little guy just flew off me like a shingle flying off a roof during a wind storm. No sooner had he hit the mat then two of Charlotte's finest rolled into the ring. He rolled out and was making tracks for the nearest exit, but they caught him before he could take more than a few steps. I'm not sure what in the world could have been going through his mind. Did he really think he could beat me when the world champion couldn't? I hope he thought better of those ideas after that.

Nikita vs Ric Flair

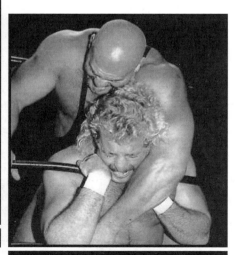

Nikita vs Magnum TA

There was another incident, this one even more bizarre, during my program with Magnum T.A. Magnum and I were battling back and forth for the U.S. title and we were wrestling in his hometown of Norfolk, Virginia. Towards the end of the match, he and I got into an altercation and, when it looked like I was on the losing end, Ivan entered the ring to lend me a hand. As we beat Magnum from one side of the ring to the other, Baron von Raschke also came into the ring to help us. It was great theater as the Evil Empire was ganging up on the American hero.

A few minutes into the melee, I saw a fan running out of the crowd and into the ring to help even the odds for Magnum. This time I was ready. I wasn't sure if there was something in his hand, but as he approached me, I gave him a boot to the stomach. He doubled over and fell to the mat and I went back to pummeling his idol.

As I was beating Magnum, I caught the guy out of the corner of my eye. He was getting up and coming at us again. I was thinking, *"Who is this guy? He's nuts!"* It's one thing to be in the ring with another wrestler, but to be in the ring with a crazy guy is a different matter altogether. I booted him in the stomach again and he hit the mat for a second time, only this time, as soon as he hit the canvas, he immediately got back to his feet. I nailed him a third time and yelled for Ivan and the Baron to hold him down while I got my chain. Ivan and the Baron held him while I hit him with the chain, in the hope that it would end the matter. Finally, the police at ringside realized the guy wasn't part of the match and pulled him out of the ring.

As the three of us turned back to finish the match, the babyface dressing room cleared out and Magnum's friends all came to the ring to help him, running us out of the ring and back to the dressing room. I got on the floor and began looking around for my chain, but I couldn't find it anywhere.

One of the policemen working ringside came up to me with the chain and said they were pressing charges against me. I know I must have looked at him as if he had lost his mind. The police escorted us to the dressing room and I started to speak to Ivan in "Russian" while pointing to the policeman. Even in the middle of all this craziness, I never broke character.

When the promoter came into the dressing room shortly before we left, I told him I didn't care what the guy or the police officer said. I had been defending myself from someone who came into the ring. What was I supposed to do, get stabbed like Ole did in Greenville? I didn't know whether the guy had a weapon or not, but I wasn't about to find out the hard way. The promoter told me not to worry about it and returned my chain to me. He thought the officer was making a big fuss in order to make a name for himself by arresting Nikita Koloff.

We left for the next town and didn't hear any more about it until I came back to Norfolk. I was told that the guy was in the military and was stationed at the base there. He was so drunk at the matches that night that he could hardly see straight. Charges were pressed that night, but not against me. When the guy who attacked me returned home from the hospital, where he was treated for a concussion, the promoter pressed charges against him.

Standing before the judge, he asked for leniency. The judge looked at him and, with a laugh, said, *"I think you've suffered enough punishment and justice was served. Don't do it again."* My bet would be that he took the judge's words to heart, if not his experience with us in the ring.

Fighting with the fans outside the ring was a bit different. We certainly had to be careful how we defended ourselves if a fan decided to challenge us when we were out of the ring. One night, after a match in Indiana, I went out to a night club with Sting, Animal, and Luger. Now I wasn't one to frequent the clubs, but on this particular night, I decided to go, if for no other reason than to get the guys off my back. They were always riding me about never going out with them, so I agreed to go just to keep them quiet. We hadn't been in the club for too long before a little guy walked up and began to provoke Lex. At the time, I weighed about 285 pounds, Animal was close to 300, Sting was about 250, and Lex hovered around 280 … and that guy couldn't have weighed more than 110 pounds.

I have no idea how many beers he had, but however many it was, it was way too many. Lex ignored him, but he kept trying to goad Lex into a fight. I just sat and shook my head, wondering, *"What can this guy be thinking?"* We all decided that discretion was not only the better part of valor, but probably the safest. We decided to get out of the club and look for another place to go and unwind.

That wasn't hard to do as we were on Rush Street where there seemed to be a bar every ten feet. We went into the next bar and, almost a soon as we walked in, the same thing began to happen. Different bar, different guy. This time, it was Sting who was the recipient of the challenge. So, we left again and ducked into the third bar. As soon as we sat down, another guy walked over to Animal and called him out to fight. Of all the people in the bar, this guy had to pick Animal to prove his manhood. That seemed to happen quite a bit. No matter who he was with, the inebriated always seemed to gravitate to the biggest wrestler around, and that was Animal. To his credit, Animal refused to engage the guy and we left. This time, we decided to call it a night.

That wasn't always the case however. One night in Charlotte, a guy came up to Animal and said, *"I'm not afraid of you. I have a black belt."* Animal tried to be nice to the guy, but he just kept on and on, obviously wanting to prove himself with one half of the "Legion of Doom." Animal repeatedly told the "black belt" to leave him alone, but the guy continued to push him. Finally, Animal had enough. He open-handed slapped the guy and sent him flying. I mean, the guy sailed about eight feet into the air and looked like he was levitating. When he landed, he slid another five feet. The manager pulled the guy to his feet and threw him out of the bar.

When we left and began getting into our car, the same guy walked up, looking for a rematch. With the car door between them, he began pushing Animal. This time, Animal had about all he was willing to take. Animal struck so quickly that nobody saw it coming. With the car door between them, Animal nailed the guy with his left hand, breaking his jaw in three places and shattering his nose. I can't imagine what would have happened if he had hit the guy with his right hand, which really had power. He had the quickest hands of anyone I had ever seen. Even now, I can't imagine why Animal always seemed to be the one those guys went after. One thing is for sure. That guy in Charlotte certainly will think twice before challenging a guy who made his living in the ring, black belt or not.

At least, I hope he does.

Chapter 13

Dressing Room Heat

The heat I received as Nikita Koloff not only lent itself to the ring and the loyal fans we performed in front of every night, but I found it spilling over into the dressing room with the boys, as well. When I first entered the business, I wasn't sure what to expect from the wrestlers who were already there, most of whom had already either had established themselves or were on their way to doing so. I wasn't sure whether I was going to be accepted, ostracized, or find myself somewhere between the two. To my surprise, and with help from Ivan and Don, I am sure, most of the veterans not only accepted me, but welcomed me with open arms. It seemed the bigger the name and the higher up on the card the wrestler was, the more they welcomed me into the fold.

It wasn't until much later that I realized the reason for much of their open-hearted acceptance. It wasn't all altruistic, as I had thought. It wasn't because they were all just good guys who wanted me to do well, although it was that way with a good number of them. Above all, everyone knew it was good business. If I did well, they would do well, and that would be reflected in their payoffs. The larger gates at the house shows and higher buy rates for the pay-per-view events would result in their pay envelopes being a little thicker and heavier.

But it wasn't that way with everyone in the dressing room. To some of the boys, I wasn't much more than a pariah. Those wrestlers viewed me as a usurper, someone who was taking or trying to take their spot. Those aspiring stars had paid their dues during the six or seven years, or more, prior to my arrival. I understood some of what they were feeling and why they disliked me and my entrée into the business. In their eyes, they saw their big break looming large on the horizon, or jockeying for the vantage point with their character, or their place on the card to move up to the main-event level. With that in place, now comes some new guy who not only ascends the corporate ladder ahead of them, but uses them as the rungs on his way up to the top. That certainly was not the case, nor had it ever been my intent. I worked hard and made the most of the opportunities that were presented to me. I wasn't going to let anything get in my way, but I wasn't going to use anyone to get to the top, either.

All in all, I couldn't blame them for being unnerved by a guy who rose to the top in a matter of months. I made mental notes and was determined to bridge those gaps, and to make sure that if and when the roles became reversed, I would remember how kind some of the veterans treated me and return that kindness to those that would follow after me.

As much as I tried to look past the obvious snubs and comments by some of the boys, it did bother me, but once again, Ivan was there to lend me his support, experience, and wisdom. *"Niki,"* he would say, *"don't let it bother you. It's just the nature of this business. Yes, they have paid their dues, but so have you. Maybe not in the ring, but you paid them elsewhere. Keep that in mind. Maybe you didn't pay them by going to a wrestling school, or by wrestling in some minor league wrestling circuit, traveling from one tank town to another, but you paid your dues in the gym, working out and paying the price with your blood, sweat, and tears. That is every bit as important as the work in the ring. You paid the price, just in another way, and when your opportunity arose, you were ready."* Ivan was always ready with words to encourage me. He had been at every level of the sport and cared deeply about those who entered it and looked to it to make a living for themselves and their families.

Ivan continued by saying, *"The way you came into the business is, in many ways, more admirable than how I, and many of the other boys, got in. We were working in the business and seeing our goals beginning to unfold. You sweated it out every day, just waiting for your chance to come and your future to reveal itself. Don't ever think that you haven't paid your dues."*

I never looked at any of the boys as being below me. I had great respect for them, but I was there to focus on my career and see my plan to fruition. I never had planned on being a wrestler, so I saw it more as a means to another end. Not that I took it lightly, but I was there for a short time, to do well for the Crocketts, the fans, the boys, and myself, in the hopes of retiring at the top of my game at age 35. I wanted fans to say, *"I wish Nikita had stayed around longer,"* instead of saying, *"Man, is he still around? When is Koloff going to retire?"*

I have seen so many other athletes that had hung around "just one more year" and ended up diminishing their status in their sport. I planned to go out on top

and leave with style. The boys used to kid me and say, *"You'll never do it. This sport gets in your blood and you won't be able to get out. We've heard it all before."* I would defend my plan and adamantly say I would be financially secure and leave the ring at 35.

Not long ago, I ran into a wrestler at the Atlanta airport that I had worked with years ago. He and his partner were tag-team superstars during the 1980s. He was traveling alone and was on his way home to see his family. He was still carrying his wrestling gear with him and he looked so very tired. My heart just went out to him when I saw that lifeless expression on his face. Wrestling was all he knew. It was the only thing he could do. He was well past his prime, but he was still traveling from one independent wrestling organization to another. The business had passed him by and he was unprepared to do anything else.

I had seen a number of the boys like that throughout the years in more towns than I can remember — wrestlers who had seen their main event status fade. They either loved the sport so much they refused to let go, they believed they couldn't do anything else, or both. I was determined that I would fare better. Not that I thought I was better than them, but I knew I wasn't going to limit myself or sell myself short. Like any athlete who makes a living with their body, I know there was only a short time for me to be able to perform and compete at a certain level. Life is full of exciting things, and when my time was through, I wanted to be ready to move on to another career.

In order to make my first steps toward my goals, I knew I had to watch my money carefully. During the time I broke into wrestling, we were traveling 2,000 to 2,500 miles a week and had to pay most, if not all, of our own expenses, so I tried to economize every way I could while on the road. A lot of the guys would spend every penny they earned as soon as they cashed their checks. They would stop at a restaurant and spend $25 or more for a meal and not think a thing about it. I would pack a small cooler with sandwiches and drinks to save money. The boys would laugh at me and give me a hard time, but I took it in stride.

You have to remember that I came from a very poor family. We lived in the projects and I learned early on to be appreciative of anything I received. When I began wrestling, I was paid once a week. There were weeks when I received $300 for a few nights' work and other weeks when I made $700. I thought that was great. I was traveling a lot, but most of my matches were lasting only a few minutes, so the hourly rate was astronomical.

At one point, it became a game to see how many checks I could accumulate without cashing them. I think thirteen was the highest number I had before Crockett's accountant called and asked me to please cash my checks because it was throwing off his bookkeeping. It wasn't a lot of money at the time, but considering where I came from, it was a small fortune.

Paydays would increase considerably during the next few years, as would my understanding of the business and those involved on both sides of the ropes. I was eager to learn and I was beginning to grow impatient for the next step in my career.

Abraham Lincoln once said, *"If I had eight hours to chop down a tree, I would spend six hours sharpening the ax."* I spent years sharpening the ax long before I ever saw a tree, but I knew that when my time came, I would be ready.

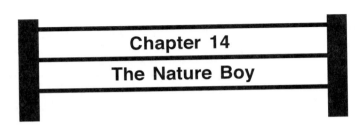

Chapter 14

The Nature Boy

It wasn't long before my single matches began to last longer than a few seconds. I was finally getting the time in the ring that would allow me to get the experience I needed to wrestle Ric Flair for the world title. The Crocketts plan was to take the Ric Flair-Nikita Koloff show on the road and draw fans to bear witness to our battles. The cold war was being reduced to two men, each of whom was willing to die in the ring for the supremacy of the wrestling world; all for the price of a ticket.

I think what made our program so compelling, especially at the beginning, was the anticipation. I would destroy opponent after opponent, while Uncle Ivan would challenge all comers and call upon the "Nature Boy" to prove he was a real champion by defending his belt against me.

To that point, Ric and I had not so much as brushed shoulders, but fans everywhere, as well as the wrestling magazines, were all clamoring for the title match. The magazine that drew the most attention to our possible confrontation for the title was the August 1985 issue of *Sports Review Wrestling*. The cover featured Ric and me with our bodies turned toward each other and our heads turned towards the camera. We were set against a yellow background so Ric's red ring robe, my red singlet, and the red USSR letters emblazoned on my headband, would stand out on the cover. Between us, the words read: "Ric Flair vs. Nikita Koloff — Why This Could Be the Match of the Century!"

On the inside, there was a four-page spread that stated, *"As a three-time NWA champion, Ric Flair has faced challenges of all shapes and sizes, styles and temperaments, and has never yet backed down. But Ric Flair has never faced anyone like Nikita Koloff."* Ironically, the story touted our upcoming title clash set for July 6 at the Great American Bash in Charlotte, while the cover date of the magazine was August, but like most periodicals, it was dated two to three months ahead.

The article compared and contrasted our strengths and weaknesses, focusing on my power, resourcefulness, and speed against the Nature Boy's skill at combining science and brawling and dubbing him the consummate wrestler. The article concluded by reminding the reader, *"Ric Flair vs. Nikita Koloff, July 6, for the NWA title. America vs. Russia. Wrestler vs. Brawler. Veteran vs. Rookie. Some matches need a lot of publicity. This one doesn't."*

As nice as that sounded, we did need a lot of publicity, as any major match does. Without it, no matter how great the match might be, without the promotion, it would be just another title defense. And just another title defense would be the kiss of death for any rematch or program for Ric and me.

As you may recall, I described part of the image I was projecting by working out in the austere "dungeon" where I trained like a mad man under the watchful eye of Uncle Ivan. We ran the dungeon angle for six to eight weeks before I ever faced Ric on camera. But it was the expectation of the match and the possibility of a Russian taking the world title that kept the *Mid-Atlantic Championship Wrestling* television program at the top of the ratings week after week.

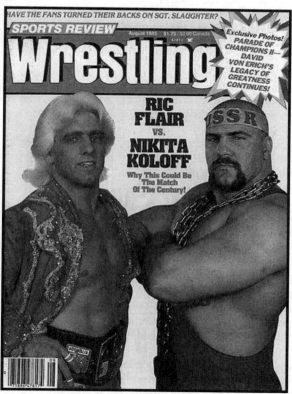

To set up our first match, I had to be elevated into top contender status and a force the world champion would have to reckon with. I may have been carving a wide swath through the Mid-Atlantic territory, but I had yet to catch the eye of Flair, so in order to vault me over the other challengers, I had to do something that would anger Ric enough that he would be willing to put up his world title in order to get me in the ring.

The angle was set up to take place during an interview, during which time I would attack David Crockett, the television commentator. While I was establishing my reputation as unbeatable, Crockett Promotions pushed the idea that David and Ric were very close friends. Each time Flair appeared in the ring or on the interview set, David would sing Ric's praises.

Once that idea was planted in the minds of the viewers, we were ready to establish the feed that would lead into the main event for the first Great American

Bash. David was going to interview Ivan and me during a TV taping after a match. During the interview, I would become enraged and nail David with the Russian Sickle, one of my signature moves. That would initiate Ric's anger and put us in the ring together for the title.

We all thought it was a great idea. Well, almost all of us. David wasn't too excited about the plan. He didn't relish being hit by a 285-pound wrestler coming at him at full speed and having to take a bump on the hard concrete studio floor. Apprehensive as he was, David agreed to go along with the angle. David was, indeed, good friends with Ric, but that friendship didn't extend to a lot of the other boys. Pro wrestling has a penchant for jealousy, and being friendly with the promotion owner just didn't set well with some of the guys, so when I hit him during the interview, the boys in the dressing room came running out to see what was going on.

We had kept everything to ourselves. Nobody but David, Ric, Ivan, and I knew what we were planning to do. When the boys saw the soles of David's shoes pointing towards the ceiling, they couldn't believe it. They came up to me in the dressing room after the incident and asked if it was for real. They thought I had finally gotten fed up with David's attitude and the way he treated the wrestlers and leveled him for real. Many of the boys considered David to be arrogant, and even I found myself chuckling at his announcing more than once, but I would say I had a good working relationship with him.

Months before we met in the ring, the fans had built up the feud between Ric and me in their minds. With little more than a year's experience under my belt, I had been elevated to the status of "number one challenger." It was the power of anticipation that made us all a lot of money. I was portrayed in such a way that it was almost a foregone conclusion that, as good as Flair was, his hope of beating such a powerful opponent was slim at best.

The Great American Bash was the idea of Dusty Rhodes, who was the booker for the company at the time. It's interesting to study what draws fans to wrestling. Wrestling is storytelling in its most direct form, much like you would see in a movie or a play. That is where the booker comes into play. The booker or booking team creates the script or storyline that keeps the fans glued to their television sets and into the arenas to see what will happen next. He determines the matches, works out the angles or storylines, and decides who holds which title and for how long. A good booker can tell a story in the ring and on the air during a specific period of time, segueing one into another without missing a beat, and bringing it to a crescendo with a championship match, death match, cage match, or any number of specialty matches. A great booker is worth ten times his weight in gold, just as a bad one can cause a company to destruct in a matter of months. Remember WCW?

Who had control of the book had as much to do with politics as it did with talent. Niccolò Machiavelli would have made it to the top as a booker for WCW if he hadn't lived in the 15th century.

Vince McMahon had been doing well with *WrestleMania*, the *Royal Rumble*, and *Summer Slam*, and the NWA needed an event in which to battle back and gain ground. Crockett already had *Starrcade*, but if they were ever going to take the upper hand in the promotional wars, they needed another show of that size, so the Bash was created to be the major card for the summer months.

In 1985, there was only one Bash, but in subsequent years, the Great American Bash became a tour that ran throughout the month of July in Philadelphia, Washington DC, Charlotte, Memphis, Cincinnati, Charleston, [WV], Jacksonville, Richmond, Fayetteville [NC], Johnson City [TN], Norfolk, Greensboro, and Atlanta. Each town received the benefit of seeing a major pay-per-view type card featuring Jimmy Valiant, Magnum T.A., the Road Warriors, Wahoo McDaniel, the Midnight Express [Bobby Eaton and Dennis Condrey], the Rock 'n' Roll Express, Ole and Arn Anderson, Tully Blanchard, Paul Jones, Ron Garvin, Krusher Khrushchev, Ivan, Ric, and me, among others.

The Bash was a lot of fun because it gave us all a chance to mix up the roster a bit and wrestle opponents we normally didn't get to wrestle. The fans also enjoyed it because they got to see a major card in somewhat smaller venues like Johnson City, Tennessee, and see us against different opponents.

At the time, Ric and I were the the perfect opponents for each other. In any title match, from the smallest regional title to the heavyweight title of the world, the challenger is every bit as important as the champion. An old adage in boxing says "styles make the match," and the same can be said for wrestling. Without a viable challenger, the champion might as well retire with the belt.

Title matches are the crown jewel of any promotion. Title matches draw more fans than non-title matches, and the more prestigious the title, the better the chance of drawing a larger crowd. Of course, bigger crowds mean more money makes its way into the box office. On the other hand, the champion can't do it on his own. The man standing across the ring, hoping to take the title, is every bit as important as the man entering the ring as the champion. Likewise, the man in position to challenge the titleholder has to pull his share of the load. If one of the combatants fails, they both fail, and so goes the match. Too many matches like that can kill a town, and too many dead towns can completely destroy a territory.

Your opponent's character and ring prowess makes all the difference in the world to the story you are telling in the ring. It dictates whether the program [the series of matches in which you are involved] succeeds or not. If the fans buy into it, you are on your way. If not, there isn't much you can do to change their minds. In many ways, your opponent is as much your partner as a tag-team partner is. You may have to wrestle the same guy five or more times a week across the territory, across the country, or across the world. "Strangler" Ed Lewis vs. Jim Londos, Lou Thesz vs. Buddy Rogers or Gene Kiniski, and Jack Brisco vs. Dory Funk Jr., all had vastly successful programs that ran for years. More times than not, they wrestled to packed houses and had the fans exhausted at the conclusion of each match … and ready to line up at the box office to purchase tickets for a rematch.

The champion is always under a great deal of pressure. He carries a large part of the promotion on his shoulders, and the more important the title, the heavier the load. In the case of the world champion, he carries the weight of the entire National Wrestling Alliance. Even in territories devoid of much talent, all promoters eagerly anticipated the arrival of the world champion into their area. That meant bigger crowds and a renewed interest in whoever the challenger might be. The champion had quite a responsibility, and it took an exceptional athlete, wrestler, and man to pull it off night after night. That being the case, the stress of Flair's world title would have been staggering to most men; but not to him. Ric did it without missing a beat. The original "Nature Boy," Buddy Rogers, who held the NWA world heavyweight title in the early 1960s, was famous for saying "when the going gets too tough for everyone else, it's just right for the Nature Boy." Ric not only received his inspiration from Buddy, but also showed the same tenacity of his namesake.

If anyone was destined to be champion, it was Ric. He personified what the world perceived the world champion should be in the 1980s. As Ric would say, *"I'm a kiss stealin', wheelin' dealin', jet flying, son-of-a-gun."* With his long,

Ric Flair

blond hair, custom-made suits, Rolex watches, and Italian shoes, Ric lived up to the title "Nature Boy." In addition to everything else, he could wrestle, and it seemed that no matter who he was wrestling, he would draw packed houses, with the fans all echoing his signature "whoo-ooo" in arenas around the globe.

Flair was, for all practical purposes, to the manor born. He was adopted as a young child by a loving couple in Minnesota. His new father was a physician and his mother a patron of the arts. After trying to decide what path to take during college, he decided to give wrestling a try. It was in the arduous journey that Richard Morgan Fliehr became ... "Nature Boy" Ric Flair.

Ric had wrestled in high school and took an opportunity to train with the legendary amateur and professional wrestling champion, Verne Gagne. He wrestled preliminaries around the AWA and in 1974, on an invitation from Wahoo McDaniel, headed south to the Carolinas. Flair became the "Nature Boy" under the advice and guidance of booker, former world tag-team champion, and promotional genius, George Scott. Up to then, he had been little more than a jobber for Verne's more established stars. To look at him then, one would be hard pressed to see the Ric Flair who helped transform professional wrestling.

According to George, Ric probably was fifty pounds or so heavier and had the idea of taking on a cowboy image, much like his favorite wrestler, Dusty Rhodes. Scott saw him through a different set of eyes. He saw a rebirth of former NWA world heavyweight champion "Nature Boy" Buddy Rogers. Ric trimmed down, let his hair grow long, dyed it blond ... and became the "Nature Boy." Buddy Rogers may have been his model, but Ric took to his new persona as he took to wrestling and began to write a new chapter in the history of wrestling.

Ric's path to the ring, the title, and our first meeting, was as unusual as my own. In many ways, Ric wasn't all that different from his in-ring persona.

At the time of our match, Ric was actually in the middle of his fourth title reign, and not the third, as the wrestling magazines were stating. He first won the world title on September 17, 1981, by defeating two-time champion, Dusty Rhodes in Kansas City, Kansas. Dusty had captured the title twice — the first time by beating Harley Race in Tampa, Florida on August, 21, 1979 and beating

Race again in Atlanta on June 21, 1981. As popular as Dusty was, he served only as a transitional champion. The first time, in 1979, he dropped the belt back to Race five days after winning it. The same proved to be true with Dusty's second reign when he dropped the belt to Flair in Kansas less than three months later.

Ric took to the title like a fish to water. If anyone was born to wear the "ten pounds of gold," it was the Nature Boy. He defended the title and took it to a level that had not been seen since Jack Brisco held the title seven years before. Ric held the title for 21 months before his reign came to an end at the hands of six-time champion Harley Race in the storied Kiel Auditorium in St. Louis on the hot summer night of June 10, 1983.

In taking the title from Ric, Harley took the wrestling world by surprise. He had a great run as champion during the previous ten years, but after losing the belt to Flair in Atlanta, the wrestling pundits considered Harley a great former champion, with the emphasis on former. With this new victory, however, he not only shocked the Nature Boy, but the rest of the wrestling world, as well. But what the wrestling world didn't know was the story behind the scenes that revolved around Race's defeat of Flair that precipitated one of the greatest cards in the history of the National Wrestling Alliance. That card would help usher in the modern age of pay-per-view and sports entertainment. It was christened *Starrcade–A Flair for the Gold*.

Starrcade was first devised as a vehicle to end the angle of Flair's "Quest for the Gold," his bid to regain the world title from Harley. The card, held in Greensboro on November 24, 1983, was a who's who of professional wrestling, where nearly every major star competed and nearly every major title was on the line. Flair did take the title back for the third time by pinning Race in a cage match with former world heavyweight champion, Gene Kiniski, serving as referee. *Pro Wrestling Illustrated* called it the "Match of the Year."

It is the champion's job to make the challenger look good. No matter who they are facing, they have to make the challenger look like he can take the title at any time during the match. That's not all that difficult if you're wrestling someone like Sting, Ricky Steamboat, or Dusty Rhodes, but to make the challengers look good in some of the territories where the world champion had to visit, the task could be daunting, if not impossible.

However, Ric was so talented he made everyone he wrestled look like a million dollars. It has been said numerous times that Ric could get in the ring with a broom stick and have a four-star match. I can't imagine anyone loving the business more than he does. As champion, he would put a challenger over by losing a fall or a non-title match, and that would bolster a territory and draw money for an upcoming match. Ric has held the world title sixteen times (or more depending on whose count you accept), but no matter how many times he won and lost the title, he is the quintessential champion.

For me to face him in a major program for the belt was beyond my wildest dreams and I will be forever grateful. After all, he won his first world title three years before I entered the ring, and thirteen months after my ring debut, I was challenging him for the heavyweight title of the world.

Ric's third title reign came about after he lost the title to Kerry von Erich in front of a huge crowd in Irving, Texas on May 6, 1984. He returned the favor eighteen days later in Yokosuka City, Japan, by reversing a rolling cradle and pinning von Erich's shoulders to the mat for the three-count.

That is where the magazines of the day ended their count, but there had been another quick title change that was not recognized for more than a decade. On March 24, 1984, Ric handed the belt over to Race in Wellington New Zealand, and took it back two days later in Singapore.

Preceding our match on the night of the Bash, the fans sat through seven matches, including Ole and Arn Anderson successfully defending the National tag team title against Buzz Sawyer and Dick Slater, world tag team champions Ivan and Krusher ending up in a double disqualification against the Road Warriors, and Magnum T.A. pinning Kamala the "Ugandan Giant." Those early matches not only gave the fans value for the price of their ticket, but gave those who were predisposed time to consume quite a lot of beer.

To say I was nervous on the night of the Bash would be an understatement of gross proportions. There were more than 35,000 fans packing the American Legion Memorial Stadium that night. The closer we came to the main event, the larger the butterflies in my stomach became. By bell time, they seemed more like bats than butterflies, and the cotton mouth I was experiencing couldn't be quenched by all the water in the Great Lakes. But when Jim Crockett stuck his head in the dressing room and said, *"You're on Niki,"* I knew I had to leave my nervousness, butterflies and all in, the dressing room.

I entered the ring first as dictated by tradition. The challenger usually enters the ring before the champion to build the expectation of the crowd and to show respect to the champion of the world. As I walked the aisle to the ring, I took slow deliberate steps, looking ahead and showing the singular resolve of a determined challenger. The fans were hanging over the security railings trying to either touch me or take a swing, depending on their disposition. A spotlight followed me as I took each step.

Arriving at the ring, I stopped, scanned the crowd, and walked up the ring steps onto the apron, where I parted the ropes and entered the squared circle. As I stood up, I threw my arms up into the air. The coliseum was well lit and 70,000 eyes were focused on me. To the fans, I'm sure I looked fierce, but inside, the "Russian Nightmare" was still feeling a bit overwhelmed. As I waited for Flair, I tugged on the ropes and paced back and forth, trying to appear as menacing as possible.

When it was the champion's turn to make his way to the ring, Ric entered the stadium in a manner befitting the world heavyweight champion — by way of helicopter. Ric, wearing one of his famous sequined robes, was accompanied by local sportscaster Harold Johnson of WSOC-TV. It was more than obvious who the fans came to see. When the crowd caught sight of Ric, they let loose with a deafening roar, and the closer he got to the ring, the louder the fans screamed. The wave of sound steadily increased from the moment Ric first stepped into view and rose in a crescendo that peaked at the moment Flair stepped into the ring.. He threw his head back, shook his long blond hair, and yelled *"Whoo-ooo"* to the crowd, which echoed his cry in response.

The announcer took the microphone and began: *"Ladies and gentlemen … the moment you have been waiting for … the main event of the evening for the heavyweight wrestling title of the world. In this corner, the challenger, from Moscow, Russia, weighing in at 285 pounds, the undefeated challenger, the*

Russian Nightmare, Nikita Koloff." I thought the cheers for Flair were deafening, but the jeers that followed my name made Ric's entrance seem like a whisper. I had no idea how much heat or anger I had built up with the fans during the previous months. I threw my fist at the crowd and waited for Flair's introduction.

"And in this corner, from Charlotte, North Carolina, he is the three-time heavyweight champion of the world, weighing in at 243 pounds, the "Nature Boy" Ric Flair." Now the crowd did go berserk. I know, with total certainty, I have never heard anything like that before or since. It was like the Beatles, Elvis Presley, and Douglas MacArthur's return all rolled up into one. *"Man,"* I thought, *"this guy is great."*

David Crockett, who was the special referee for our match, called us both to the ring, gave us the instructions, and showed me the belt, emblematic of the world's title. He then held the belt up over his head and slowly turned, facing each side of the ring to show the crowd the valued prize that would be awarded to the winner. He walked to the edge of the ring, handed the belt to the timekeeper, and called for the bell. With the peal of the bell, all the months of buildup and expectation had subsided, and within the hour, the preeminence of the ring would be decided.

We tied up in the referee's position and I began the match with power moves to establish superiority and control of the match.

I already described the incident involving the fan who entered the ring and attacked me during the match. In retrospect, I guess I was somewhat proud that my character was over so well that it brought fans to their feet and, in this case, into the ring with such raw emotion. I must say that it's quite an accomplishment to be voted by the fans as the number-one hated guy in wrestling. I didn't necessarily enjoy having that reputation, but I did take great satisfaction in doing my job so well. At the time, however, I thought, *"This is crazy. What a way to make a living; putting your life at risk in front of a bunch of wacky people."* Certainly, not all the fans were like that. I'm sure all in all, only a small percentage of them were of the mind to actually attack me or any of the boys, but as Ole Anderson can attest, it only takes one.

I believe my first match with Ric made my career, even though I didn't win the title that night. He was probably as responsible, if not more so, for me doing as well as I did so early in the game, and that set the stage for what I would accomplish in the weeks and months that followed.

If two or more wrestlers were involved in a program that drew money, we would work it for seven to eight months. I worked with Ric at least that long. We would build up the house shows on television and take the world title match into a town like Greensboro. The first night we were in the town, we would do a 60-minute broadway, and a week or so later, we would have a return match with a no-disqualification and no-time-limit stipulation. In the weeks that followed, we would continue to build the story. When it began to cool off with the fans, I would get a non-title win over Flair in a tag-match and we would be off and running again. It was the anticipation of what might happen next that kept the fans tuning in and lined up at the box office.

But a program can last only so long, and as much fun as it was wrestling Ric, the fans eventually wanted to see him defend his belt against other contenders. I was ready to seek other opponents, as well, and possibly capture a singles title of my own.

Chapter 15
The Mama's Boy

Next to the world title, the belt with the most prestige was the United States heavyweight title. In fact, it was actually more insidious for me to go after the U.S. title than the world title. It was one thing for the "Russian Nightmare" to win the world title, but it was a different matter altogether for a man from the Soviet Union to hold the most important title in America. In fact, it wasn't unusual for a Russian to hold a world title in any sport, but for a Russian to be brazen enough to travel to America and capture the title of the United States was unthinkable.

The history of titles billed as the United States heavyweight title is as varied and colorful as the narration of the world title. It has been, since its inception, believed to be the precursor, in many cases, to the world heavyweight title. In the mid to late 19th century, there were three major titles in the country which could be considered to be "United States" heavyweight titles.

The earliest known wrestling title was the American Collar and Elbow. It was first won by James McLaughlin in Newark, New Jersey in 1867. Over the next 17 years, he lost, and then regained, the title four more times.

In 1880, the legendary William Muldoon defeated Thiebaud Bauer in New York City to capture the first American Greco-Roman title and went on to defeat Edwin Bibby of England in San Francisco to claim the world title in 1883. Muldoon kept a strong hold on both titles, retiring undefeated and leaving the titles vacant upon his departure from the sport in 1891.

After winning the world catch-as-catch-can title in 1887, Evan "Strangler" Lewis (not to be confused with "Strangler" Ed Lewis, the great five-time world heavyweight champion of the 1920s and 1930s) set his sights on the American Greco-Roman title and took the laurels in March 1893 by beating Ernest Roeber in the best of five falls. Having both titles and seeing the growing popularity of the new American style, Lewis combined both titles into the American title. Over time, that title would pass through the hands of the immortals of early wrestling: Martin "Farmer" Burns, Dan McLeod, Tom Jenkins, and Frank Gotch (who held the title three times). On April 3, 1908, Gotch defeated George Hackenschmidt for the world heavyweight title in front of a sellout crowd in Chicago and unified both titles.

In the years that followed, there were dozens, perhaps hundreds of claimants, to the United States heavyweight title.

The first high-profile and most prestigious version of the U.S. title appeared in Chicago when Verne Gagne held the belt in 1953. During the next 15 years, many other versions of the title would pop up in various territories, including Denver, Kansas City, Hawaii, Toronto, Detroit, Texas, and San Francisco.

The claim to being the heavyweight champion of the United States was too good to leave to the NWA and one champion. It was a big country and a big title, so why not share it? In 1960, repeating what they did with the world tag team title, the California promotion crowned Ray Stevens as their first United States heavyweight champion, claiming he had defeated Bobo Brazil in November 1960. The title would change hands 55 times before the promotion closed in 1981 with Dusty Rhodes as their final champion,

As strange as it seems, Toronto had its own version of the title, with Johnny Valentine as their initial champion in 1962. In 1981, when Crockett started promoting in Canada, the Mid-Atlantic version of the title was brought into play when Sgt. Slaughter defeated Ricky Steamboat in a tournament final.

Hawaii also had a version of the U.S. title in 1962 with Nick Bockwinkel as their initial champion. In 1968, the title was rechristened as the North American heavyweight title.

Perhaps the most well-known version of the title was the one in Detroit, which was defended on and off for more than 15 years and traded countless times between the Sheik [Ed Farhat] and Bobo Brazil.

The most bizarre adaptation of the United States heavyweight title was defended in Giant Baba's All Japan Pro Wrestling promotion. Dick Beyer, of Syracuse, wrestling as the Destroyer, was billed as the champion upon arrival in 1970 and held the title on five different occasions during a period of eight years.

When George Scott took over as booker in the Carolinas and began rebuilding the crumbling territory, he knew he needing an established star and a new title. Prior to that, the Atlantic Coast and Eastern championships had been featured as the primary titles, but the area relied heavily on tag team matches, rather than singles competition. Scott brought in Harley Race as the champion and billed him as having won the U.S. title by defeating Johnny Weaver in a tournament. As with many wrestling storylines, the tournament was fictitious, but in order to give the title instant credibility, it was necessary to bring in someone with the stature and reputation of Harley Race. On July 3, 1975, Johnny Valentine took the title from Race in Greensboro. Scott's intent was to use Johnny Valentine to transform the territory into one that would place more emphasis on single matches.

Valentine was a great champion and the Carolinas were on fire. It looked like Valentine would hang onto the belt like Franklin Delano Roosevelt hung on to the presidency … until he was seriously injured in a plane crash in October of that year and was forced to quit active wrestling.

Not to be derailed by the tragedy, George quickly put together a 16-man one-night tournament to crown Valentine's successor. On November 9, 1975, one month after the plane crash, Terry Funk defeated Paul Jones in the final match of the tournament. Crockett gave the belt credibility by bringing in someone of Funk's stature, but it was only intended for Terry to be a short-term champion. Terry was in line to win the NWA world heavyweight title on December 10, just four weeks later, so he held the title for just two weeks before dropping it to Jones.

Some of the greatest wrestlers that ever laced up a pair of boots have held that version of the U.S. title, including Blackjack Mulligan, Bobo Brazil, Ric Flair, Ricky Steamboat, Mr. Wrestling [Tim Woods], Jimmy Snuka, Greg Valentine, Roddy Piper, Wahoo McDaniel, Sgt. Slaughter, Magnum T.A., Lex Luger, and Tully Blanchard.

When my quest for the U.S. belt began, it was held by Terry Allen, or as he was known by the fans in the Mid-Atlantic area, Magnum T.A. Terry grew up in Chesapeake, Virginia, and had followed wrestling since he was a young boy. He spent many Saturday afternoons watching the *Mid-Atlantic Championship Wrestling* television shows and attending live matches with his grandfather. Terry's interest in professional wrestling led him to take to the amateur mat in high school, where he won the 167-pound state title and a spot on the wrestling team at Old Dominion University. He did well as a college freshman, but gained thirty pounds over the summer and came back weighing 215 pounds. Not being too excited about cutting back to 167, and not being big enough to wrestle as a heavyweight, he decided to leave the mat and look for other things to fill his time.

Magnum TA

To earn extra money, Terry took a job at one of the popular Virginia Beach night clubs, the Rogues Gallery, where he first came into close contact with the wrestlers he watched on television. As he was getting to know them, he read an article in a local newspaper that said some of the top wrestlers made $100,000 or more. Terry decided that was the path he wanted to follow. He wanted to be a professional wrestler.

He began his training under the tutelage of Gene Anderson. A few weeks into preparation, he came to the realization that Gene didn't seem to be very interested in seeing Terry and his group break into the professional wrestling business, so he decided to quit.

A short time later, he was approached by "Mad Dog" Buzz Sawyer, who offered to train him one-on-one. Agreeing to his offer, he set off to Don Owen's territory in the Northwest. After parting ways with Buzz, Terry moved on to the Texas, Florida, and Louisiana territories. It was there he was told he resembled the popular television star, Tom Selleck, of the hit show, *Magnum, P.I.* And so, Magnum T.A. was born.

Arriving in Charlotte for Jim Crockett, Magnum was an immediate hit with the fans. He had some fantastic matches with Ric for the world title and captured the United States heavyweight title within a few months of his arrival. When I came onto the scene, Terry still held the U.S. title, having regained it from Tully Blanchard on November 28, 1985 in Greensboro. Magnum had lost the belt five months earlier to Tully after winning the belt from Wahoo McDaniel in March of that year.

Magnum defended the title against all comers until May 29, 1986 when Bob Geigel, president of the National Wrestling Alliance, stripped the title from him after an altercation on television where an angry Magnum attacked Geigel. Geigel had a colorful career in wrestling and won the NCAA amateur championship before entering the professional ranks. He won more than his share of regional titles before buying into the Kansas City territory to become a partner and booker. One of his partners in the company was none other than "Handsome" Harley Race.

The story of how Magnum was stripped of the belt was the perfect entrée to our battle. After a number of victories, I was deemed the number one contender for the title. To illustrate the importance of our first match, the Crocketts held a formal contract signing between the two of us. Magnum and I, along with Sandy Scott, Ivan, and Magnum's mom, appeared on the studio set. Sandy was there as the official representative of the NWA, Ivan was there as my second, and Magnum's mom was there to second him and show how proud she was of her son.

It was the perfect scenario for any heel, but the best of all possible worlds for a heel from the Soviet Union. During the signing, I kept making remarks to Uncle Ivan about the mighty heavyweight champion of the United States being nothing more than a "Mama's Boy." I referred to the fact that I brought my uncle, coach, and advisor, the former heavyweight champion of the world with me, while Magnum brought his mother. That was an insult, not only to the champion and his mother, but to all American mothers everywhere.

When Magnum couldn't take it any longer, he jumped over the table to get at me, knocking over Sandy Scott in the process. Ivan and I took advantage of the attack and hit Magnum with one of the chairs, and then continued to stomp him while Sandy lay prone on the floor and Magnum's mom watched in horror. When Ivan and I left the set, Magnum was lying "unconscious" on the floor with the U.S. belt draped across his chest and his mother hovered over him, weeping.

The next week on television, they replayed the incident while NWA president Bob Geigel watched the monitor. At the conclusion, he called out Magnum. Of course, Magnum and the fans all thought Geigel would side with him and fine me or suspend me from competing, but Geigel had other ideas. He began to berate Magnum, telling him his conduct during the signing was disgraceful and unbecoming to a champion. Magnum began to argue with Bob, and the longer the conversation went, the more heated it became. Once again, Magnum lost his temper and nailed Geigel, "knocking him out" and sending him sprawling to the concrete floor. When he recovered, a heated Geigel stripped Magnum of his title and ordered us to wrestle in a match which would determine whether Magnum or I would be the champion.

But our match would have a different slant to it. In fact, it was an angle that, to my knowledge, had never been tried before. Instead of one match to decide the new U.S. champion, Magnum and I were scheduled for a best-out-of-seven series with the winner walking away with the belt. It was dubbed the World Series of Wrestling.

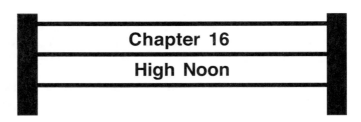

Chapter 16

High Noon

Of all my matches throughout my career, the ones in our "best-of-seven" series seem to etch themselves in the minds of the fans. The match up was a natural. The fans loved Magnum as much as they hated me, if not more. You have to remember that the Cold War was still raging and a lot of Americans were greatly concerned about the possible aggression of the Soviet Union against the United States. To the wrestling fans, I was the personification of that "Red Menace." I not only wanted to conquer the world, but I wanted to take their United States heavyweight title in the process, and the closer I got to winning the title, the more deep-seated their anger became.

A foreign heel taking the beloved U.S. belt worked well in the 1950s and 1960s. The Japanese villain Kinji Shibuya held the San Francisco version of the NWA U.S. title three times from 1964 to 1968, and Tiger Jeet Singh defeated Johnny Valentine for the Toronto version of the title just before the turn of the decade.

One of the most famous (or infamous, depending on your preference) was Jack Adkisson, who wrestled as the goose-stepping Nazi, Fritz von Erich. Fritz, the patriarch of the famous von Erich clan of the 1980s, held the Detroit version of the U.S. belt twice Fritz took the title from fellow heel (but American) Dick the Bruiser [Richard Afflis] in 1961 and two years later from Lord Athol Layton. It had been a scant 15 years since the end of World War II and the Allied victory over the Axis powers led by Nazi Germany. The thought of this "jack-booted" heel holding the championship of the United States was a lot more than patriotic American fans could stomach. What it did do, however, was turn that music major and football star from Southern Methodist University into a top draw in wrestling, and he became a very wealthy man in the process.

When Fritz pulled up stakes and left the Detroit territory for Dallas, he established a new title in Texas that would easily mirror the U.S. title. It was too good of an angle to let fall by the wayside. The "Iron Claw" wielding Nazi character was gold at the box office in Texas and the fans there were not that different from the fans in Detroit. Besides, a good angle is a good angle. On June 6, 1966 (6-6-66, as if the angle wasn't bad enough in the eyes of the fans), Fritz defeated Brute Bernard to become the first NWA American heavyweight champion.

Establishing the American heavyweight title gave Fritz's new promotion a major title and a goal for the American wrestlers in the territory — to take the

American title from the German heel. It was a great idea and storyline, especially for the time. No matter who was challenging, the crowd would always root for the American. It didn't matter if it was hero versus heel or heel versus heel. Fans would crowd the arenas hoping to lay witness to von Erich's demise. The venues were full each week and so were Fritz's coffers.

Perhaps the most nefarious foreign heel to hold the U.S. heavyweight title was a former mail carrier from Michigan, Ed Farhat, who transformed himself into the Sheik, a "fire-throwing" Arab. The Sheik, who eventually secured ownership of the Detroit territory, held the Detroit version of the title twelve times between 1965 and the close of the promotion in 1980. Interestingly enough, 46 of the 47 title changes from 1958 to 1980 took place in Detroit, rather than one of the other towns in the territory.

It's a given that professional wrestling promoters will stick with a tried-and-true formula until they see crowds begin to wane. When that happens, they will reshape the angle with a modern twist and revive the basic emotions and interests of the fans as the good and righteous do battle with the darker side of mankind. That formula worked in the 1930s and it still works today. Veer too far away from it and make the storylines too convoluted or disjointed, and you would be ... well, WCW.

A secondary reason for the best-of-seven series was to have it be a major part of the Great American Bash, which was touring the country in July and August 1986. My first match with Magnum took place at Veterans' Stadium in Philadelphia on July 1, 1986, the first night of the Bash tour. The purpose of the match was to build me up as an unstoppable wrestling machine. I defeated Magnum in a good match, especially for the fact that it established me as the more dominant competitor. In the eyes of the fans, Magnum did well, but I was just too strong that night for him to prevail.

Losing the match didn't harm his reputation. He was only down one match and he had plenty of time to even the score. As far as the fans were concerned, he was still the champion because he didn't lose his belt in the ring.

Our second match was held a week later on July 9 at Riverfront Stadium in Cincinnati. Like the first match, Magnum fought with his back against the wall in an effort to come back from being one match down. He fought valiantly in an attempt to even the series, but I was the strongest and took control of the match. Once again, I defeated him in the middle of the ring. The score: Koloff, 2 – Magnum, 0. Magnum had lost two in a row, but the fans rallied behind him more strongly than ever. It's true that everyone loves a winner, but that doesn't hold true if they hail from Moscow and are bent on taking the U.S. title. Magnum not only got the sympathy of the fans, but he personified all their hopes.

The fans came out in droves for our third encounter. We headed back south to Magnum's home state of Virginia and battled in the Roanoke Civic Center. To Magnum's legion of fans, being down two matches was nothing more than a detail. In their eyes, he was sure to take the third one and then the rush would be on. I would be lucky if I even came close to winning another match.

To the fans chagrin, I defeated Magnum once again. He had his moments, but as in the previous two matches, I proved to be too strong and beat him, despite Magnum making a better showing and coming close to winning the match on several occasions. Koloff, 3 – Magnum, 0. All I had to do was win one more match and I would sweep the series. The U.S. title and belt would be mine.

Now here is the genius of effective wrestling promotion. With a three-match advantage, the fans attitudes were beginning to change. They were still behind their hero, but they couldn't help but wonder if I was going to take the series 4-0, vanquish their champion, and win the U.S. belt. I came off the first three matches as such a relentless, unstoppable force that it seemed all but inevitable that I would win match four and walk away, not only as the champion, but as Magnum's conqueror.

We came together for our fourth match at the Greensboro Coliseum on July 26. It had been 15 days since our last match. During that time, the Bash had continued to run in other cities. Magnum and I were on those cards, but we didn't wrestle each other in single matches. On July 3, we were in Washington D.C. where I teamed with Uncle Ivan and Krusher Khrushchev against Magnum and the Road Warriors. On July 4, we were in Memphis where I put the Nature Boy over in the main event for the world title. On July 5 in Charlotte, I teamed with Ivan again against Hawk and Animal. On July 10, Ivan, Krusher, and I faced Dusty and the Road Warriors in a cage match in Charleston, West Virginia.

When I walked into the ring that night in Greensboro, I had my head held high, showing confidence that by the time I left the ring, the title would be mine. Throughout the match, I battered Magnum from pillar to post. I purposely missed pinning him on a number of occasions, playing with him like a cat played with an injured bird. I was going to defeat him in my own time and only when I was ready to do so. I was well on my way to victory when Magnum surprised me with a belly-to-belly suplex and pinned me.

As soon as the referee slapped the mat for the third time, I jumped up. I thought the roof was going to come off the Coliseum. The fans were dancing in the aisles. I had never seen a reaction like that. It was as if Magnum had won a title. He didn't, but he did take one match in the series and kept hope alive. Koloff, 3 – Magnum, 1.

The genius behind the best-of–seven series was the psychology behind it. As the matches progressed, the excitement and electricity grew and the crowds swelled. I made appearances on all the syndicated wrestling shows and vowed to crush Magnum. His one victory over me was no more than a blip on the radar screen. I would crush him and end the series as I should have done in our previous match.

Magnum, of course, also appeared on television, vowing to take the next two matches and even the series. He promised not only to even the series at three matches apiece, but he would take match seven and regain the title that had been wrongly taken from him. The fans hung onto his every word. Not only did they freely hand over their hard-earned dollars, but some drove hundreds of miles to cheer him on.

On August 2 in Atlanta, Magnum and his fans experienced the emotion of his second victory over me. Once again, I was the aggressor throughout the match and had Magnum on the verge of defeat at least a dozen times. At each juncture, however, he reached inside himself and found the strength to break free or to kick out of my pin. I continued to take the battle to him, only to have him catch me off guard and pin me for the win. The score now was: Koloff, 3 – Magnum, 2.

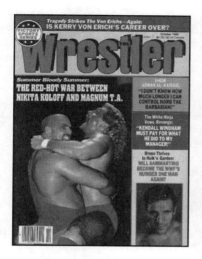 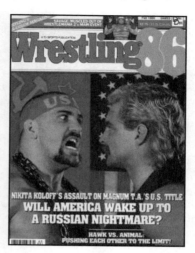

Magnum was on a roll, but he still had to win two matches to regain the belt, while I had to win just one. On the other hand, even though the odds were in my favor, the momentum belonged to him. For match number six, we entered the ring in the Asheville Civic Center on Sunday, August 10. This was a regular wrestling card since the Great American Bash had ended with the show in Atlanta. As in most of our matches, Magnum spent a great deal of time fending off my relentless attacks. Just when I had victory in my grasp, Magnum nailed me with his suplex and won the match. The fans were overjoyed. In three consecutive matches, Magnum went from a 3-0 deficit to being one match away from, once again, strapping the U.S. belt firmly around his waist. The score was now even: Koloff, 3 – Magnum, 3.

It was high drama as the seventh match became our "High Noon." Crockett gave us the week to build up the final match of the series and Terry and I played it to the hilt. The match was held on August 17 at the Charlotte Coliseum with the "best-of-seven" series and the U.S. title hanging in the balance. That actually was our second "seventh match." We had wrestled the night before in Philadelphia with both of us being disqualified. That was planned, of course, to finish the series in front of the "home crowd" in Charlotte. At the time of the series, our match held such importance that, the following week, Crockett dedicated the entire television broadcast to the match. He had his television crew there to tape it and they aired the match on TV in its entirety, which was rare for wrestling at the time.

I think it was the best match of the series with the advantage see-sawing back and forth. At the end of the match, Magnum had victory in his grasp, as he did numerous times during the match, and was well on his way to what the fans thought would be impossible — coming from three matches down to winning four in a row and taking the series.

Each of us garnered several near falls during the 45 minutes we wrestled and we had the fans standing up and sitting down for the duration of the match. Towards the end of the match, Magnum left the ring and gave "Uncle" Ivan a piledriver to render him unable to assist me, a tactic we used often to give me an advantage and help me win my matches. With Ivan down, Magnum dropped me with his signature move: the belly-to-belly suplex. Meanwhile, Krusher had made his way to the ring and distracted referee Tommy Young. Magnum had me covered for a lot longer that the required three-count; reminiscent of the Tunney-Dempsey infamous "long count" as they battled for the world heavyweight boxing championship in Chicago in 1927. The fans counted out loud 1-2-3-4-5-6-7, but Tommy was too busy with Krusher to pay attention. As the crowd counted seven, Magnum stood up and walked over to get Tommy's attention. As he turned his back and walked away, I wrapped my chain around my arm. When Magnum turned back around, I lunged and nailed him in the forehead. When Tommy turned around, he saw me holding Magnum's shoulders to the mat. As Tommy made the fatal 1-2-3 count, the fans' worst nightmare came true. I became the U.S. heavyweight champion.

One of the most dramatic parts of the match came after the pinfall, and it couldn't have happened better if it had been scripted. After I hit Magnum with the chain, I tossed it into the corner of the ring. The chain slid to the side of the ring apron and enough of it fell over the side to pull the rest of it to the arena floor. As if to underscore my treachery and sinister victory, it slowly slid to the floor like a snake slithering into its hole. Sometimes things just work out that way.

There have been occasions when I have heard people say they believed there was actual heat between Magnum and me, that our battles in the ring were an extension of our true feelings about each other, and that the professional rivalry between us brought us to physical altercations in the dressing room. I am here to say that nothing could be further from the truth. The angle between Magnum T.A., the "All-American Boy," and me was confined totally in the ring and the minds of the fans. When the angle began, I didn't know Magnum well. I always stayed pretty much to myself and tried to keep things in the dressing room on a professional level. As a result, I didn't have a lot of close friends in the business. I never was really buddy-buddy with anyone or intruded into their business. I was there to do a job, so I tried to stay away from the locker room politics. It wasn't that I was aloof. I just thought it was better not to blur the lines between the professional and personal sides of the business.

I had read that during his days with the Cleveland Browns, the great running back, Jim Brown, would arrive to practice each day wearing a suit and carrying a briefcase. To him, football was a business. He was a professional on and off the field and he made sure he conducted himself in that manner. I tried to do the same. From the moment I entered the business, I decided I would keep it just that — a business. I had a plan for my career and knew there would be a life for me after I left the ring. Please don't take me the wrong way. I wasn't a prima donna and I didn't keep to myself in the corner. I enjoyed the camaraderie with a lot of the boys and still count a number of them as friends, but while I was active in the ring, I tried to keep my business and personal life separate.

Egos in our sport can be larger than the wrestlers themselves and I tried to keep mine in check. I never called anyone on the phone and said, *"Hey, watch me on TV tonight,"* or, *"Guess where I wrestled last night?"* I was there to do a job and to put forth every effort I could, no matter the angle or what I was called upon to do. As they say, "business is business," and my job was to wrestle and give both the fans and the promoters their money's worth.

Chapter 17
The Soviet Ambassador

Jim Crockett was an ambitious promoter and businessman. He saw dollar signs everywhere in the country and the possibility of even more profits throughout the world, so in 1986, Jim booked us in Kuwait, Japan, and Puerto Rico. My last match in the States before leaving on the tour was in Charlotte on September 28.

I had never been out of the country before and really didn't know what to expect. I had heard that fans overseas were very different from those in America. They could be as polite and reserved as those in Japan or as volatile and dangerous as those in Puerto Rico. The boys who had been around a while told me not to worry about it. I was told to be careful, do what I usually do in the ring, and once the match was over, get to the dressing room as quickly as I could.

Kuwait was one of our first stops and turned out to be the site of one of the most bizarre experiences I could ever have imagined. I kept expecting Rod Serling to appear and say, *"That's the sign-post up ahead. Your next stop ... the Twilight Zone."*

There was a lot of promotion that preceded our arrival. Huge posters were pasted on what seemed to be every available wall all over the country. I'm not talking about the regular-sized window cards that we used in the States. I mean six to seven-foot posters reminiscent of the big circus billboards that Ringling Brothers were so famous for during the past century.

I was prominently featured on quite a few of those billboards. Of course, word had gotten out that a Russian who had been wrestling in the United States and defeating almost everyone was coming to Kuwait to continue the carnage. That was all well and good for me to get over with the fans, but it was about to put me and Jim Crockett Promotions in a potential international incident involving the governments of Kuwait, the United States, and the Soviet Union.

Upon my arrival, the Russian Embassy contacted the promoter and informed him that if a Russian athlete was in Kuwait, either to visit or to compete, he had an obligation to stay at the embassy as long as he was in the country. The promoter politely declined and suggested it would be better all around if I remained with the other wrestlers. As much as it made sense to us, it had the opposite effect to the Soviet ambassador. The ambassador replied with indignation to the promoter's declining of his offer. His refusal, and mine as it was inferred, was an insult to him, the Russian Embassy, and to the Soviet Union and its people. The only answer the ambassador would accept would be a grateful and humble "yes" — and the sooner the better. As funny as this sounds today, at the time, it had some serious implications. The "Cold War," even though weakening, was still going on and nothing could have been seen as more of an affront to the Russian officials than to be snubbed by an American wrestling promoter and a Soviet athlete.

The promoter sent a message to the Soviet ambassador and asked if the two might be able to meet to work something out before things got out of hand. The Kuwaiti government seemed to be somewhat sympathetic to the Soviet Union. They certainly didn't want to upset the emissary assigned to the country and cause hard feelings between the two countries over a wrestler of whom they knew nothing about. When the ambassador and the promoter met, the promoter explained that I really wasn't a Russian and that I actually was from Minnesota in the United States. At first, the ambassador didn't believe him, but the more he insisted that Nikita Koloff was just a gimmick, the more incredulous the ambassador became. *"If he is, indeed, a Russian, he must stay at the embassy,"* the envoy demanded, *"and if he is not, as you say, then why is he wearing CCCP on his headband and singlet?"*

The promoter did finally convince him that Nikita Koloff was just a character, but even then, the ambassador did not like it. He took it as a tremendous personal insult, as well as one to his country. He demanded that any pictures of me with wrestling gear bearing the CCCP initials be removed immediately. The promoter explained that he would do everything he could to honor the ambassador's request, but he had spent tens of thousands of dollars promoting the arrival of his wrestlers, and without the posters, the tour would be a disaster. Not only he, but the country of Kuwait, would not only be embarrassed, but could possibly lose a lot of money.

I am sure the Russian ambassador could not have cared less about any embarrassment or financial loss that Jim Crockett Promotions or the local promoter would incur, but as a diplomat assigned to Kuwait, he must have thought he had some obligation to his host country. He agreed to let the posters remain, but required Jim to black out any reference to the Soviet Union. Jim had to hire someone to block out the CCCP on my pictures.

On the first night of the scheduled matches, the ambassador and his wife were sitting at ringside with a few others from the embassy. I guess they were there to either keep an eye on me, to see what all the fuss was about, or to see how the fans would react to me. It was probably one of the times I was the most nervous about being in the ring. There were a number of reasons for my fears, and not all had to do with the embassy.

One was the fact that the local media was working us pretty hard due to an incident that had occurred a few months or so earlier. We were told that wrestlers from the WWF had been on tour and took some of the matches outside the ring. The fans weren't sure how to react when the wrestlers began fighting on the floor. They got scared and pushed to get out of the way, resulting in a number of people being trampled and injured.

The media continued to play up that story while we were there and we had to make sure we were on our best behavior inside and outside of the ropes. I was also very nervous about the press conference in which we all were participating because I had a responsibility to protect the gimmick and character of Nikita

Koloff, and with all the turmoil surrounding the Russian embassy, I was concerned that some of the reporters would start asking me questions in Russian. And, of course, if that happened, I would be staring back at them with a look that would denote, *"I have no idea what you are saying."*

I sweated through the entire press conference, but fortunately, all questions directed at me were in English, and the press didn't let the prior incidents with the fans get out of hand during their questioning. I was also worried about the ambassador's representatives at ringside trying to force me to stay at the embassy. A few of them came into the dressing room and I thought they might be there to take me back with them. I was concerned to the point that I met with the local promoter and impressed upon him that I was just fine at the hotel and I wasn't going to stay at the embassy. Fortunately for me again, nothing transpired and we finished the tour without any incidents.

Probably the strangest thing of all was, every time I walked to the ring, I was cheered. I had never been cheered before. I was used to having the fans at home hate me with a passion, and here I was a hero. I was scheduled to wrestle a man who was billed as an "All-American Hero," Sgt. Slaughter. Of course, here in the United States, Sarge is loved and cheered for like mad. But in Kuwait, they were jeering him from the moment he stepped out of the dressing room. I was standing in the ring thinking, *"I don't know how to wrestle as a good guy. What am I going to do?"* As we locked up, I shared my apprehension with Sarge, and he just laughed. *"Don't worry about it, kid. It will work itself out."* He was right. It did, and we had a great match.

Kuwait wasn't exactly what I would call a vacation destination. It was mostly brown buildings with a little patch of green here and there. It seemed like everyone wore black clothing and the women were clothed everywhere except for their eyes. The country was also alcohol free, which most of the boys didn't like. The one thing they did have was a mall. The mall held our interest more than it would in other towns because there was literally nothing to do during the day, so we would all go to the mall to kill time. There wasn't a lot of variety in the stores at this particular mall. It seemed like they had four clothing stores and about a hundred jewelry stores. I know that might be a bit of an exaggeration, but not by much.

Now, it wasn't unusual for us to draw a crowd when we were on a tour, but I had never, even to this day, seen a crowd like we saw in Kuwait. Hundreds of fans, or just curious onlookers, followed us everywhere we went. When we went into a store, the fans would gather around the windows and press their faces against the glass to get a better look at us.

Superstar Billy Graham was on the tour with us and we hung out a lot together. One day, we broke away from the larger group of the boys to do some jewelry shopping. We went into the first store we came to and walked directly to the counter. In no time at all, the store was completely packed with Kuwaitis. There were so many fans in the store that they had us pinned against the counter. As we looked out over the heads of the crowd and into the mall, all we could see were the heads of rows and rows of more Kuwaitis. The funniest part of this was that Superstar suffered from a bit of claustrophobia. As the crowd pressed in upon us, Billy gave out a loud yell. Everyone in the store slowly backed away and opened a path for us to work our way through.

We never did find any souvenirs to take home with us. I guess it shows my naiveté at that time in my life to actually think I could find a coffee mug or key chain that had "Kuwait" embossed on it. It was my first time experiencing their culture and, somehow, I expected it to be more like some of the other countries we visited. I sure was wrong, but in retrospect, I really don't know if I wanted to be reminded of my trip to Kuwait every morning as I drank my coffee.

One of the most popular countries we would tour was Japan. Professional wrestling had been a big draw for the country in the decade following the end of World War II. Its popularity grew thanks to its first international star, Rikidôzan, who, with the help of Lou Thesz, popularized the American catch-as-catch-can style in Japan.

Born Mitsuhiro Momota in Korea, a fact that wasn't revealed until after his death due to the fact that he and his business partners feared it would damage his popularity and hurt business in Japan, had begun his career as a sumo wrestler. In 1950, Rikidôzan left the Sumo ranks and became enamored with pro wrestling, which was growing in popularity in Japan. Wrestlers from the United States began visiting Japan shortly after the American occupation in 1945 and Rikidôzan saw a gold mine and a lucrative future for himself in the ring. With the help of Bobby Bruns, an American wrestler from the Midwest, Rikidôzan traveled to the Kansas City territory to learn the American style of professional wrestling.

Proving early on to be a colorful performer in the ring, he headed out for the west coast territories and Hawaii, taking the Pacific Coast tag-team title with Dennis Clary in 1952 and traveling back and forth to Japan. In 1954, Rikidôzan captured the heavyweight title of the Japanese Wrestling Association, the governing body of Japanese wrestling that he founded in 1953. He reached international stardom in 1958 when Lou Thesz put him over in Los Angeles for the NWA International title and defeated "Classy" Freddie Blassie in Los Angeles for the WWA world heavyweight title in 1962. With those prestigious titles in hand (although he lost the WWA title back to Blassie four months after winning it), his promotion took off in Japan.

Rikidôzan ruled the roost until his tragic death in 1963. His death not only shocked the country, but the entire wrestling world. By that time, Rikidôzan had a penchant for liquor and his habit grew worse when he purchased a popular night club and bar named the Chez Paree from some reported mobsters in Tokyo. One evening when he was drinking and holding court in his bar, a minor member of the mob became drunk and belligerent. Rikidôzan, being intoxicated himself, physically threw the 150-pound mobster out of the bar to the amusement of all who were there. Apparently, the mobster sobered up, but stewed about the altercation for some time. One evening, about six months later, he returned to the Chez Paree, walked up behind Rikidôzan, and stabbed him repeatedly in the kidneys with a stiletto.

Rikidôzan turned to his assailant, beat him within an inch of his life, and threw him out into the street. He then returned to the bar and continued drinking, showing his patrons and admirers that he was as invincible in real life as he was in the ring. It was not the stab wounds that killed him as much as his bravado. He drank with his friends for another couple of hours until he became so weak from the loss of blood that he agreed to go to the hospital. He died of blood poisoning the next day. He was 35 years old.

Professional wrestling in Japan would have died with Rikidôzan if it hadn't been for his star pupil, Shohei Baba. Baba, who stood about 7-foot-4, had a promising career as a professional baseball pitcher in his homeland until a fall and ensuing elbow injury brought an abrupt end to his career on the diamond. Japan was hungry for a new hero — one that could carry the banner and the NWA International title that Rikidôzan still held at the time of his death — and Baba was just the man to fill the bill. He returned from a tour of the United States and assumed the mantle of champion and promoter. He took what Rikidôzan had started and created a sports empire that would have made his mentor proud.

I made three tours of Japan [January 1986, October 1986, and October 1987] and worked for Baba each time. I knew him to be a first-class businessman with an incomparable mind for the sport. A three-time NWA world heavyweight champion (beating Jack Brisco once and Harley Race twice), Baba knew how to get over with the fans. He brought top card American wrestlers over to do battle with his top stars and would treat us like kings. We were given first-class airfare, driven everywhere we went, and were assigned a personal attendant to carry our gear and make sure everything we needed was provided. We traveled on beautiful coach buses and rode the bullet train from city to city. I remember eating steak and rice — lots of rice. It seemed that everywhere we went, there were hundreds of cameras with fans, magazine, and newspaper photographers taking pictures at every turn.

During my tours of Japan, like most of the boys from America, I wrestled the top talent Baba had to offer: Riki Chôshû, Masahiro Chono, and Jumbo Tsuruta. One thing different about my stay was that I went over [won my matches], rather than Baba's guys. This was pretty unusual in itself as Baba not only brought the American boys over for the fans and to draw bigger crowds, but also to show how Japanese wrestlers were superior to those from the west. After all, Baba wasn't bringing Americans halfway across the world to beat his boys. Of course, in most cases, the opposite held true when the Japanese wrestlers came to America.

One thing the Japanese wresters did was test us in the ring. They would push us as far as they could physically and would do so until we pushed back. When we did, the tone of the match changed. It would still be physical, but they would show us a level of respect. They never tried to injure me, or any of the other boys for that matter, but they wanted to show us that there was no doubt that we were in their country.

When I first got to Japan, Baba asked me to put his wrestlers over in my matches. I thought about it for a minute or two and said respectfully, *"No, I can't do that."* It wasn't a matter of pride, and I wasn't trying to be difficult. I just thought it wouldn't be the most believable thing to happen to Nikita Koloff at the time. I was being promoted as the indomitable "Russian Nightmare," and being beaten night after night wouldn't do me any good, no matter what country we were wrestling in or who I was wrestling.

Baba wasn't the type of man who was used to being told "no." He tried to convince me, but I held my ground. He then turned to Krusher and asked him to appeal to me to at least drop a fall. I told Krusher the same thing I told Baba. Baba stood silent for a moment, looked at me, nodded his head, said *"Okay,"* and walked away. I'm not exactly sure why he relented. I suppose it may have been a combination of him rethinking what he wanted to see in the ring, or knowing that I was steadfast in my decision, but whatever it was, he agreed. Above all, Baba was a businessman, and he was known for making quick, but thoughtful, decisions and moving on without wasting time.

The only thing negative about my tours of Japan was the food. I enjoyed my tours more and more each time I went, but I don't eat seafood. I never cared for it and the thought of eating it raw made it all the worse. Each tour lasted about two weeks, and each time, I wondered what in the world I was going to eat for that period of time. I do like rice, so I figured I would probably eat quite a bit of that, but upon arrival, we found a number of Kentucky Fried Chicken franchises, so we spent a lot of time eating there.

When we made trips to the smaller islands, finding something palatable to eat was more challenging. The restaurants would make up plates of food from what they had displayed in the window or display cases. We would take the waiters or waitresses up to the cases and point out the food we wanted, hoping it tasted close to what our less-than-sophisticated American palettes could handle.

The thing I enjoyed the most was touring the country on the Shinkansen — the bullet train. Seeing the Japanese countryside, Mount Fuji, and visiting the cities of Hiroshima and Nagasaki gave me a much more historical viewpoint of our host country and all they did to rebuild their homeland. But the best part of my visits to Japan was meeting the wonderful people throughout the country.

My last trip to Japan ended quite badly. It wasn't because of anything I did, in or out of the ring, but rather because of the guy I was assigned to babysit. Through the years, there have always been a few of the boys the rest of us would have to look after, especially when we were out of the country. Terry Gordy was one of them.

Terry had a meteoric career that began when he was only 13 years old and he was well on his way to being a major star by the time he was 18. I liked Terry. I think everyone did, but he had too much success too quickly and it was difficult for him to handle. Terry dropped out of high school after his freshman year and was wrestling main events by the time he was sixteen. He gained his biggest measure of fame as one of the Fabulous Freebirds, and later, as a single star capturing nearly every regional title in the sport. Terry's star shone in every territory in which he appeared, but nowhere brighter than in Japan. His work ethic in the ring was phenomenal, but Terry also was known in the business for his partying and out-of-control antics while away from the arenas. He was a big kid, and even in his late twenties into his thirties, he made decisions you would expect a kid to make with no regard for anyone else or the consequences they might bring.

On that particular trip, I was asked to keep an eye on Terry and to keep him out of trouble, and if not out of trouble, out of jail. I learned that keeping him from getting arrested may have been possible, but keeping him out of trouble wasn't.

One night, he was adamant about going to one particular club. I knew I wasn't going to have any success in dissuading him, so the best I could hope for was to tag along and keep the madness to a minimum. That night, Terry had way too much to drink, and sometime during the evening, he ripped a fire extinguisher from the wall. He began spraying the photographers who were following us and everyone else in sight. I don't know if Terry listened to reason, got tired, or just ran out of foam, but he finally put down the canister. It was three in the morning and we headed back to the hotel.

About eight o'clock the next morning, we heard a pounding on our door. It was some of Baba's executives, who had heard about what happened at the club. The club's owners had said they wouldn't press charges if we paid for the damages. That's "we." Not Terry, but both of us. I told them I wasn't going to pay for half the damages for something I didn't do. They said I was supposed to keep things like that from happening, so I was responsible for half the cost to repair and clean the club. I told them they were out of their mind and if they were waiting for me to pay, they would be waiting for a long time.

After some discussion, they finally realized that I meant what I said, so to save face, they asked us to leave the tour that day. I was sorry they had asked us to do that with only a few days remaining on the tour, but they paid us in full and Terry and I were on our way back to the States.

Terry died of heart failure fourteen years later. He was only 40 years old. It was a tragedy for the world of wrestling and all who knew him.

Regardless of how things ended, to this day, I can say without any hesitation, that the Japanese people are some of the kindest, most humble, and most courteous people I have been fortunate to meet anywhere in the world. I am certainly blessed to have made those trips and have had those memorable experiences. But as I was to find out a short time after that, not all the places we visited were like Japan.

Puerto Rico was one of those places. It was as different from Japan as I could imagine, even though the popularity of professional wrestling was on the same level as it was in the Orient. The sport revolved around Puerto Rico's perennial champion, Carlos Colon, who is the father of WWE superstar Carlito.

Carlos was not only the promoter and owner of the World Wrestling Council [WWC] promotion, but also held the WWC Universal heavyweight title more than a dozen times since defeating his arch rival, Abdullah the Butcher, in San Juan in 1982. Trained in Antonino Rocca's wrestling club in New York in the early 1960s, Colon wrestled throughout Canada, the United States, and his native Puerto Rico, where he set up his own promotion in the early 1980s.

San Juan may be a beautiful place to visit, but not if you wrestle as a heel. If you wrestle as a heel in Japan, you are still respected as a wrestler and an athlete. In Puerto Rico, you were lucky to escape with your life. I visited the country three times and vowed after the third time that I would never come back. At least, not as a wrestler.

The fans there had to be the most serious fans I had ever encountered, to the point where kids would sell bags of rocks to the fans entering the arena to hurl at the heels in the ring. Sadly, I was one of their targets, and the fans never wasted an opportunity to practice their aim on me.

The first time I visited the island, the promoters sent a van in which we would travel to an outdoor stadium where we were booked to wrestle. When we arrived, there were thousands of fans waiting. When they saw the van approaching, they rushed us like a swarm of bees to a hive. They surrounded the van and packed in so tightly we couldn't move. The driver kept trying to inch ahead, but was getting nowhere. Military police armed with machine

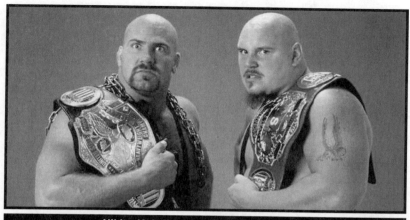

Nikita Koloff and Krusher Khrushchev

guns finally arrived and forced the crowd back so we could drive up to the entrance. The line "nobody told me there'd be days like these" from the John Lennon song, "Nobody Told Me," kept going through my mind. When I was booked in Puerto Rico, nobody had mentioned anything about what I was seeing take place. More than likely, it was because they suspected that if they did, I most likely wouldn't have gone.

I was booked in a series of matches with local babyface and strongman Hercules Ayala, who had held the WWC Caribbean and Puerto Rican titles. The fans loved him and his popularity with the fans only made them hate me all the more.

When it was time for me to go to the ring, I was escorted by armed guards who carried military-issue machine guns. As we left the dressing room, they surrounded me with a cage. I'm not talking about a panel of a chain-link fence. They put an actual cage around me to get me safely to the ring. As I walked to the ring, I saw that it, too, was surrounded by a cage. At first, I thought that, unbeknownst to me, I was scheduled to wrestle Hercules in a cage match, but I soon came to the realization that the cage wasn't to keep us in, but to keep the fans out and the wrestlers safe.

With every step, I kept wondering what I had gotten myself into. As I walked to the ring, fans on all sides threw rocks, bottles, and anything that wasn't nailed down. Hercules was nearing the end of his career and was still playing up his strongman gimmick, so the match wasn't anything to write home about. It lasted about fifteen minutes and I put Ayala over. I was more than happy to give him the win. All I could think about was getting out of there alive.

We wrestled several other times in different parts of the island with pretty much the same results. In one venue, the ring was set up with a few chairs around it with most of the seats located in the balcony. This time, there was no cage surrounding the ring. I didn't know it at the time, but during the match, someone from the balcony threw a whiskey bottle at me. It missed and hit a little boy sitting in the front row, cutting his knee open. In yet another match, the fans aim was better and I was hit with a spark plug. It sliced open my arm and gave me quite a scar which is still visible today. Is it any wonder that I vowed my third trip to Puerto Rico would be my last?

Chapter 18
The Secret

When I returned home from my overseas tour, I had to immediately pack and fly to Philadelphia for a scheduled October 18, 1986 house show. That may seem like a pretty heavy schedule, but you have to understand that it was always like that. There was no off-season in professional wrestling. We went where and when we were booked. If you are top card and working main events, you wrestle even when you are sick or injured. No matter what condition we were in, or how we were feeling at the time, we had to get into the ring. It's what we were expected to do. If we didn't want to do that, there was a long line of guys just waiting to step in and take our spot. Our fear of losing that spot was great motivation for us to show up. I do have to say that most of the boys of that era showed up to wrestle, not only because they worried about losing their place, but due to their commitment to the fans. In wrestling, as in any other sport or form of entertainment, "the show must go on," and it does.

Jesse Ventura certainly exemplified that attitude and tenaciousness when he was wrestling in the Portland territory. On October 15, 1976, when he was scheduled to wrestle Terry Funk for the NWA world heavyweight title, Jesse was battling the flu and had a temperature of 103 degrees. Jesse and Terry were scheduled to do an hour broadway. He approached Terry in the dressing room and explained his situation, saying he didn't think there was any way he could wrestle for an hour. He suggested they go fifteen or twenty minutes and then Terry could pin him.

Terry knew how important the match was to the territory and to Jesse's career. *"Just follow me,"* Terry said, *"We'll get through the hour."* Jesse agreed and tells the tale that they made it through the hour without any difficulty, and at the end of the match, he had the champion in his signature finishing hold, the full nelson. As the final bell rang, the fans were on their feet and screaming as they believed they were about to see a new champion being crowned. Jesse relinquished the hold as Terry slumped to the mat unconscious. When the referee called for the belt, Ventura walked across the ring to claim it, only to watch the official hand the belt to the prone champion and declare the bout a draw. Jesse protested and played to the crowd, yelling, *"I heard him quit, I heard him quit."* That was a great match that fans still talk about. More than that, it is a testimony to the skills of Terry Funk and the skills and determination of Jesse. The show must go on, and so it did.

So, exhausted or not, I flew into Philadelphia and took a cab to the arena.

When I walked into the dressing room, Jim Crockett and Dusty Rhodes were already there waiting for me. They said they wanted to talk with me and took me to a small room in the back of the arena. I assumed they had thought up a new angle for me while I had been overseas and they wanted to fill me in and get my thoughts. When they told me to sit down, I began to think they wanted to talk to me about something a lot more serious than a new program.

"Niki," Dusty said. *"I guess you heard."*

"Heard what?" I asked. *"I've been overseas and we don't get much news on the road."* Jim and Dusty looked at each other and Jim continued. *"Niki, Magnum was in a serious car accident and may never walk again. In fact, he may be a quadriplegic for the rest of his life."*

I couldn't believe what I had just heard. In fact, I *didn't* believe it. As cruel as it sounds, I thought Jim and Dusty were ribbing me. Wrestlers are known for pulling practical jokes that know no boundaries. Yes, this would have been a rib of the cruelest magnitude, but nevertheless, I hoped it was a joke. *"You are kidding me, right?"* I asked.

"I wish we were," Dusty said. *"I'm afraid it's true."*

And it was. The accident happened on October 14, 1986 in Charlotte. I kept seeing Magnum in my mind's eye and recalling the amazing athlete he was. All I could do was to sit there and stare at the floor, shaking my head.

"Niki," Dusty continued. *"That leaves us with another problem. I know this may seem like a bad time, but we have to make a decision."*

Before I left for the Orient, my feud with Magnum was still hot, but at the same time, Magnum and Dusty were involved in a feud against the Four Horsemen, comprised at the time of Flair, Ole Anderson, Arn Anderson, and Tully Blanchard. As a result, Magnum's career-ending injuries left a huge void to fill in the lineup.

The problem Dusty and Jim were referring to was a match scheduled for the following night, October 19, in the Charlotte Coliseum with Dusty and Magnum in a cage match against Ole and Tully. Advertising had already gone out for the card and it would be a huge blow to the business if they cancelled or changed the main event. They had already pre-sold a large number of tickets and business was good. In fact, business at that time was *extremely* good. We were running neck and neck with the WWF and drawing bigger crowds each week. The Rhodes-Magnum battle with the Four Horsemen had hit a responsive chord with the fans and they loved it. Dropping the angle would have set the company back months and it wouldn't have been a smart move. We also knew Magnum would have been the first to encourage us to move ahead with the program if he had been able to be there.

"What do you have in mind?" I asked.

"I want you to team with Dusty," said Jim.

That took me completely by surprise. I was still dealing with the news about Magnum … and now this? A jumble of thoughts began to rush through my brain. Would this go over with the fans? I had never wrestled as a babyface and I wasn't sure I could pull it off and sustain a good-guy version of the Russian Nightmare.

Jim explained the concept that would shock the fans and turn the wrestling world on its ear. At the time, Dusty was one of the most popular men in the ring, and all the fan polls in the magazines attested to that. Strangely enough, the same magazines listed me as one of the most hated, if not *the* most hated, wrestler in the world. *"That's the beauty of the angle,"* said Jim. *"Nobody will expect it."*

It seemed like a long shot, but I had faith in their judgment. After all, Dusty had been around the block more than a few times, while Jim had been brought up in the business and knew a great angle when he saw one. That was enough to convince me. If two of the best minds in the sport were telling me this was the way to go, then this was the way to go. I talked a bit with Dusty and that pretty much sealed the deal. So that night, in the dressing room in Philadelphia, the "City of Brotherly Love," the "American Dream" Dusty Rhodes and the "Russian Nightmare" Nikita Koloff became the "Superpowers."

As far as anyone else knew, I would team up with Ivan and Krusher in Charlotte, as had been planned all along. The Crocketts would also continue to feature the cage match, only they would have a "mystery partner" in the place of Magnum. *"When we say no one will know, we mean no one,"* Jim insisted. *"The only people who will know are the three of us, period. None of other boys will know. You are not to tell the other wrestlers. You can't even tell Ivan. You don't tell anyone. I'm telling you, Niki. I really think this will work. We will do some business and draw some big crowds."*

That idea was one of the best-kept secrets in wrestling. That never would have made it today with all the media outlets, industry newsletters, websites, and hotlines. I'm sure word would have leaked out in some fashion.

Kayfabe is one thing when you are protecting the business from outsiders, but to kayfabe the boys in the dressing room is another matter altogether. It was an interesting time, to say the least. I had to work heel in Philadelphia while I knew I was going to turn babyface on the following night. My mind was flooded with questions: Can I make it as a babyface? Will the angle go over? What will the fans and the wrestling world say?

The new buildup was based on who Dusty's mystery partner was going to be. Speculation ran rampant as nearly everyone on the Mid-Atlantic roster was, at one time or another, the "smart" pick. There was even speculation that one of the Horsemen might turn and join Dusty. I think *everyone* was suspect … but me. I wasn't brought into the program at all and totally ignored the situation. I was still wrestling heel and was being billed as the Russian Nightmare.

In the dressing room, the boys got the idea that the office hadn't yet picked anyone for the part. Everyone was on their best behavior and did some of their best work in the ring, hoping they might be the one tapped for the role.

Nobody had any idea.

The matches in the Charlotte Coliseum began at eight o'clock. I always tried to arrive as early as possible, but on that particular night, under the orders of Jim Crockett, I didn't get there until nine o'clock. I parked a block away and went in through the back door. I wasn't booked on the card, so I entered after the matches had begun when the fans would be in their seats watching the action in the ring and the boys would be in their dressing rooms getting warmed up for their bouts. I put a towel over my head, tucked it into the collar of my jacket, kept my head down, and tried to keep as close to the wall and in the shadows as possible.

Normally, I would have headed to the heels' dressing room, but this time, I made a beeline for the babyface dressing room. There were strict rules about keeping the babyfaces and heels separate in those days. If heels and faces were ever seen socializing together in public, they would be severely reprimanded or fired.

The dressing rooms at the Coliseum were on opposite sides of the building. That kept the wrestlers apart and allowed them to enter the ring from different sides of the arena. When I entered the dressing room, the boys all looked at me and said, *"Niki, you're in the wrong dressing room."* I told them I wasn't, but they didn't seem to catch on to what was going down. Some of them began to argue with me. *"No, I really am supposed to be here."*

Remember, no one knew who Dusty's partner was going to be that night, and they all were still hoping that Crockett would choose one of them at the last minute to walk to the ring beside the "American Dream." Most of the haze dissipated from their thoughts when Jim Crockett entered the dressing room and walked over to me and said, *"Niki! Good to see you, man."*

If there wasn't much animosity towards me before, there certainly was now. The usual inane chatter of the dressing room stopped abruptly and all eyes became focused on me. If there was any time in my career when you could cut the tension with a knife, that was it.

I had begun to hope the days were over when the boys resented me for my early push and subsequent success, but this decision by Jim and Dusty brought back in full force whatever feelings and thoughts may have lain dormant. Everyone in the dressing room had hoped to be picked to take Magnum's place as Dusty's partner. If they did well, it would move them into the stratosphere of the NWA.

Wrestling is a sport of moments and chances. Opportunity and success are not only dependent on what you can accomplish in the ring and during interviews, but also by what happens around you and to other wrestlers. The loss of a talent like Magnum could have sent Jim Crockett's business into a tailspin. Decisions had to be made quickly in order to curtail a loss of fans and revenue. I never met anyone in the business who wanted anyone else to be injured, or to see someone's career destroyed, but when mishaps occur, or someone left for another territory, a spot was opened up. When that happened, there were more than an ample number of applicants waiting to fill the position.

I could understand their feelings because, once again, many of them had been passed up when the role went to me. Not only had I been given a great opportunity when I broke into the business, but now, after I had been in the business for just fifteen months, I was being handed an even bigger opportunity … I was going to be Dusty Rhodes' partner. More than that, since Dusty was the booker, I was going to be the *booker's* partner. Once again, I felt like I had the weight of the world on my shoulders, and a number of my fellow wrestlers were sitting on top of that weight just in case it wasn't heavy enough. But I was there to do my job and business is business.

One thing I don't think a lot of my detractors in the dressing room ever realized was that if I had been asked to do a job, or if Jim and Dusty had told me I was being relegated to a popcorn match or a lower place on the card, I would have done it without a second thought or the first complaint. When you take a job and you accept the pay, you do what is asked of you. If you don't like what you are being told to do, you have the option to move on. This time, the request was in my favor. It wouldn't always be that way, but at that particular time, it was.

I had my share of popcorn matches during my career. Outside of what we call the "curtain-jerker" or opening match, the "popcorn match" is probably the least-desirable position on the card. To the fans at large, the popcorn match is usually referred to as the semi-final match, which is the match preceding the main event, although it could be the first main event on a double main event card. In any case, it's the match that takes place after intermission.

Most of the boys didn't mind working the opening match because it was first match of the night. They could wrestle and be headed for home, or the next town, early in the evening. The problem with the curtain jerker is that the fans are still making their way into the arena, so there is a lot of commotion and noise and few people are watching the matches.

The popcorn match is seen in almost the same light. Although it is part of the upper card and pays extremely well, it has the same difficulties as the opener. Fans are returning to their seats after making a visit to the concession stand and there is just as much disturbance as when the people were first coming into the building. The wrestlers in the ring derive a lot of energy from the reactions of the fans in the seats, and if the fans are filtering in from getting their beer, soft drinks, and popcorn, it can be tough to get into the match until everyone settles down.

As I prepared to go to the ring that night, I had a moment of déjà vu, like the first time I walked the steps into the ring in Raleigh against Barry Horowitz. This time, however, the butterflies in my stomach felt like bats. There was a lot more at stake than there was in my debut. Thoughts ran through my head like a freight train. I had been booed everywhere I went … and now I was going to the ring as a babyface. They hadn't given the fans the customary buildup, in which they would build a slow turn from heel to hero. Would the fans accept the angle? Would this turn out to be a good idea? Only time would tell … and that time was rapidly approaching.

The moment came. The timekeeper rang the bell for the main event.

I'm sure that when 17th century English poet and preacher, John Dunne, first wrote, and when Ernest Hemingway echoed in his 1940 novel *For Whom the Bell Tolls* — and therefore never send to know for whom the bell tolls; it tolls for thee," — more than likely, they were not thinking about the "Russian Nightmare" walking to the ring in Charlotte, North Carolina. And the bell they referred to was not signaling the main event and calling the combatants to battle. But nonetheless, when I heard the bell, there was no doubt for whom it was tolling. That night, it was indeed tolling for me.

I don't mean to wax poetic here, but that night in Charlotte will always be remembered by me as one of the most memorable nights of my career and one of the most remarkable events of my life.

The way the match was set up was that our opponents would be the first to enter the ring. That would build up Dusty's entrance and pique the fans' expectation and curiosity as to who the mystery partner was going to be. Of course, speculation by the fans ran the gamut, from any number of wrestlers who were then competing (even those in the WWF and the AWA) to the possibility of one of the Four Horsemen. I'm sure my name was brought up in the mix somewhere, but probably was dismissed as soon as it came up in conversation.

We were booked to face Ole and Tully that night, but Tully had been injured a few nights before, so their manager, James J. "JJ" Dillon, was substituting. Tully did appear at ringside that night, but he was relegated to an onlooker position.

A chorus of jeers and catcalls were still being directed at Ole and JJ when Dusty's theme music began to play over the sound system. As soon as the first note sounded, the crowd went berserk. As Dusty and I walked through the curtains, we were met by security guards, who escorted us to the ring in the beam of a dazzling spotlight. When the fans saw me trailing behind Dusty, much of the cheering and commotion stopped as abruptly as it had begun. It was like a truck driver hitting the air-brakes on his eighteen-wheeler. It was amazing how 15,000 fans could become that quiet so quickly. It was so quiet, in fact, that for a moment, I thought I had lost some of my hearing. It was almost surreal. My nervousness became enhanced by a bone-chilling eeriness. Dusty walked to the ring without ever looking back at me, which led me to believe many of the fans thought he was oblivious to my presence behind him. They seemed to be wondering if I was going to attack him.

When I reached a position in the arena where the fans could see me, I stopped and looked around, heightening the effect of my presence. At the same time, Dusty stepped over the ring barrier, ascended the steps, and entered the ring through the cage door. As soon as he stepped foot in the ring, Ole and JJ began flailing away at Dusty. The crowd broke their silence and began to scream at the Horsemen, and then cried out for help for their embattled hero. As I climbed up on the ring apron and took stock of what was happening inside the cage, I looked at the crowd one last time. Ducking through the ropes, I stood in the corner with the harsh glare of the spotlight shining on me. As far as the Horsemen knew, I would always be in their corner. I had as much disdain for Dusty as they did. After taking a few slow paces towards the three men, I ran towards Ole and hit him with a forearm to the back, after which I laid into him with fists and feet.

The crowd went completely nuts. The alternating cheers and silence were just a quiet prelude to the sound that ensued when I decked Ole. Pulling him off the mat and to his feet, I continued to beat him. Ole was unable to put up any defense whatsoever. I knocked him towards the door of the cage and threw him out of the ring and onto the arena floor, slamming the door and locking him out of the battle.

During my onslaught on Ole, Dusty found his second wind and began to repay JJ in spades. I joined Dusty and picked up JJ, whose face was now nothing more than a crimson mask from being thrust face-first into the cage by Dusty. While Dusty climbed to the top of the turnbuckles in one corner of the ring, I put JJ in a bearhug. As I bent JJ backwards, Dusty used his famous finishing move, the "bionic elbow," on JJ's head. I stepped back and allowed Dusty to cover JJ as the referee, Tommy Young, dove to the mat and counted "1-2-3." The match was over, but the fun was yet to begin. If there ever was a time that the "roof came off the building," it certainly was happening that night in Charlotte.

As I stated before, it always was important to me (and most of the boys for that matter) to give the fans more than the price of their ticket. That night in Charlotte, the fans not only received their money's worth, but received the total value of their entire seating section. When the referee, Tommy Young, declared us the winners and raised our hands to symbolize our victory, the two remaining Horsemen, Ric Flair and Arn Anderson, came running down the aisle to join the fallen Ole and Tully at ringside.

Dusty and I decided to place an exclamation point on the end of the match. To the fans' delight and the dismay of the Horsemen, we slammed JJ headfirst into the cage and threw him out the door. The expression on Flair's face was classic. He drew back his fist and called me a few expletive names. With the veins popping out on his neck, he ripped off his coat and attempted to climb the cage while the other Horsemen held him back. Once again, Ric proved himself to be the master of ring psychology.

In retrospect, it was one of the most amazing things I have ever witnessed. The crowd, who only minutes before would have crawled over broken glass to spit on me, to throw whatever they could find, to call the office of Jim Crockett Promotions to issue death threats, or to risk their safety by getting into the ring to attack me, were now chanting my name: *"Nik-it-ta, Nik-it-ta."* I have never experienced, either before or since, the feeling that came over me that night. The 15,000 fans chanted my name for almost ten minutes. All I could do was think, *"Well, what do you know? Jim and Dusty were right. This is unbelievable."*

As the chanting continued, Dusty stood in the center of the ring leading the cheers. Men and boys in the stands were taking off their shirts and doing the "most muscular" pose I had used as part of my gimmick, complete with sticking out their tongue, which I did at the conclusion of my television interviews. I turned from heel to hero in a matter of moments. It was a new era in the career of the "Russian Nightmare."

An interesting note was the fact that even though I was listed as the "most hated" in the wrestling magazine polls and was looked at as one of the top heels in the business, my t-shirts and other merchandise sporting my image were selling like crazy. I was outselling everyone except the "Nature Boy." It surprised a lot of people in the office when the sales figures came in listing me as a strong second. I would like to think the fans appreciated the dedication I had put into the business and my training. However, as a babyface, my popularity soared to heights none of us could have imagined.

After the match, Dusty and I went back to the dressing room and cut our first interview as the "Superpowers," the name originally given to the United States, the Soviet Union, and the British Empire in 1944.

It didn't take me long to realize that I not only had to change my attitude in the ring, but outside it, as well. No longer could I allow the "Russian Nightmare" to ignore or growl at the fans as I passed them by. As a babyface, I had to win the fans over on both sides of the ring ropes. When the fans approached me for an autograph, or just to say hello, I greeted them with a smile and a handshake. I wonder how many fans noticed how dramatically my English improved when I made the turn from heel to babyface. My biggest transformation, however, had to take place on the inside. When I said earlier that I didn't have any trouble looking mean and angry in my earlier incarnation of Nikita Koloff, I wasn't kidding. My attitude during that time of my life was pretty nasty. I was a real-life "Stone Cold" Steve Austin.

As a good guy, I was now expected to morph from a growling monster into someone who kissed babies and signed autographs. Don't get me wrong. In the ring, I would still clothesline my opponents, but the recipients of my handiwork were the heels, so instead of hearing catcalls from the audience, I was cheered. I was dressing in a different dressing room, but I was still the "Russian Nightmare." My style didn't change, but my attitude began a slow transformation … one that would culminate in a life-changing event in later years.

I came to the realization, more than ever, that it was the fans who put the bread on my table and I had a tremendous obligation to them. Without them, there would be no need for either version of Nikita Koloff to exist.

Nikita Koloff and Dusty Rhodes

Chapter 19

The Four Horsemen

The team Dusty and I faced that historic night in Charlotte was part of one of the most fabled teams in the annals of wrestling. In my opinion, they rank among the very best.

Throughout wrestling history there have been tag teams with names like "Murder Incorporated," the "Minnesota Wrecking Crew," and the "Road Warriors." A different slant came about in the 1980s in Atlanta with the "Freebirds," a three-man team comprised of Michael Hayes, Buddy Roberts, and Terry Gordy. Opposing teams may have found themselves facing any two of the three, while the third member became a distracting obstacle at ringside. But as innovative as those teams were, there was nothing like the Four Horsemen.

Even with my babyface turn, the formation of the "Super Powers," and the business we were doing, the Four Horsemen was an alliance that would transform the wrestling business as we knew it at the time. The Horsemen were not just another team or group of wrestlers who had banded together. They were considered a "corporate" team. They were all champions and top-flight competitors. Ric Flair, of course, was still the king ... and rightfully so. He was the world heavyweight champion and the cornerstone of the group. Ole and Arn Anderson were the reigning world tag-team champions, while the final member of the team was Tully Blanchard, the United States heavyweight champion. To give them even more credibility, they were managed by James J. Dillon, a man who not only had managed many main-event caliber wrestlers during his career, but as a wrestler, had been a top-tier talent himself during the '60s and '70s.

I inadvertently had something to do with the formation of the Horsemen, but only from a peripheral perspective. On September 29, 1985, I wrestled Ric for the title in a steel cage match in Atlanta and put him over. After he defeated me, Ivan and Krusher ran into the ring to exact their revenge on the Nature Boy. As Ric was getting the worst of it, Dusty came running to the ring, sending everyone scattering out of the ring. As Dusty approached the prone champion in an effort to help him to his feet, it appeared to the fans that their battles in the past were just that ... in the past.

Instead of reconciling, Arn and Ole stormed the ring and began to dish out to Dusty what they had been doing to Ivan, Krusher, and me only minutes earlier. The angle was great. They "broke" Dusty's ankle and fought off the cleared dressing room of babyfaces who besieged the cage in an attempt to rescue

Dusty. It brought the fans in the Omni to a near riot and helped establish this championship clique that would later be named the Four Horsemen.

The one thing about being involved in a successful tag-team program is that it leads to all types of combinations for other matches. With four opponents, any combination of single matches would draw, after which we could revive the tag-team wars and set up returns for other tag matches. If the Horseman versus the Super Powers began to grow stale, Dusty or I would take off on our own for a while to battle Ric, Arn, or Tully in a series of one-on-one matches, culminating in the revival of our tag-team battles. At times, we would add the Road Warriors or the Rock 'n' Roll Express into the mix, giving the fans a change of pace. At other times, we would team with the Road Warriors in an eight-man tag-team match against the Horseman. It was those eight-man tag matches that set the stage for the infamous *WarGames*.

It's ironic that the concept of the Horsemen was Dusty's idea. He was the one who took the beating to get the angle over. That goes to his credit and shows what he was willing to do for the business.

Now that the group was established, the only thing lacking was the name. As I said, the idea was Dusty's, but Arn gets the credit for coining the name.

Arn began his career a few years before I did. He learned his craft in Georgia under the tutelage of journeyman wrestler, Ted Allen. Arn had been a wrestling fan since he was a youngster, idolizing Dick Slater, who wrestled on the old Georgia Championship Wrestling circuit.

Wrestling as Marty Lunde, his given name, Arn made his entrée into the ring as a preliminary wrestler. In his first match, he wrestled veteran "Bullet" Bob Armstrong in his first match. Arn left Georgia and hit the road, doing stints in the Louisiana territory for Bill Watts and Florida, where he teamed with Jerry Stubbs to win the NWA Southeastern tag team title. Leaving Florida, Arn moved on to Charlotte where he became fast friends with the Nature Boy. During this time, Marty became the "cousin" of Ole Anderson, and thus, the "cousin" of Ric Flair (who had been brought into the Mid-Atlantic territory as a cousin of Ole and Gene).

Now, as a full-fledged star and a member of this elite group, he described the carnage that he and his partners were leaving in their wake as being likened to the devastation predicted in Revelation by the Four Horsemen of the Apocalypse. During a television interview, he made a comment along the lines of, *"The only time this much havoc had been wreaked by this few a number of people, you need to go all the way back to the Four Horsemen of the Apocalypse!"* The name stuck and the angle remained one of the most successful of all times. When the fans began to grow tired of a particular combination of Horsemen, Ric and Arn would turn on one of them, fire them, or find some other reason to extricate them from the group, opening up spots for new horsemen and a fresh feud with the former members. But Dusty and my battles with them were just beginning.

During my time in the ring, Arn and I never got along too well. I'm not really sure why. I can't recall any particular incident between us that caused a falling out. We just didn't get along. We found ourselves "ribbing on the square," which really isn't a good thing. "Ribbing on the square" is a way of telling your true feelings under the guise of kidding. As GK Chesterton said, *"I am never more serious than when I'm kidding."* As the years went on, we got along

The original Four Horsemen: Ole, Arn, JJ, Ric and Tully

better and I'm glad we did. Arn is a good guy. Even when we weren't getting along, I had nothing but the greatest respect for Arn and always considered him the consummate wrestler, tactician, and master of psychology in the ring. He had a creative mind and could tell a story in the ring like few others.

Besides Ole, Ric, and Arn, the fourth member of the original Horsemen was veteran and second-generation wrestler, Tully Blanchard. Son of legendary San Antonio wrestler and promoter, Joe Blanchard, Tully began his wrestling career at age ten when he placed window cards of his dad's upcoming events on cars at the local mall and selling concessions at the matches.

Wrestling wasn't the only sport that caught Tully's interest. He earned a football scholarship at Southern Methodist University and later transferred to West Texas State. As quarterback for West Texas, Tully gained and kept the starting position for three years, despite a near career-ending car accident that injured his throwing arm prior to his first season.

Being 5'10" and about 200 pounds, the NFL didn't exactly come clamoring for his services, so he decided to join the "family business," Southwest Championship Wrestling. He came into the business in 1975 around the same time as two of his West Texas State teammates, Ted DiBiase, who played defensive tackle, and Merced Solis, better known as Tito Santana, who played tight-end. Tully did well and held every major title in the promotion. When the territory began to falter, as so many were as the 1980s unfolded, Tully moved to Charlotte just as the sport and the territory began to explode.

He teamed with Arn to take the NWA world tag team title and they later headed north to work for the WWF as the "Brain Busters." Tully won the United States heavyweight title from Magnum in 1985 and the NWA world television title twice, the first time from Mark Youngblood in May 1984 and the second from Dusty Rhodes on Thanksgiving night 1986 in Greensboro. He held the title as if he owned it, defending it for more than eight months before I lighted his load a bit by relieving him of the belt in Fayetteville on a steamily hot night in August 1987.

Tully, by his own admission, let the fame and money go to his head. He listened to the inner demons that hounded him and he became as much a part of the world of drugs and drink as he was the world of wrestling. Failing a drug test closed the career of this great wrestler. It was a wakeup call that resulted in him turning his heart and mind to the peace he had been seeking for so long. Today, as an evangelist, Tully still stands in front of crowds, but the harsh lights of the ring are replaced by the soft and powerful glow of the Holy Spirit. Trading the ring for the pulpit and the championship belts he once sported around his waist for a cross, Tully has become every bit a champion of Christianity as he had been of wrestling in the ring.

The final member of the Horsemen was their manager, mentor, and consultant, James J. Dillon. Born Jim Morrison, Jim was a wrestling fan from boyhood. While still a Trenton, New Jersey high school student in 1958, Jim was the president of the Johnny Valentine Fan Club. Upon graduation, Jim's love for wrestling continued to grow, and in 1960, he began to referee local bouts for the WWWF. He took to the ring as a wrestler in 1962 and began traveling from territory to territory, landing in Charlotte in spring 1971.

In 1975, he shifted his talents to managing other wrestlers, although he continued to put on the tights and wrestle occasionally. Nine years later, he returned to the Carolinas to work as an assistant to Dusty in the office of Crockett Promotions. He also managed Ron Bass and Black Bart, known collectively as the Long Riders. But where Jim hit his zenith was in 1985 with the formation of the Four Horsemen as he became the manager of the premier tag team in modern history.

Landover, Maryland was one of the most memorable towns in which I recall having a great match with the Horsemen. We were moving along with the "Superpowers" angle and business was booming. That being the case, Jim Crockett made the decision to head north and invade Vince McMahon's territory. The date of the first show was July 2, 1987. By going into Landover, the NWA was invading enemy territory and boldly going where other promotions either feared to tread or upheld the old agreement to respect the traditional territorial lines. It served notice that Crockett was not about to back down or remain a regional promotion. A top town for the WWWF for many years, Landover had been the scene of countless battles and title defenses by erstwhile champions such as Bruno Sammartino, Pedro Morales, "Superstar" Billy Graham, and Bob Backlund, each of whom drew tremendous crowds and did the sport proud. I would have loved to have had a program with any of those legends, but I was a bit too late. However, I did have one opportunity to wrestle Bob Backlund.

Bob and I were wrestling in a cross promotion called Pro Wrestling USA. The promotion was the idea of Jim Crockett and Verne Gagne and their intent was to exchange talent and work together to strengthen their position against McMahon's movement into traditionally NWA and AWA strongholds. We wrestled in Altoona, Pennsylvania at the Jaffa Mosque on March 13, 1985. It was a cold, blustery winter night and the card was "make-shift" at best. There was no angle or storyline between us, but the promoter thought it would make a good match to pit the villainous "Russian" (I was still a heel at the time) and the "All-American boy." The most interesting aspect of the match was that it involved two participants who most fans thought they would never see in the ring together. Bob was into his Army character and came running to the ring wearing fatigues and an army helmet. As in all his matches, he was full of energy and was bouncing around the ring. It was one of the few times that I broke character in the ring. I just couldn't maintain the "evil-empire" look when Bob looked like Howdy Doody in fatigues. We had the classic good guy vs. bad guy match and it wasn't hard to get the crowd to chant, *"USA, USA."* I have to say that everything I had heard about Bob in the ring was true. He is an amazing scientific wrestler and he had unbelievable stamina. I would have loved to have had more matches with him. Bob is one of the best; a great athlete, wrestler, champion, and gentleman.

On the main event in Landover, Dusty and I were booked in the main event with the Horsemen. We were all a bit apprehensive as we didn't know what to expect in this new town, offering a different product than what the fans were used to seeing in person. Our numbers were good for the television shows we were airing up there, but whether or not anyone would venture out to the arena, and if they did, how we would be perceived, was anyone's guess. To top it off, not only were we wrestling in a stronghold the WWF had promoted for the past 25 years, but we were doing it two days before the Fourth of July holiday. Would the foray of the National Wrestling Alliance into Vince's backyard be enough to make fans alter any holiday plans they may have had? We were all anxious to see. It was actually Vince who allowed us into the Capital Center that night. He had a lock on the building contract, but probably figured we wouldn't draw during the holiday and relished the idea of seeing us fall flat on our faces.

I don't believe things turned out the way he expected. Nearly 15,000 fans came to see the Superpowers and the Road Warriors face the Four Horsemen in a one-fall cage match. The Horsemen on this night were Tully, Arn, Ric, and Lex Luger, who had taken the place of Ole, who had left the Horsemen. Dusty opened the match against Arn, while Animal, Hawk and I waited outside the ring for our turn to do battle. As I was standing on the apron waiting for the tag, the crowd began chanting my name, just as they had done in Charlotte, encouraging and almost willing me into the ring to replay what I had done a few weeks before when I first teamed with Dusty. The eight of us milked the match for all it was worth. Dusty took a beating and sold everything the Horsemen did on the offense. The crowd went crazy.

When Dusty finally made it to our corner, he gave Animal the "hot tag" and he entered the ring. The crowd was in frenzy. A hot tag is the tag your partner gives you after he has taken a beating and finally manages to make it to the corner for the tag. His partner then comes in and lays the other team to waste. In many cases, at that point, he wins the match.

Arn milked the crowd for all it was worth and then tagged Luger. Lex made Animal shine for the next few minutes as chants of *"Nik-it-a"* continued to rumble through the crowd. Animal, after battering Lugar, tagged his partner Hawk. At the same time, Lex made it to his corner and tagged Tully, who followed Lex's lead and sold everything Hawk did, making him look like a million dollars. For fifteen minutes, the Horsemen put us over as only they could. They made us look like supermen, putting over everything we did — Dusty's "bionic elbow," the Road Warrior's press slams, everything.

I had yet to enter the ring, and as the chanting rose to fever pitch, Hawk pointed at me and gave me the tag. I jumped through the ropes and motioned for Tully to get out and tag anyone he wanted. Of course, he slapped the Nature Boy's hand. When he did, the building almost exploded. Like the trooper he is, Ric put me over like never before.

The fans in Landover that night never sat down during the main event. For twenty-three minutes, we entertained them like never before, and even though they paid for seats they didn't need, they got more than their money's worth. Opponents, as I have said, make the match, and if you were fortunate enough to see the Horsemen, or Dusty for that matter, in action, you would have no doubt why they worked top card everywhere they wrestled for years. My hat was off to them then and remains so today.

Chapter 20

Leaving on a Jet Plane

I am grateful to have started my career with Jim Crockett. I know my perspective may seem somewhat skewed in that I came into his territory at the right time. Yes, it's true that Jim moved me into main event status quickly and I drew well from the beginning, which was making him a lot of money, but he treated me well from the outset and gave me the chance of a lifetime. Anyone with half a mind would be thankful.

When Jim took over the promotion in 1973 after the death of his father, he began to make changes, and one of the first of those changes was hiring George Scott as his booker. George had a creative mind and did innovative things in the ring with storylines and characters. He was responsible for rebuilding the territory when the veteran performers began to retire or leave for other territories and business fell on hard times. With only a handful of the stars that made the promotion what it was during his father's time, Mid-Atlantic Championship Wrestling was in a free fall. George came in and created new titles, such as the Eastern heavyweight title, and turned the predominantly tag-team-oriented territory to one in which singles competition was the standard.

By the late 1970s, Jim Crockett Promotions was the hottest promotion in the country, boasting a roster of top stars that rivaled any promotion anywhere in the world. Already proven stars with track records of success, like Jack and Jerry Brisco, Ric Flair, the Road Warriors, the Anderson Brothers, Dory Funk Jr., Paul Jones, Blackjack Mulligan, Roddy Piper, all plied their trade in the territory.

By the 1980s, the wrestling business was changing, moving in a direction towards something called "sports entertainment." Jim and George were smart enough to realize they had to change the way in which they ran their business. Until that time, the boys all traveled from town to town in their own cars, easily putting 100,000 or more miles per year on them. It wasn't at all unusual to see a wrestler buy a new car every year due to the wear and tear on them. Jim thought that was an antiquated way to make the trips and also hampered his ability to expand into other areas of the country. He decided it was time to take Jim Crockett Promotions into the 1980s.

One of the first things he did was to purchase two private planes to make travel a bit easier. We still traveled by car quite a bit, but with Jim's plan to expand his territory into Detroit, Oklahoma, Canada, and spot shows in the Northeast and New England, a better and quicker way of travel was needed.

Jim purchased a Gulfstream G-1 prop plane that would seat sixteen to eighteen passengers and a Falcon Jet which would seat ten. We enjoyed the easy, comfortable trips, but in another sense, we paid the price for the luxury. With the shortened travel time, Jim saw the opportunity to add more towns and more shows in one day. Many times, we would have to wrestle twice in one night, often in different states. We would do a TV taping in Detroit on Friday afternoon and then travel to Cincinnati, Lansing, or Saginaw that evening for a house show. That wasn't all that bad, but then we would be booked on Saturday afternoon and evening in Charleston, South Carolina or Savannah, Georgia.

While most people look forward to a relaxing weekend at home with their families, we knew that Saturdays and Sundays were almost always two-a-day matches, and if we did a television taping, it wasn't unusual for us to wrestle six or seven times in a two or three-day period. Once a month on Sunday afternoon, we would wrestle in Asheville, North Carolina, and then head to Atlanta, Charlotte, or even Toronto. With the bell time set at three o'clock in Asheville, the only way we could make the second town was by air.

Asheville, a beautiful town situated in the heart of the Smoky Mountains, has always been a great wrestling town, hearkening back to the days of Jim Crockett Sr. During the '60s and early '70s, the good folks of western North Carolina would have to choose between attending the Wednesday night church services or cheering on their heroes at the Asheville City Auditorium, a small building located downtown across from the beautiful St. Lawrence Basilica. When it was renovated in 1974 and renamed the Asheville Civic Center, wrestling was moved to Sunday afternoon,

Asheville's wrestling history goes back even farther than the days of the weekly cards in the old Municipal Auditorium. In 1905, the eyes of the entire sporting world was on the mountain town as two of the top grapplers in the world both found themselves living in Asheville. One of the top professional wrestlers of the era, Charles Olsen, and Professor Akitaro Ono, the top Kodokan Judo master in the world, who was doing exhibitions and lessons at the YMCA, both chose Asheville as their base of operations after touring the country.

With both champions extolling the benefits of their own discipline, the town, and soon the sporting world, began clamoring for the two to meet in the ring. On Friday, September 15, Olson met Ono at the Grand Opera House in what was billed as a "blood match, with tickets priced from $1.50 to $3.00 — a pretty hefty price to pay in 1905. There was also a special section reserved for the ladies attending.

Olsen won the first fall of the highly-contested match after an hour and ten minutes of battle. Ono was so badly beaten that he refused to return for the second fall, giving the match and $10,000 cash to Olson. Ono was so incensed over the verdict that he and his manager traveled to Washington, D.C. to appeal the decision to the Japanese ambassador and the President of the United States, Theodore Roosevelt. The decision stood as it was rendered, but for a time, the world's interest, including that of Roosevelt, was on a wrestling match in Asheville.

Another thing the planes did was give me a realization of where I stood in Crockett's plan and in the pecking order of the company. One of the highest compliments I received during my career was never addressed directly to me, but to the pilots Jim employed. It was sort of like my mom never telling me directly how proud she was about me wrestling, but she sure told the neighbors, and in turn, they told me. Jim told the pilots that no matter how long they had to wait, they were not to leave the ground until four particular wrestlers were on board. The wrestlers he named were Ric Flair, Dusty Rhodes, Magnum T.A. … and Nikita Koloff. Anyone else scheduled to fly with us had to be on time. If they were late, even by a minute or two, the plane took off with no questions asked. If they missed it, they missed it. Not many did, because if the plane left without them, they had to find their own way to the next town.

Jim's decision to include me in the four with special air privileges certainly spoke well for how Jim Crockett Promotions viewed my worth to the company and the confidence he placed in me. Jim and I didn't always agree, but we did respect each other. He knew that every time I entered the ring, or was on camera, he would have my utmost effort.

Most of the people who had dealings with Jim saw him as all business. With Jim, as far as the promotion was concerned, business came first, but, on occasion, he would let his hair down and take some of us along for the ride. One night after we finished wrestling in Ontario, Jim, Dusty, Barry Windham and I boarded the plane and flew to New York City. When we landed, a limousine was waiting for us and we spent the entire night touring the "Big Apple." We visited restaurants and clubs, all on Jim's dime.

When I said I didn't establish a close friendship with many of the other wrestlers, I need to make one particular exception, and that's Virgil Runnels, better known as Dusty Rhodes, the "American Dream." Dusty had been in the business for almost twenty years before I became Nikita Koloff, and even the most casual fans know the lore of the plumber's son from Austin, Texas.

Early in his career, Dusty gained a measure of fame teaming up with fellow Texan, Dick Murdoch, as the Outlaws. He eventually broke away from tag matches and set out on a course in single matches that would garner him many singles titles, including the United States heavyweight title and three runs as the NWA world heavyweight champion.

Dusty first came into prominence as a singles wrestler when he went to work for Eddie Graham in Florida. He took the state by storm and hit his stride by challenging then world champion Jack Brisco. While Jack was in the ring for a television taping, Dusty came onto the set wearing a top hat and tails and began to criticize the champion and question his skills, courage, and choice of opponents. After Jack's victory, Dusty hit him from behind and pinned him, with "Dirty" Dick Slater coming in to count the fall. Dusty grabbed the belt and made his way back to announcer Gordon Solie, where he proclaimed himself to be the new world champion and said that only in America can a plumber's son from Texas beat the great Jack Brisco and become the heavyweight champion of the world. *"I truly am the American Dream,"* Dusty proclaimed. And the legend was born. He would have to wait until 1979, however, to actually win his first world title.

Probably the most emotional time I had during my career was when Dusty and I teamed together for the first Jim Crockett Sr. Memorial Cup tag team tournament.

The Crockett Cup was held in Baltimore on April 10 and 11, 1987. Prior to the tournament, Dusty and I dedicated the tournament to Magnum T.A. and vowed to win the trophy and the million dollar prize for him. Magnum surprised the crowd by making his first appearance since his near-fatal accident. Leaning on his walking cane and with one arm in a sling, he was escorted to ringside by wrestling legend Sandy Scott. As he made his way to the ring prior to our first match, there honestly wasn't a dry eye in the house, including Dusty's and mine as we stopped and hugged our friend as we walked to the ring.

Nearly every tag team imaginable was entered. Competing in the first round were the Thunderfoots, Arn Anderson and Kevin Sullivan, Bobby Jaggers and Rocky King, the Barbarian and Bill Dundee, Mike Rotundo and Tim Horner, Shaska Whatley and Teijo Kahn, Jimmy Valiant and Lazertron, Jimmy and Ronnie Garvin, the Italian Stallion and Ricky Lee Jones, Todd Champion and Denny Brown, Bill and Randy Mulkey, Steve Keirn and George South, Nelson Royal and Mike Graham, Bob and Brad Armstrong, the MOD Squad, Wahoo McDaniel and Baron von Raschke. The teams of Dusty and I, Rick Rude and Manny Fernandez, Ivan Koloff and Vladimir Petrov, the Road Warriors, the Midnight Express [Bobby Eaton and Stan Lane], Shohei Baba and Isao Takagi, the Rock 'n' Roll Express, and Tully Blanchard and Lex Luger, all received byes.

Dusty and I took our match in the second round from the Barbarian and Bill Dundee, while on the following night in the quarter finals, Dusty and I beat the NWA world tag team champions, Manny Fernandez and Rick Rude, when Dusty pinned Manny after nearly ten minutes. That win put us in the semifinals against the Midnight Express, who had upset the Road Warriors, the defending Crockett Cup champions, when Animal was disqualified. We defeated the Midnight Express after I dropped Eaton with the Russian Sickle.

That put us in the finals against Tully and Lex. Without a doubt, that was the finest match we had in the tournament, with the advantage going back and forth. I was still wearing the neck collar from injuries suffered when I was attacked by the Four Horsemen, so Lex and Tully zeroed in on my neck and tried to wear me down. The four of us went 17 minutes, 29 seconds with Dusty and me taking the brunt of the abuse before we finally made a comeback and Dusty pinned Tully. The crowd was ecstatic as Dusty and I were presented with the giant cup and the million-dollar check. For those who might be wondering, we did get to keep the cup. I don't believe I have to explain the rest.

WarGames probably was the most fun I ever had in the ring, and that's saying a lot. I really enjoyed my time between the ropes. Even the bad days and less-than-perfect matches had an upside to them, but *WarGames* was as much fun as it was intense and exhausting.

WarGames was created by Dusty as part of the Great American Bash tour. It was set up to showcase the Four Horsemen in a match in which they would all team together, rather than breaking them up into singles or tag matches. *WarGames* weren't a part of every Bash. In fact, it was part of only two in 1987, but they proved to be so popular that they featured them on 28 events, including *WrestleWar* and several *Fall Brawl* shows.

How the games worked was what made them so much fun for the fans and all of us. A *WarGames* match consisted of two teams of five men, each facing off against each other in staggered entry format. The match began with one member of each team entering the cage. After five minutes, a coin was flipped to decide which team would send another member into the cage to have a temporary advantage. After two minutes, a member from the other team would

enter to even the odds. Wrestlers from each team would then alternate entering the ring until all five members of each team were in the ring.

At that point, the second part of the match began. Called "The Match Beyond," we would all beat each other silly until one member of either team gave up, giving the other team the victory. I did think it was kind of funny when the announcers would say, "The Match Beyond, submission or surrender." I suppose they left their thesaurus at home. Otherwise, I'm sure they would have noticed that "submission" and "surrender" meant the same thing.

It wasn't only the concept that made the match unusual, but it also was where it took place. We didn't wrestle in just one ring. We wrestled in two that were set up side by side. The rings were surrounded by a steel cage which included fencing over the top. Doors were at opposite corners of the rings so neither team would confront each other until we entered the cage.

The first *WarGames* event took place in Atlanta on July 4, 1987. I was teamed with Dusty, Hawk, Animal, and their manager, Paul Ellering, against Flair, Arn, Tully, Luger, and their manager, JJ Dillon.

Dusty and Arn were the first two wrestlers in the ring and went after each other as if it was the last thing they would do on earth. They put on a great match for the first five minutes, at which time referee Tommy Young tossed a coin and pointed a signal flag at the Horsemen, indicating that one of them should enter the cage, giving them a two-on-one advantage. Tully entered the ring and he and Arn double-teamed Dusty, with the American Dream fighting back valiantly. After two minutes passed, it was our turn to even the odds. Animal stormed into the ring and, being the freshest guy in the ring, cleaned house on Arn and Tully. The Nature Boy was the next contestant to climb in, followed by me, Lex, Hawk, JJ, and finally, Paul. With all of us in the cage, the "Match Beyond" began and we gave everything we had to the battle. It was a brilliant concept.

I was scheduled to drop the U.S. title to Lex the next week at the Bash in Greensboro, so the match gave us time against each other to continue to set the stage. It also gave JJ what he needed as well. He had been scheduled to undergo shoulder surgery for some time and needed an "out" to take a few weeks off to recover. To end the match, we kept the Horsemen at bay in one ring, while the Road Warriors beat Dillon senseless. Of course, they "injured" his shoulder in the process, forcing him to concede the match. The heroes won, the Horsemen saved face since none of them had to submit to any of us, and JJ was rewarded with time off for his surgery. Add to that the fact that we all had a great match, the fans loved it, and we had wrestled less than thirty minutes. Granted, it was an intense thirty minutes, but all and all, it was a good night.

We repeated the *WarGames* on the last stop of the tour in Miami. This time, we faced the Four Horseman with the "War Machine" taking JJ's place. The War Machine was the late Ray Traylor, who had a great career as Big Bubba and the Bossman. He came to the ring wearing Dusty's old Midnight Rider outfit [which Dusty wore in Florida in 1983]. I'm not sure how Ray got into the mix, but he was a good worker and he could fit into the Midnight Rider costume.

As they did in Atlanta, Arn and Dusty started the match. The Horseman won the toss (Gee, what are the odds of them winning the toss for the second time in a row?). After the initial five minutes, we all entered the ring in turn in two-minute intervals. The War Machine, Hawk, Flair, me, Tully, Animal, Luger, and Ellering climbed into the cage in that order. While we contained Flair and company, Animal used a spiked wristband brought into the ring by Ellering to lay waste to the War Machine. Ray gave up and, once again, the good guys won over the Horsemen without them actually losing. All was well with the world.

I had a great rapport with Dusty and I was as close to him, if not closer, than with anyone else in the business. When we became the "Super Powers," we spent a lot of time together, not only in the ring, but traveling from town to town in either his red Mercedes convertible or my gold Corvette convertible. I didn't do this to garner any special favor from Dusty. In fact, there were many occasions when Dusty had to wait on me for ten to fifteen minutes before we hit the road.

My friendship with Dusty continues to this day, and while he and I were working together, it caused more than a little jealousy in the locker room. Dusty was in charge of the booking at the time and I'm sure more than a few of the boys thought I was just "sucking up" to the boss to enhance my opportunities to wrestle on the top of the card. Nothing could be further from the truth. Dusty and I have an authentic friendship and we enjoyed hanging out together.

One thing I tried to do outside of the ring was to establish a level of respect with other people in the business. It was no different with Dusty. Even though he controlled the book, I never hesitated to speak my mind. To this day, I believe that was part of what helped establish and maintain our friendship. He knew he could trust me and that I wasn't a "yes man" who was only going to tell him the things he wanted to hear.

Besides the Crocketts, Dusty was the most important man behind the scenes in Jim Crockett Promotions. In fact, that's true about anyone who holds the head booking position. The head booker sets up the matches, the storylines, and the programs between the wrestlers. He decides who wins, who loses, and how those results are facilitated. Most of the boys walked around the booker like they were treading on egg shells, trying their best not to upset him, and stepping and fetching for them at every opportunity. Everything they did was done in the hopes of currying favor and moving them up the ladder. That was something I never did. Not to Dusty, not to anyone. I treated everyone with the same respect and I hoped that respect was returned. No matter who was in charge, who held the belt, who was in the curtain jerker, the popcorn match, or the main event, I treated them all as I wished to be treated.

Trips on the road could be onerous at best, but with Dusty, the miles seemed to fly by as we spent time on the road talking and having a good time. We would set up a time to meet and head out to whatever town in which we were booked to wrestle. Even though we had an appointed time to meet, I would, from time to time, be running late for one reason or another. If we were supposed to meet at five o'clock, I wouldn't arrive until 5:20 or 5:30. When I pulled up, Dusty would be waiting for me. I know a lot of guys who would have gone to great lengths to be thirty minutes early and be waiting for Dusty to arrive. After all, you should never be late for an appointment with the guy who holds your career in his hands. On the other hand, I knew Dusty was the boss, but I didn't want Dusty to think the only reason I was traveling with him was to get ahead in the business. In fact, the funny thing about it, not only would I be late, but I would ask Dusty to drive. A lot of the boys would chauffer him around and be happy to do so, but Dusty loved to drive, and that was just fine with me. There would be occasions when I would drive, but most of the time, it was Dusty behind the wheel.

It wasn't that I was taking advantage of Dusty. It was more of a testament to our friendship. I was very casual and his position as booker didn't interfere with our friendship. Love him or not, Virgil Runnels left a legacy in the sport of wrestling that certainly won't be forgotten anytime soon.

Chapter 21

Cockroaches

I was honored to be the U.S. heavyweight champion, and in the days before I turned babyface, holding the title of the best wrestler in the United States made me a bigger heel in the eyes of the fans, especially in respect to the method I had used to win the vacant title from Magnum. I had the title, I had the belt, I had the notoriety and the crowds that accompanied it, but the one thing I didn't have during my title reign was an ongoing program.

I defended the belt against just about everyone in the upper tier of the promotion. I put the belt on the line at house shows, television, and pay-per-view, against talent like Arn Anderson, Tully Blanchard, Vladimir Petrov, Rick Rude, Ivan Koloff, and Dick Murdoch. It was somewhat of a throwback to the prior days of the sport when a champion would travel to various territories and put his belt on the line against the top contenders in each area. Now, however, we were traveling to cities across the U.S., Canada, and Puerto Rico, where I would defend the U.S. belt against a variety of different contenders. They just all happened to be part of Crockett's roster.

Traveling up and down the roads to make towns could be an adventure in itself. Volumes of books could be filled with tales of the road and I certainly had more than my share.

There were so many days when I would arrive with just enough time to change and get into the ring. On one particular night in Chicago, Ivan and I were running late on the way to our match in the UIC Pavilion. Our plane had been delayed and it took us a little longer than usual to rent a car, so we were leaving O'Hare International Airport around the time the bell rang for the opening match. I have always said that I loved the fans in the Windy City, but I wasn't too crazy about the city itself. It's not that I dislike Chicago. It just seemed that every time I was there, I got lost, and on this night, it was worse than ever. I'm usually good with directions and, in most cases, I could wrestle in a town for the first time and, when I returned years later, I could find my way to the arena without a second thought. Not so in Chicago. The town just drove me crazy.

The time seemed to fly by as Ivan and I tried to make our way to the UIC. Eventually, Ivan and I thought we had better stop and ask for directions. We took the directions and headed off with new hope that we might actually make it on time for the main event. Lewis and Clark had an easier time on their expedition across the west than we had driving across Chicago. We were more like Rocky and Bullwinkle than Lewis and Clark, so we stopped for directions again and again. Each time we stopped, we were given totally different directions from those we had been given previously, or the people refused to give us directions at all.

In desperation, Ivan suggested that I pull over and ask a policeman who was writing a ticket. I stopped beside him and said *"Excuse me, officer. Could you please tell me how to get to the UIC Pavilion?"* The officer didn't even look up from his ticket book as he said, *"Get lost."*

"I am lost," I said. *"That's why I'm asking you for directions."*

I couldn't believe it when the officer turned towards us and, without saying a word, gave us a look like "figure it out yourself" and turned to finish writing the ticket. We drove off and eventually, by pure chance, found the Pavilion. We had driven around Chicago for more than two hours! We did make it on time for our match, but just barely. That was probably the worse time I ever had when it came to finding an arena. Thinking back, during all the time we spent driving around, Ivan was as calm as anyone could be, while I got more and more frustrated. Come to think of it, I don't remember Ivan ever losing his temper about anything.

All in all, I was pretty fortunate to do as much driving as I did without having an accident or getting a ticket. There are more than a few of the boys who could easily wallpaper their entire house with the tickets they received on the road. In fact, some of the boys had pleading their way out of a ticket down to an art. The master of this was Don Kernodle. Ivan, Don, and I got stopped for speeding late at night after a show in Columbia, South Carolina, on July 3, 1984. We were on our way to the next day's show in Myrtle Beach. Don was driving, so the officer asked him to get out of the car and told Ivan and I to remain seated. Don began talking to the officer and used every trick in the book to avoid getting a ticket, but to no avail. My jaw dropped to the floor when Don got down on one knee, right there on the interstate, to plead with the policeman. Don said he couldn't believe the officer would give a ticket to the "Pride of the USA" (Don's ring nickname) on the eve of the birthday of our great nation.

Ivan and I howled at the scene of Don on one knee invoking the patriotic spirit of the officer. When Don finished his stellar performance, the policeman said, *"I won't write you a ticket, but I would like to see your championship belts."* He turned out to be an avid wrestling fan, as many of the law enforcement officers throughout the South were. By the time he finished looking at the belts, we had four other state trooper cars parked behind us as "South Carolina's Finest" sought a look the belts and asked us for autographs. It was one of the rare occasions, and one of the very few exceptions, in which I broke my heel character, and for good reason. It never hurts to have state troopers on your side. It was definitely an Independence Day I will never forget.

I didn't receive any speeding tickets, but that doesn't mean I was free from trouble on the road. My car "gave up the ghost" on at least two occasions while I was traveling to a match. During one, I was making an independent shot (one that wasn't affiliated with one of the major promotions) in West Virginia. Somewhere near the northern border of North Carolina, my car engine rumbled to a stop. I had just pulled into a small town, the kind where they roll up the sidewalks after four o'clock in the afternoon. I don't mean to insult the town or the people who live there. It's just the kind of a town it was; the kind that makes Mayberry look like Gotham City. I still had a good three hours to make the match, but I was told my car couldn't be repaired, at least, not at the service station where I was.

It was definitely a dilemma of some magnitude. I had never missed a match and I was booked for the main event. Since the entire card usually revolves around the main event, it would be devastating to the program and to the promoter who put on the show. Besides, I didn't want to lose the $1,000 guarantee I was due. So I began to talk to the folks around the service station, telling them of my plight. I approached them and said, *"I know this may sound crazy, but if anyone here is interested in driving me to West Virginia, I'll be glad to pay you for your time. I'm a wrestler and I have to get to a match tonight. I don't know if any of you are fans, but if you would like, I can get you into the matches and it won't cost you anything."*

One guy took me up on the offer and said he would be happy to help me out. I offered him a hundred dollars to drive me the two hours to my match and he gladly accepted it. It was either that or disappoint the fans, let down the promoter, and lose $1,000. He turned out to be a great guy and he had the time of his life. It was certainly worth the $100. All I can say is, *"God bless the wrestling fans."*

Sometimes we had to deal with unpredictable things that happened when we got to our venue. We were booked in Texas in a small town near the Mexican border. Everything seemed fine until I went to baggage pickup to get my bag, only to learn it hadn't arrived. All my wrestling gear was in the bag, so I had nothing to wear in the ring that night. I used to wear a black singlet and big, black "stomper-like" boots, the kind that fastened on the side instead of lacing up the front. I had fostered that look for the "Russian Nightmare," so I couldn't just borrow anyone's gear.

But that's exactly what I had to do. Dick Murdoch let me borrow an extra pair of trunks he had brought along, and just before it was my time to hit the ring, Arn Anderson handed me his red-and-white lace-up boots. I entered the ring wearing Dick's trunks, Arn's boots, and a pair of kneepads I borrowed from someone else. It was probably the most uncomfortable I had felt in the ring since my first match. Besides the fact that nothing fit well, I didn't "feel" like Nikita Koloff. That was the first and the last time that happened to me, but it made me realize how much I had become Nikita Koloff and how the look was as much the character as the character itself.

My run as U.S. champion lasted one month shy of a year. By July 1987, it was time for me to work another program and to pass the torch and belt to the next champion. Lex Luger was tapped to fill that role.

The title switch was scheduled for Greensboro on July 11, 1987. To set up the switch, I had to develop a weakness that Lex could exploit so he could become the new champion, albeit by way of a tainted win. That "weakness" came about during a match in March when Dick Murdoch "injured" my neck by dropping me with a brainbuster on the concrete floor. We sold the injury by having me wrestle while wearing a foam collar for a number of weeks. A week or so prior to my match with Lex, the neck injury was "aggravated" when Ric Flair, Arn Anderson, and Tully Blanchard repeatedly drove my head into the mat with the piledriver move and left me lying prone in the ring.

Lex Luger, the "Total Package," in reality was Larry Pfohl, who began his career on the gridiron playing for the Canadian Football League and the United

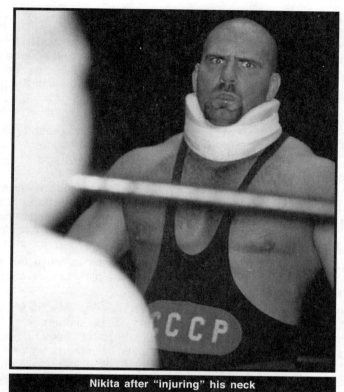

Nikita after "injuring" his neck

States Football League. He began wrestling professionally in September 1985 after training with Hiro Matsuda in Tampa.

I liked Lex. We got along well and even traveled together occasionally. He was the type of guy who paid close attention to his looks, and to say he was a bit vain would be somewhat of an understatement. After wrestling, we would all shower and get dressed. As soon as we were finished, we were ready to hit the road. Lex, on the other hand, would take his time (and a lot of ours) to make sure he cooled off before leaving the dressing room. He would towel off carefully to make sure no beads of water remained on him before dressing. He then had to cover his arms and chest with lotion and make sure every hair was in place before leaving the building. It was pretty amusing to us, except for the times we rode together and we had to wait until the "Total Package" was perfect.

I have to admit that we had more than a few laughs at Lex's expense. During the time when I was riding with Lex, Sting, and Animal, we were traveling through a town in Iowa. It was a small town and not much different than hundreds of others in which we wrestled. Every now and then, we would hit a town where there were no vacancies in any of the hotels. I don't recall why we hadn't made reservations that night, but for some reason, we didn't. The only hotel we could find with a vacancy was way out in "no man's land," and it was as far from being a four-star hotel as anyone could imagine. Animal and I decided to share one room, while Sting and Lex would share the other.

When we hit the road again the next morning, all Lex could talk about was how terrible the room was, and how he didn't get any sleep because he was up all night killing cockroaches with his shoe and swatting flies with a fly-swatter. He complained for hours about how bad the hotel was and how he couldn't believe we made him stay there. We kept laughing at him as he continued his tirade. He swore he wouldn't stay in a motel like that again for all the money in the world. To the rest of us, it was just part and parcel of the business we chose. To Lex, it was worse than staying at the Bates Motel.

To make matters worse for Lex, we decided to eat at a little country restaurant next to the motel. We were all certain that Lex was famished from his all-night battle against the killer cockroaches and needed to get something to eat. What we learned was that Lex was just as particular about his food as he was about his appearance. When the waitress brought out his food, it was saturated in cooking oil, which to him was like kryptonite to Superman. When she placed the plate in front of him, he didn't say a word. All he could do was stare at it, slack-jawed, for several minutes. Sting, Animal, and I couldn't stop laughing. Poor Lex. He just wasn't built for life on the road.

On May 1, 2003, Lex's world fell apart when he was implicated in the accidental overdose death of Liz Hewlett, better known to wrestling fans as the beautiful "Miss Elizabeth."

Elizabeth became involved in wrestling after meeting "Macho Man" Randy Savage at a local gym. They married in 1984 and she accompanied Randy to a WWF ring for the first time on July 30, 1985. Elizabeth became a star in her own right as she became the central character in numerous storylines that focused on Randy and Elizabeth's supposedly roller-coaster ride of a romance, which culminated in Randy "proposing" to Elizabeth on television and "marrying" her in the ring at *SummerSlam 1991*. They had actually been married for seven years at the time of their nuptials in the ring, but it gave the fans a great story to follow.

Unfortunately, their marriage took the route of so many others in a business that seems to prey upon relationships and they divorced in 1992. After their breakup, Elizabeth withdrew from wrestling, only to appear in 1996 with the rival World Championship Wrestling promotion where she worked again with "Macho" in the NWO angle.

I suppose that was where she got to know Lex because the two eventually moved in together. Sad to say, they seemed to have their ups and downs, as well. Sometime around 5:30 in the morning on Thursday, May 1, 2003, paramedics were summoned to Lex's townhouse in Marietta, Georgia, after a 911 call was made concerning Elizabeth's reaction to the combination of vodka and painkillers she was taking for back pain. When paramedics were unable to revive her, she was rushed to the WellStar Kennestone Hospital emergency room. Elizabeth Ann Hulette, the beautiful, petite woman from Kentucky, who lit up so many lives as "Miss Elizabeth, the First Lady of Wrestling," was pronounced dead at the age of 42 in Cobb County, Georgia.

Getting back to the subject of my series of matches with Lex, I was more than happy to drop the U.S. title to him. I had no desire to be a perpetual champion — U.S. or otherwise. There were more worlds I wanted to conquer and Crockett was ready to program me against other wrestlers. I was looking forward to new challenges and opportunities.

Chapter 22

David Copperfield

In 1985, Jim Crockett Promotions began to expand its territory into other parts of the country and Canada. Our television shows were being seen in the other territories, most of which were beginning to falter due to the combination of increasing debt and sparse crowds. The other reason for the company's expansion was to stem the onslaught we saw coming at a distance led by Vince McMahon and the World Wrestling Federation. This brought us into an agreement with Bill Watts to bring in some of the wrestlers from the Universal Wrestling Federation, which was formerly known as the Mid-South territory. It was with that move that I had my first encounter with Bill Watts.

The Mid-South promotion had a fairly good roster of its own, including Ted DiBiase, "Dr. Death" Steve Williams, Terry Taylor, "Hacksaw" Jim Duggan, Eddie Gilbert, Dick Slater, and a stable of other superstars that ran the gamut from the Iron Sheik to the Junkyard Dog [Sylvester Ritter]. Their territory covered Oklahoma, Louisiana, Mississippi, Arkansas, and parts of Missouri and Texas. It had been a strong region for years and grew stronger when Watts took over the helm in 1979 from former world junior heavyweight champion, LeRoy McGuirk.

Bill enhanced the prestige of the main title, the North American heavyweight title, which he held on five different occasions from 1970 to 1977 and a brief angle for two days in 1980. He elevated Ted DiBiase, Mr. Wrestling II, the Junkyard Dog, and Magnum T.A. (before his accident) to main event status and promoted a version of the United States tag team title, the Mid-South Brass Knuckles title, the Mid-South tag team title, the Mid-South TV title, as well as the Louisiana, Arkansas, and Mississippi state titles.

Mid-South was doing well and really hit their stride when they syndicated a second wrestling show called *Power Pro Wrestling*, which was picked up by TV stations outside their area. Seeing the opportunity and a much wider audience base through nationwide syndication, he pulled the plug on Mid-South Wrestling and, in 1986, renamed his promotion the Universal Wrestling Federation.

To compete for the fans' attention on a nationwide scale, Bill had to drop his regional and state belts and create more compelling titles, and what can be more compelling than the world heavyweight championship? So Bill dropped out of the NWA and crafted his own world title. On May 30, 1986, Terry Gordy defeated Jim Duggan in Houston and became the first person to strap the new belt around his waist. The title, along with the UWF version of the world TV and world tag team titles, had a short run as they were abandoned in 1987 when the UWF was taken over by Crockett.

Like many of his peers, Bill had come to professional wrestling by way of the autumn battles on the college gridiron in Oklahoma. A high-school standout on the mat, as well as the football field, Bill attended the University of Oklahoma and went on to play for the fledgling Houston Oilers and the Minnesota Vikings in the early 1960s. Wrestling during the off-season, Bill decided his fortune was to be better made in the ring, so he took to the squared-circle and began what would become a storied career.

Trained by fellow Okies and world champions Leroy McGuirk and Danny Hodge, Bill had a tremendous run throughout Texas and the region promoted by McGuirk. He invaded the east coast to challenge Bruno Sammartino for the WWWF title and drew well, selling out Madison Square Garden and other venues graced by the World Wide Wrestling Federation. He was a top contender for the NWA and AWA titles as he picked up regional tag team and single belts everywhere he appeared. As his in-ring career came to a close, Bill turned to the promoting end of the business and took over the Mid-South area.

Of course, he wasn't the only person with dreams of going national as McMahon and Crockett both set their sights on controlling wrestling and taking in or destroying all others in their wake. The UWF had a great product, but not the cash it needed to survive, so in 1987, Watts threw in with Crockett and set the stage for a series of title versus title matches.

This took place before Jim actually bought the territory from Watts, during a time when we were trading talent back and forth. We were doing shots in his territory and some of his boys were doing shots in ours. My first impression was not favorable at all. The way he talked to the wrestlers under his employ and the subsequent way he treated them was like something out of Charles Dickens' *David Copperfield*. He treated them so poorly and demeaned them by instituting some of the most ridiculous rules I had ever heard. It bordered on Draconian. I thought to myself, *"Man, I could never work for this guy."* Little did I know what was in store for both of us within a few years, but in the dressing room at the time, we saw a huge difference between what Watts' boys were experiencing and what we were experiencing back in the Carolinas.

One time I remember when I was told I would be working for Bill was the time we were working with his promotion in Philadelphia. While I was changing into my wrestling gear in the dressing room on the third floor with some of the boys, we heard Bill berating some of his boys for what he thought was a lousy match. He talked down to them like they were less than human. We couldn't believe our ears and we all just stared at each other in disbelief. None of us saw the match, but there was no way we could imagine that the match, or any match for that matter, could be so bad as to warrant that kind of treatment. The humorous part of the story was that the dressing room Bill and his wrestlers were in was on the first floor. He was two floors below us, and we heard every word as if we were in the same room.

As in any profession, if the employees are happy and believe they are being fairly treated, they will respond in kind and give their employers all they have. If they are treated like dogs, they will respond in kind. The latter is what was taking place with the boys in Bill's territory. They seemed so preoccupied with the mental battle and constant conflict they were having with Watts that they didn't have the camaraderie we had in the NWA. There was more of an edge, and not much joking or the mindless chit-chat that goes on between the boys in the dressing room. There were no ribs, no laughter. Just an attitude of *"Let's get out there, get this over with, and go home."* I'm not saying the boys in the UWF didn't go out in the ring every night and give it their all for the fans. There was no doubt that the fans received their money's worth before Crockett's group arrived. Some of their top stars could have easily headlined cards anywhere in the world. In fact, most of them did, both before, during, and after Watts.

I had the opportunity to wrestle most of the boys in the UWF, but one of the most talented wrestlers I faced was Terry Taylor. As the cross-promotion ended with Crockett's buyout of the UWF, a decision had to be made about what to do with their titles. Usually, when a promotion goes out of business, the titles are just abandoned, but this was a unique situation, and as the old saying goes, "Make hay while the sun shines." And Jim Crockett knew how to make hay.

Terry grew up as a wrestling fan in West Palm Beach, Florida, and attended the local matches with his brother. While in college at Guilford in Greensboro, he became friends with Steve Travis [Steve Musulin], who had a tryout match with the old International Wrestling Association, a short-lived promotion that Pedro Martinez and Johnny Powers had set up to run against the Crocketts. Steve had the size, weighing in around 300 pounds, but very little knowledge of wrestling, so upon telling Terry of his opportunity with the IWF, Terry offered to show Steve what he knew from watching the matches. Steve's tryout was successful as he did get the job and, after working with the IWF as Stonewall Jackson, he worked for the WWF and the NWA for a number of years.

Years later, Terry ran into Steve at a card in West Palm Beach and Steve invited Terry to join him the next night in Tampa. That night at the Fort Homer Hesterly Armory, a wrestler named Chick Donovan didn't show up for his match and they asked Terry to fill in for him. Terry borrowed some wrestling gear, got into the ring, and began his career.

Terry was in his second run as the UWF world television champion when Crockett acquired the UWF. I had just won the NWA world television title in August 1987 from Tully Blanchard in Fayetteville, so it was a natural to have the two men who claimed the world television title meet and decide who the rightful champion was.

Now, the television title was different from all the other titles in wrestling. It had, in numerous variations, been around almost as long as television itself. As first, it was designed to only be defended on television, so the folks who couldn't get to the live matches could see a title defended while sitting at home. The challenge of this particular title is that you had to defend it all the time. Every time you were on television, you had to put the title on the line, so if you did three TV tapings in one day, you would have to defend the belt three times. Eventually, the NWA changed the parameters of the title so the belt was up for grabs for the first 15 minutes of every match at house shows. Whoever held the television title was an awfully busy man.

The Mid-Atlantic version of the NWA world television title had been another one of George Scott's ideas. It was introduced in 1973 as the Mid-Atlantic television title and was first held by Ole Anderson, followed by Danny Miller,

Ivan, Paul Jones, Ric Flair, Angelo Mosca, Tim Woods, Greg Valentine, Ricky Steamboat, Baron von Raschke, Johnny Weaver, Roddy Piper, and Rocky Johnson, to name a few. The title was elevated to the "world" television title when Dusty held the belt in 1985.

I won the TV title on August 8, 1986 in Fayetteville by pinning Tully Blanchard as part as my running feud with the Four Horsemen. Tully had held the belt for almost a year after defeating Dusty at *Starrcade* in Greensboro the previous year.

Terry and I were scheduled to meet at *Starrcade* in the UIC Pavilion in Chicago on Thanksgiving night, November 26, 1987. We were in the first main event on the card that saw Tully and Arn beat the Road Warriors by disqualification, Dusty taking the U.S. belt from Lex, and Flair regaining the world title he lost a month earlier to "Hands of Stone" Ronnie Garvin.

The buildup was somewhat different as it had been some time since two titles were on the line with the intent for one man to walk out with both. Terry was a consummate professional. He always had excellent ring psychology, had a great feel for the crowd, and had a lot more experience in the ring than I did. Knowing that, I trusted Terry to call the match. In other words, lead what was going on and call the holds and spots. It was important that he shine in the early part of the match since I was going to walk out of the ring with both titles, so I put him over at every turn. One reason was, the better he looked during the match, the better I looked when I beat him. Even though the match was a "work," it was important, especially when a title was at stake, to not make it look like you won too easily. It didn't mean as much to win a match if it looked like you haven't worked for it.

We went about fifteen minutes and he put me over to retain my TV title and to take his. On that particular night, we worked well together, but at times, it seemed he was a bit hesitant in the ring. I found out why years later when Terry told me that Arn Anderson had told him I was going to destroy him "like a jobber" during the match. To this day, I have no idea why Arn would say something like that, but Terry kept apologizing to me. I told him to forget it. I didn't know anything about it then and it certainly was of no consequence years later.

What neither of us knew was that events were in motion that would change the wrestling industry forever.

Chapter 23

Sports Entertainment

While we were bouncing back and forth across the country, Vince McMahon was beginning an expansion of his own. He began raiding Verne Gagne's American Wrestling Association, enticing Hulk Hogan, Gene Okerlund, Bobby Heenan, and Jesse Ventura to jump to the WWF. He also took some of the NWA's best, including "Rowdy" Roddy Piper, Jack and Jerry Brisco, Paul Orndorff, and "Superfly" Jimmy Snuka. He even captured the coveted Saturday afternoon spot on Ted Turner's WTBS, replacing the long-running *Georgia Championship Wrestling* with his own program. His vision and moxie took the old-time promoters by surprise, but most of them refused to believe Vince McMahon's son would be able to pull it off. Little did we know how much he would change the face of the wrestling business in the years to come.

One question I am frequently asked is if I ever talked to Vince during that time, or if I had been approached by him directly and asked to move north and wrestle for the WWF. The answer to that question is no. Barry Darsow received an invitation from the WWF to join their ranks and he thought it would be a good move for him. He thought his Krusher Khrushchev gimmick had pretty much ran its course, so it might be a good time to move on and take advantage of Vince's generosity. Barry left the Mid-Atlantic territory and his Krusher persona behind with it. His new character was called Ax, and along with Bill Eadie (formerly the Masked Superstar) as Smash, they took on the persona of Demolition, an imitation of the Road Warriors, and quickly became the WWF's world tag-team champions.

Barry approached me with the idea of going with him to Stamford, Connecticut, as his partner. I did give it some consideration and discussed it at length with Barry, but after awhile, I thought it better to stay and continue to wrestle for the Crocketts. It was not a decision I took lightly and I carefully looked at all the pros and cons on where I was in my career and the direction in which I wanted to go at that time. The biggest factor that convinced me to stay with Jim Crockett Promotions was my character — Nikita Koloff. I had worked extremely hard to perpetuate my persona and I didn't want to lose that in another incarnation. Nothing had been said to me about that, but I knew that if Barry's character was going to change, there was a good chance I would have to say goodbye to the "Russian Nightmare."

Another reason I stayed with the NWA was the loyalty I felt to Jim Crockett and his company. After all, Jim gave me my start, took care of me, and gave me an opportunity I never thought I would have been given, even in my wildest dreams. I was happy for Barry. He had a great run as Ax and later wrestled as the "Repo Man," but I was confident that I made the right decision for my career at the time.

There was one other time that I was intrigued about trying my skills in the WWF. Many of the magazines at the time were pushing the idea of a match between Hulk Hogan, the WWF world heavyweight champion, and me. We both were known for using power moves and the meeting between us for the heavyweight championship of the world served as fodder for the imaginations of fans everywhere. It's too bad it never came about. I would have loved to have worked with Hulk and I think it would have been a great angle.

I did watch the WWF's programs during that time whenever I could. Their shows were quite a bit different than ours and, at the time, I thought their characters were a bit over the top and somewhat cartoon-like. They had as many skits on their programs as they had matches, which was totally different from the direction Crockett took. In fact, for awhile, the NWA promoted their shows as "This is the NWA. We wrestle." That was a direct slap at what Vince was doing. Not that it really mattered much. McMahon had a different vision and was reinventing the industry, while we were holding on to the tried-and-true methods. We soon learned that many of them had been tried, but no longer were true.

The thing about the WWF that amazed so many in the Crockett promotion is that they were going over like crazy. Both companies were doing good business, but the WWF was not only doing good business at the box office. Vince's vision encompassed marketing the WWF and his wrestlers in ways that have never been done before that time. Lunch boxes, notebooks, ice cream bars, Saturday morning cartoons, record albums, action figures. You name it, there was a license for it. It would probably be easier to list items that did not carry his logo or the visage of one of his superstars. Someone once said that the

NIKITA KOLOFF 217 Series I

- Height: 6' 4" ■ Weight: 265
- Color of Eyes: Blue
- Color of Hair: Bald
- Hometown: Moscow, Russia
- Number of Years in Pro Wrestling: 3
- Favorite Wrestling Hold: Sickle
- Toughest Opponent: Ric Flair
- Titles Held: NWA World Tag Team, World Six-Man, US Heavyweight, World TV
- Favorite Old Time Wrestler: None
- Amateur Wrestling Experience: Trained for 1984 Olympics
- Favorite Pro Sports Team: CCCP National Wrestling Team
- Favorite College Sports Team: None
- Favorite Vacation Spot: Cayman Islands
- Favorite Recreational Activity: None
- Hobbies: Weightlifting
- Favorite Food: Borscht & Vodka
- Favorite Dessert: Ice Cream
- Favorite Color: Black
- Favorite Song: None
- Favorite Singer: Billy Joel
- Favorite Movie: Rocky II
- Favorite Actor: Sylvester Stallone
- Favorite Actress: Sigourney Weaver

LICENSED BY: JIM CROCKETT PROMOTIONS
DISTRIBUTED BY: WONDERAMA INTERNATIONAL®

Nikita Koloff trading card

best way to predict the future was to invent it, and invent it was exactly what Vince McMahon did.

George Scott had moved to the Northeast to work with Vince and helped him navigate this new era of wrestling. For the first time since the '50s, professional wrestling aired on network television. The show *Saturday Night Main Event* occasionally took the place of the popular NBC show, *Saturday Night Live*, while we [WCW] were still doing local, syndicated TV.

With all of their innovations, there is one thing Vince did that did more for the transformation of the sport than anything else. He took wrestling out of the small smoked-filled arenas and took it to major networks such as MTV with the "War to Settle the Score." He also combined wrestling with rock and roll and transformed our sport into "sports entertainment."

We were looking straight at it and never saw it coming. The WWF was no longer a regional promotion that was actually a member of the National Wrestling Alliance (in fact, for a brief time, the WWF version of the world title was reduced to being recognized as a regional championship). It had become a monolithic sports corporation that ruled from the pinnacle of the industry it created. It was akin to *Prometheus Unbound*, but this time, the creator successfully controlled his creation.

It always struck me as somewhat strange that as wrestling evolved in the 1980s, there was little acknowledgement of the sport's rich and storied past. If the sport of wrestling is adept at one thing, it is the ability to reinvent itself to the present times. As the WWF was gaining momentum, the NWA began to tout its history and traced the lineage of Flair's world title back to Frank Gotch in 1908. It served its purpose, even if it was somewhat inaccurate.

The current NWA actually began in 1948 when Orville Brown was named its first champion. His reign was short-lived as he was injured in an automobile accident and the belt was awarded to the number one contender, Lou Thesz, who was scheduled to meet Brown in November 1949. Lou then went on tour and, by 1957, he single-handedly defeated all other claimants for the world title and unified the title. This, indeed, may have given the lineage and credibility to the NWA, but we were living in a new era and Vince was catering to an entirely new generation of fans who couldn't have cared less. They came to be entertained, to cheer and jeer to their hearts content. Vince knew this; we didn't. We were entering the nuclear age armed with a slingshot, fighting a 20th-century war with 19th-century weapons, and we still couldn't understand why the WWF was beating us to the punch at every turn.

Of course, the WWF did have a history of its own. It might not have reached as far back as the National Wrestling Alliance, but it was just as interesting. As with all the major promotions at the time, the World Wrestling Federation began as a part of the National Wrestling Alliance. Promoting out of the Northeast, the "Gold Dust Trio" (comprised of Joseph "Toots" Mondt, Billy Sandow, and then world heavyweight champion "Strangler" Ed Lewis, along with Jess McMahon, the grandfather of WWE CEO, Vince McMahon Jr.) put together a force to be reckoned with in the world of sports and put professional wrestling in a hold that would not be broken for years. In fact, they were attributed to be the ones who began programming wrestling. That is to say, not only pick the winners and losers, but determine how the matches would go and the story particular rivalries would tell.

When Lewis and Sandow retired, Toots brought Vince McMahon Sr. into the fold, and eventually turned the promotion over to him. New York not only became the Great White Way, it also became one of the favorite haunts of then NWA world heavyweight champion, "Nature Boy" Buddy Rogers. Buddy preferred the larger cities, bigger crowds, and subsequent larger payoffs to the smaller venues of the Midwest. So, in essence, Mondt and McMahon not only controlled wrestling in the northeast, but controlled the world heavyweight title.

This, of course, drove the president of the NWA, Sam Muchnick, crazy. Headquartered in St. Louis, Sam controlled the bookings of the champion and received three percent of every gate where the champion appeared. Sensing a coup by his New York colleagues, Sam and the board of the NWA decided Buddy had held the title long enough and asked five-time champion, Lou Thesz, to take the belt from the Nature Boy and put it back in secure hands.

On January 24, 1963, Lou pinned Buddy with the "Thesz Press" in a one-fall match in Mondt's backyard — Maple Leaf Gardens in Toronto. McMahon and Mondt were not happy with Muchnick regaining control of the belt, so they discounted and nullified Lou's win, claiming it came by way of one fall and not the usual two-out-of-three fall match. They may have had a plausible claim, but they ignored the fact that Lou, in a return match a few weeks later, defeated Buddy again, this time in a two-out-of-three fall match.

Mondt and McMahon formed Capital Wrestling and the World Wide Wrestling Federation, picked Buddy as their first champion, and claimed he won the title by defeating long-time rival, Antonino Rocca, in the finals of a fictitious tournament in Rio De Janeiro. They only

Nikita Koloff figure

planned to use Rogers as a transitional champion before having him lose to the Italian strongman, Bruno Sammartino, on May 17, 1963 in Madison Square Garden before nearly 20,000 fans. It was from those somewhat meager beginnings (Buddy wore his old NWA U.S. heavyweight title belt when he lost the new WWWF world title to Bruno) that the WWF became the monolithic organization it is today.

From time to time, I find myself pondering about what might have happened if I had jumped to the WWF. It's always easy to second guess yourself and the decisions you made as the years begin to slip away and memories start to fade. If I had left Mid-Atlantic Wrestling with Barry for the WWF, my career may have taken an entirely different path and Nikita Koloff may have ended there. And with the fact that the two major promotions refused to acknowledge the existence of each other, if I had wrestled in New York, there would have been more than a good chance I would have been forced to become someone else. Maybe if I had, I would have been lifted to another level. It's something we will never know.

Chapter 24
The James Boys

There is another group of people in the wrestling industry that fans may have some peripheral knowledge of, but may not realize the important role they play. They are responsible for calling the shots, directing what is going on in the ring, critiquing the matches, and setting the schedules. They are the ones with whom the power lies; not about what goes on in the ring, but with what goes on in the dressing room and the office behind the scenes. The men who yield this power are the bookers, local promoters, and road agents.

I have talked quite a bit about the importance and the role of the bookers, but the local promoters and road agents are just as important in running a profitable wrestling company. Without them, things would come to a screeching halt. With so many towns running at once, a booker, or for that matter, Jim Crockett, could not be everywhere at once. A strong support system had to be in place so when we hit town, everything was set for us to wrestle and head out to the next town. They comprise something akin to middle management for a wrestling company. Many of them had been wrestlers and were no longer active in the ring, while others were old business partners of the Crockett family who watched over their respective territories like feudal lords.

I believe I got along well with all the road agents and promoters, but I did have my moments. One in particular that comes to mind is an altercation I had with Bill Watts and Grizzly Smith. Earlier in my career, I vowed that I would never work for Watts, but after he sold his territory to Crockett, he was hired as the booker and pretty much called the shots.

I had been in a six-man tag-team match in Norfolk, Virginia, and when I opened my pay envelope the following week, it was $1,000 short. I found Bill in his office and asked him why my payoff was missing $1,000. Bill accused us of slacking off during the match and that he wasn't going to stand for it, and to make sure we understood how serious he was, he was levying a $1,000 fine on everyone in the match. I'm not sure where the money went, but I had a feeling it didn't go to charity. It probably went back to the bottom line.

I was stunned by the accusation. That was the first time I had ever been accused of not giving one-hundred percent of my effort in the ring, so I took it as more of a personal affront than a professional critique. If there was one thing I was proud of above anything else, it was my work ethic in the ring, or what the boys call our workrate. I demanded to know why we were being accused of having a poor match. When I asked Bill if he had seen the match and why he thought we did less than our utmost, he said he didn't see the match himself, but Grizzly Smith, the road agent, had told him of our infractions and for him to hand us the reprimand and the fine. I asked Bill for us to get together with Griz right away and have him tell me to my face that I did less than my best. Bill agreed and, in short order, found Grizzly and asked him to come meet with us.

To his credit, Griz met with all six of the people involved in the match. When I questioned him, he admitted that he didn't actually see the match, either, but one of the boys told him he didn't think much of my match that evening. So, based on another wrestler's opinion, whose veracity I surely question, Grizzly believed we had slacked off and should be fined. I was more than adamant that I, as well as everyone else in the match, gave it our all, and I couldn't believe he would just blindly fine us on somebody else's word. After our conversation, he apologized and rescinded the fine he had levied on us. To my knowledge, once a fine had been imposed, it was never rescinded. That was one thing about Bill Watts that I did admire. Whenever I went to him with a concern, he heard me out and tried to make things right.

Promoters are a different breed than the boys who are battling in the ring. In the days of Jim Crockett Promotions, Jim ran the ship, but he couldn't be in every town all the time to take care of all the details that needed to be attended to prior to the matches. That's where the local promoters came into the picture.

Each region in the Mid-Atlantic area had a local promoter who would oversee ticket sales, interviews, security at the matches, and countless other details necessary to put on a card. I'm sure, as in any line of work, there are various degrees of honesty and people you can trust, but in wrestling, the scales seemed to tip more towards the negative than the positive. There were some great ones, however. Don Owens in the Northwest was one of the best. He treated everyone with respect and paid the boys well. I liked working for Don, as did most of the boys. Gary Juster, a promoter for a time in the Baltimore area, was also very good to the wrestlers. He was an attorney by trade, loved wrestling, and did some promoting on the side. We would always kid him that he would never make it in the business because he was too nice. He was a lot like Don Owens; he paid well and the boys liked him.

On the darker side, there were guys who would sell their grandmothers if it would help them make a buck, and then they would send her C.O.D. I was amazed at the lengths some of them would go to seek out the low road, even when the high road was right in front of them. There was one particular promoter in South Carolina the boys had nicknamed "High Pockets." It wasn't because he wore his pants particularly high, but because he was known for helping himself to the till before he paid the boys. One night after a match, Tully Blanchard walked into his office and saw him stuffing his pockets with cash. "High Pockets" indeed. There also was a brother team that promoted in Virginia and parts of North Carolina. It seemed like every time I went to one of their towns, we were shorted on the payoffs. On their best day, the James boys couldn't compete with those guys. In fact, that's what I called them — Frank and Jesse.

Since they were in charge of the ticket sales, they were in charge of all the cash in what was a predominantly a cash business. We would do a show where there might be 20,000 fans, but when the promoters would come into the dressing room, they would tell us the house was down and their count was only 12,500. I was always amazed at how, with business being so "down" in their towns all the time, they were constantly driving new Mercedes, buying condos on the beach, and always talking about their investments.

One night after a match, Frank came into the dressing room and went into his act of how the house was down and our payoff wasn't going to be as good as he thought. That night, I decided I had had enough of them cheating us. A few nights later, we wrestled in Dorton Arena in Raleigh. The dressing rooms in Dorton felt like a dungeon. They were at the bottom of a flight of stairs with a small door at the top. As expected, the "James Boys" opened the door and stood on the landing high above to give us the bad news. Even though it looked like a good crowd, the receipts were down and our payoffs would be less than what they had originally agreed to pay us. I lost it. I jumped up from the metal folding chair I was sitting on and lunged towards the stairs. Frank disappeared from the doorway. Fortunately for them, and for me, too, I suppose, Ivan was in-between us and held me back, saying, *"Niki, calm down. I will take care of this."* I told him that what they were doing just wasn't right. *"I busted my tail tonight wrestling Flair for almost an hour, and to give me half of what my take should actually be is not right."* I must say I can't remember having seen anyone move as fast as those promoters in Raleigh.

That was nothing new in the business. Promoters skimming off the top in the box office had been woven into the fabric of professional wrestling since the earliest days of the sport. Depending on the territory he was working, Chief Jay Strongbow would hire a local kid to stand by the front entrance with a grocery clicker and count the crowd as they came into the building. Jack Brisco once made the comment that you would know how bad you were going to get cheated by looking at the booking sheet and seeing what towns you were scheduled to wrestle.

I talked to Dusty about it once. *"Dusty,"* I said, *"This just isn't right. There has to be something we can do about this."*

"Keed, don't worry about it. That's just the way it is. It all works out." He then went on to explain that when he was working for Eddie Graham in Florida, he went to Eddie with the same concerns. He said Eddie told him just what he had said to me. A few days later, an envelope containing $10,000 in cash was delivered to his house. That was the end of that conversation. It may have worked for Dusty, but I checked my mail diligently for months and I never did get my envelope.

But even with all the political subterfuge and personal agendas, business was booming, and with that comes the heady feeling and bravado. Of course, many times, that success leads you to have the comfort of opinion without the discomfort of thought. A case in point was one particular night when Flair and I were working a program for the world heavyweight title.

On February 6, 1987, Ric and I were booked in the main event in Richmond. That alone was nothing unusual, other than the fact Ric and I were also booked in the main event that same night in Baltimore, Maryland. Jim thought he could pull off what had, to my knowledge, never been done before.

We had all wrestled a number of matches in one day. Television tapings, tournaments, and weekend shows where we wrestled in one town in the afternoon and a different town later that evening. Tim Woods, the late and erstwhile champion of the mat and ring, once told me that on one Christmas Day, he wrestled eleven times in two tournaments, winning them both.

Jim Crockett Sr. knew that Christmas was a great day for wrestling. He realized that by the afternoon, people begin to look for something else to occupy their time. Once the presents had been opened, Christmas dinner was consumed, and the obligatory nap over, folks begin to get bored. That being the case, there was no better place to spend the rest of the afternoon or evening than at the matches. Thus, he always presented a star-studded wrestling show on Christmas night.

Charlotte hosted the late-afternoon tournament, which gave the boys plenty of time to travel the 100-plus miles to Greenville, South Carolina to do it all again. It may have been rough on the boys, but Mr. Crockett and his company had a very Merry Christmas. I don't know if the boys pay envelopes were any heavier on those days, but I do hope so. All of this was part and parcel to what we had chosen as our profession, but again, Jim Crockett Jr. was going to venture into the unknown and promote two shows on the same night in two different cities in two different states. That all was fine as far as Jim and the brass was concerned, but then again, they weren't the ones in the ring.

When Jim explained his plan to me, all I could think of was back in the late 1800s when the notorious Dalton Gang decided to rob two banks simultaneously in Coffeyville, Kansas. Whether it was greed, arrogance, or Wild West daring that prompted the endeavor, it didn't work. When the townsmen took up arms against them, one of them was seriously wounded and the other four killed. I know our lives weren't on the line, but I was beginning to wonder if our sanity was.

As Jim explained it, in order to maximize revenue, he would run the two shows almost simultaneously. In other words, the matches in Richmond would begin at 7:30 and the show in Baltimore would begin at 8:00. Now that may not seem like a big difference, but with what we were going to attempt to do, every second was a precious commodity. After our match in Richmond, Ric and I would be spirited away to the airport, where we would fly to Baltimore in one of Jim's private planes, and then be driven to the arena in separate limousines.

Even though the main event was traditionally the last match on the card, Ric and I entered the ring early in Richmond. I'm sure the fans were somewhat surprised when Ric and I entered the ring about halfway through the card. We went about forty-five minutes with both of us being disqualified. As soon as the bell sounded, signaling the end of our match, Ric and I made our way to the dressing room as fast as we could without any semblance of hurrying. Once there, we packed our gear and, without the benefit of a shower, left the arena and headed to the airport.

As much as we tried to keep the craziness on schedule, we still arrived in Baltimore later than Jim had planned. That being the case, the promoter in Baltimore grew worried and decided to put the second main event on first as he waited for us to arrive. That shouldn't have caused any difficulty at all, other than the fact that the match was a cage match. The cage, of course, is nothing more than a specially-created chain link fence set up around the ring. All in all, it isn't difficult to set up and dismantle, but it does take a little extra time.

I remember looking at the clock in the upper balcony at the far end of the arena when Ric and I entered the ring. It was 12:00 midnight. If we ever owed the Baltimore fans a five-star match, it was that night, or should I say, that morning. So, for the second time that night, the Nature Boy and I went at it with the heavyweight title of the world at stake. We battled for 55 minutes and I don't think the fans sat down for one of those minutes. Ric and I gave it everything we had. When the timekeeper rang the bell, signaling the end of the match, the sellout crowd, as well as Ric and I, were exhausted.

The clock now read one o'clock on Saturday morning. The Baltimore fans had been there for more than five hours. The fans certainly received their money's worth and Ric and I earned our paychecks that day. Above all, that evening cemented the fans of Baltimore in my heart, where they still remain to this day. That night in Richmond and Baltimore didn't turn out to be our Coffeeville, but it still was crazy.

I wrestled Ric more than one hundred times in singles and tag team matches; so many, in fact, that most of them run together in my memory. However, there are some that stand out. One series, in particular, remains at the forefront of my series with the Nature Boy. Not because of a particular outcome, or due to it being a major pay-per-view, but because of the toll it took on my body at the time.

As I have mentioned before, Ric could go and go every night and make a one-hour broadway look like a walk in the park. I remember nights when he wrestled for an hour and he wasn't even breathing heavily when he came back to the dressing room.

In this particular program, Ric and I were doing a series of broadways. We had wrestled in Norfolk on January 9, 1987, the following night in Richmond, and after the match, headed home to Charlotte. On Sunday morning, I awoke about five o'clock with the most excruciating pain I had ever experienced. It was worse than the pain I had felt the two times I had broken my legs in college, but this time, it was in my lower back.

I called an orthopedic specialist, Dr. Joseph Estwanik, who treated wrestlers. He agreed to meet me at Urgent Care right away. When I got out of bed, I couldn't stand. The pain was bad that I dropped to my knees. I crawled on my hands and knees to the living room, where I laid on the floor and tried to stretch out my back. It was all I could do to fight back the tears as I tried to turn one way and another in an attempt to alleviate the searing pain running through my body. No matter what I did, nothing helped.

When I finally arrived at the clinic, the emergency physician had me lay on my back with my legs in the air; I looked like a big dog laying there, but once I was in that position, no matter how ridiculous I looked, I didn't want to move. He said he couldn't find anything wrong and gave me a prescription for pain. He was sending me home when Dr. Estwanik arrived. He asked me where I was going, and when I told him what the other physician had said, he told me to get back inside right away. When he examined me, he told me my lower sacroiliac was out of place on one side. He gave me some exercises to do that would help stretch out my back muscles, gave me some muscle relaxers, and sent me home.

That would have been fine if I had a week or so off to recuperate, but I had to make a living, and I made that living in the ring. I told him I was booked to wrestle Ric Flair that afternoon in Charlotte, after which I had to take a private plane to Atlanta where I would wrestle him again that night. The doctor looked at the floor and shook his head. *"I don't see how you're going to do that,"* he said. I explained that I had no choice. In the world of professional wrestling, if you are in the main event, you have to wrestle whether you are hurt or not. It means that much to the card, the company, and the fans. There was no other option.

I made it home and did the exercises the best I could. I tried to determine the best time to take the muscle relaxers so they would kick in by the time I walked to the ring. I was still in terrible pain when I left for the Coliseum. I had never before, or since, driven in such an awkward position, but I had to contort myself to keep pressure off my back. Thankfully, it was Sunday and there weren't a lot of people on the road. I can only imagine what I looked like to the people passing me on the highway.

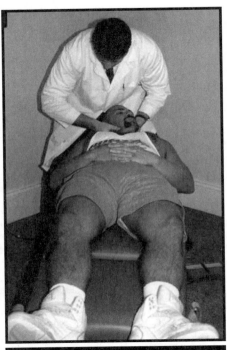

Dr. Jeff Cook works on Nikita

Once in the dressing room, I attempted to stretch out my back by doing the exercises the doctor had given me, and tried to time my next dose of the muscle relaxers to coincide with the main event. To this day, I'm not really sure how I put on my wrestling gear. I couldn't bend down to put on my singlet, let alone my socks and boots.

Ric did his best to carry me during the first part of the match. The first five minutes of the match was terrible, but the longer the match went, the better I felt. I don't know if it was the muscle relaxers, the fact that my muscles were loosening up as they grew warmer with activity, or a combination of both, but I was feeling a lot better. We went 45 minutes and concluded the match in time to get to the airport and head to Atlanta. As my body cooled, the pain came back full force … and then some. It was like a train had crashed into my lower back. I was in agony. The fact that we were flying on a private plane didn't help because there was no room to move around, let alone stretch out on the floor.

The match in the Omni went pretty much the same as it had in Charlotte. The first five or ten minutes were awful, but as the match progressed, my muscles began to loosen up. Once again, Ric and I went 45 minutes to a draw. The return flight to Charlotte was as bad as the flight to Atlanta. Somehow, I managed to get back to my apartment, where I collapsed. Fortunately for me, and thanks to the promoter's generosity, I was given the next two days off to recuperate. I was scheduled to wrestle, but I wasn't in the main event either night, so one of the boys substituted for me.

On Monday morning, I went to the chiropractor, and again that afternoon. I went twice on Tuesday and again on Wednesday morning. By Wednesday afternoon, I was back to normal. It was as if nothing had ever happened. That night, I was battling Flair again. If I hadn't been a believer in chiropractors and acupuncture before, I certainly was then.

Whether a lot of fans and other observers of sports believe it or not, injuries loom large in most athletes' lives, and that is especially true for wrestlers. It always troubles me when someone approaches me and imparts their "wisdom" on how wrestling is "fake." I could never understand how some people can see a gymnast tumble on a mat and rightfully cheer their athleticism, but when a 250-pound wrestler dives off the top rope and lands ten feet away on a concrete floor, they call it fake. Even knowing how to take a fall, there is no way to fake the effects of a body being slammed or suplexed every night. Multiply that over a period of years and a heavy toll is taken on the body.

The first injuries I suffered in the ring weren't serious, but they seemed to be almost as painful as the more serious ones I would receive later. Outside of bruised elbows, knees, and wrists, the most prevalent injury a wrestler faces is cauliflower ears. In fact, cauliflower ears are a badge of honor to those who have them. They're like a rite of passage, or point of entry, into the club. They are painful, too. Cauliflower ears are caused by headlocks or forceful blows to the ear. The stress breaks down the cartilage and the ear fills with fluid. If the fluid isn't drained, it calcifies and gives the ear its misshapen appearance. That's why high school and college wrestlers wear headgear. They prevent cauliflower ears. Lou Thesz used to say, *"You don't get cauliflower ears from sleeping on hard pillows."* If anyone would know, it would be Lou.

A good worker can pretty much protect his ears and those of his opponents by the way they take and give a headlock, or a slap or punch to the head. But in my early days in the ring, I knew none of this, so almost on a nightly basis, my ears would swell up. Ivan would take syringes and draw all the fluid out of my ears, and then I would hold ice packs on both of my ears to prevent the swelling. That might have worked well if I would have had a week or two to recuperate, but the next night, we would be in another town. One shot to the head, or a misplaced headlock, and they would puff up again. When I left the ring, my ears looked like those of John Merrick, the "Elephant Man," so Ivan sticking those large hypodermic needles in the back of my ears and drawing out two or three large syringes of fluid, followed by lying on my hotel bed with ice packs on both ears, became a nightly ritual for a long time. They stayed sore for as long as I can remember. But as I would learn, as did many of my colleagues, the pain in my ears could be likened to a splinter in my finger compared to what was to come.

There is an old saying that friends come and go, but enemies accumulate. The same can be said for injuries. There is nothing fake about them. Just ask Ivan. After all the years in the ring, he is now in retirement, dealing with the aftermath of his ring battles. His neck, back, knees, ankles, and shoulders are in terrible shape. But that is the nature of the game and the road we had chosen. Wrestling has exacted a great price on Ivan's body, on mine, and on everyone who has ever made a living in the ring.

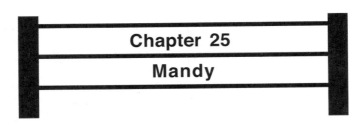

Chapter 25
Mandy

One of the aspects of my career that seemed to get almost as much attention as my battles in the ring had very little to do with wrestling and everything to do with my personal life. It is difficult at times, no matter how hard you try, to separate your public and private life when you make a living in full view of the public. We all owe so much to the fans. Without them, a professional athlete would not be able to make a living doing what we love to do. But when it crosses over into our lives beyond what the fans should respect as private, our lives take turns and we have to make decisions we would never expect to take.

I met Mandy Smithson in Atlanta in 1986 through some mutual friends. On August 8, 1988, we had been dating for about a year when she called me while I was in Las Vegas. Sting [Steve Borden] and I had just finished a match against Arn Anderson and Tully Blanchard. Mandy told me she had just seen a doctor and had been diagnosed with Hodgkin's disease, a potentially fatal form of cancer that affects the body's lymphatic system, which helps filter out infections. She said she had not been well for some time and had been hiding the symptoms from me.

When Mandy told me the news, I just stood there with the phone in my hand, trying to compose myself and sort through all the emotions that flooded through me. The news took me completely by surprise. She had certainly hid it from me well and I knew she had to have known about it for a long time before the call. I was shocked and I didn't know what to say. For a moment, I was speechless. When I regained my composure I tried to encourage her by letting her know that everything would be all right. Mandy was only 24 years old and now could be facing the end of her life. It was impossible for me to comprehend that this beautiful young woman, who was so full of life, may not live another year.

I knew practically nothing about cancer other than the bits and pieces I had heard or read. I would soon learn how much I didn't know. Up to that point in my life, I had been pretty carefree. I enjoyed being on the road and entertaining the fans in a different town every night. I loved the stories of the road from the boys who logged in more miles in a week than most folks do in a year. I was the "Russian Nightmare" and I was having the time of my life.

But Mandy's call changed all of that. It never ceases to give me pause when I think of how your life and those lives around you can change in an instant.

You are going along without a care in the world and, five minutes later, your life, thoughts, and priorities all change.

Please don't think I'm setting myself apart from others who have experienced, or are experiencing, what Mandy and I faced. Everyone's story is important, as are those of their families, friends, and loved ones. I'm reminded of the scene in the movie *Blackhawk Down* when the commander ordered a soldier to drive a vehicle. *"But, sir,"* the soldier said. *"I've been shot."* *"We have all been shot,"* the commander replied. *"Get in and drive."* Indeed, we all *have* been shot. Everyone's story is important. This one just happens to be mine.

At first, Mandy attacked the disease that was attacking her with a vengeance, as if to say, *"How dare you do this to me? This is far from over and you are not going to win."* She took her chemotherapy treatments and fought off the vomiting, hair loss, and loss of weight. She and I had difficulty deciding what was worse; the disease ravishing her body, or the aftermath of the treatments.

We soon received some unbelievable news. Mandy's cancer was in remission, but the doctor wanted to follow up with radiation treatment. Mandy was delegated to wearing wigs because of her hair loss due to the treatment and the onslaught of her illness. She had had enough of radiation and what ensued and decided not to do any more. We discussed it at length and the possibilities of the cancer returning if she didn't continue to receive treatment, but she had her mind set and was determined not to finish the treatment. I told her it was her life and her decision and that I would support her in whatever she decided to do.

But for the time being, we had hope again, rekindled. We decided to reclaim our lives and marry. We headed to Florida, chartered a boat, and, on September 20, said our vows in front of a few close friends and family.

We both were cautiously optimistic about Mandy's health, but with the news of her remission, we set off to continue our lives and put her illness in the past. We wouldn't even discuss it unless we had a reason to do so.

It wasn't long before we had that reason. Two months after our wedding, Mandy went to her oncologist for a routine checkup, and was told that the Hodgkin's disease had returned. I don't believe man has coined a word that could describe all the emotions we felt upon hearing the news, but we resolved to fight it as we did before ... together.

I have often heard people say that it is difficult to do the right thing. I don't believe that. I do believe that it is difficult, many times, to know what the right thing to do is, but once you know, it is not difficult to do. And I knew exactly what the right thing to do was. I left wrestling to take care of my wife.

The first thing I had to do was drive to Atlanta to meet Jim Herd and his staff in the CNN Center, which the boys referred to as the Ivory Tower. Crockett had sold WCW to media mogul Ted Turner and the company was in transition. Herd had once run KPLR, a television station in St. Louis that had carried Sam Muchnick's *Wrestling at the Chase* television program. He landed his job by way of his friend, Jack Petrik, who Ted Turner had appointed to take over WCW after he purchased the promotion from the Crocketts in 1988. Most of the boys called Jim the "Pizza Man" because he had more recently been an executive with Pizza Hut. It quickly became apparent to the boys that he knew more about pizza than he did about wrestling. Choosing Jim to run a wrestling company because he once had run a television station that carried wrestling is like hiring a guy to run General Electric because he once turned on a light. But that's exactly what WCW did ... and they would end up paying dearly for it.

I will never forget getting into the elevator and riding up to the office suite. We talked for almost an hour and I explained why I was walking away from a top, main-event position. I was straightforward in my decision and my explanation: my place was with Mandy and not in the ring. Even if I had agreed to stay, even on a limited schedule, my heart and my mind would not have been in the right place. It wouldn't be fair to the fans, those who were paying me, or my opponents. It was time to go. Although they appeared understanding, I had the feeling they weren't happy with my decision. They were corporate guys and I don't think they understood my priorities. They looked confused, as if they didn't believe anyone could, or would, just walk away and not place business ahead of a personal issue. But that's exactly what I did. I left the ring and a guaranteed seven-year contract. It wasn't difficult to tell what they were thinking. *"How could you walk away when you are on top? This won't be good for your career."* However, it didn't matter what they thought. Mandy did. I did promise them, however, that I would return, but it took a lot longer than any of us would have imagined.

A number of the wrestling magazines at the time were quick to pick up on the story and describe Mandy's battle and my decision to leave the ring. They reported it as heroic. Well, I may have been a hero in the ring, but not in that situation. Mandy was the one with the courage. My decision was easy. With Mandy's cancer progressing, the doctors wanted Mandy to undergo more chemotherapy and radiation treatments. Knowing what she went through the first time, I couldn't even consider being on the road. My place was with her, not traveling from arena to arena.

Nikita and Mandy

In the weeks that followed, the cancer continued its onslaught on Mandy's body and took a toll on our spirits, as well. We both tried to be optimistic about her heath and our future, but with the treatments not working and the Hodgkin's disease continuing to grow, our hopes began to dim.

During that time, I got quite an education in the area of medicine, or rather the "business" of medicine. With Mandy's treatments failing to garner results and the disease in an advanced stage, the doctor's were now recommending a bone-marrow transplant. We knew that was typically the last resort in battles like ours.

Wrestlers, as you may know, are independent contractors, and finding insurance can be a challenge, if not an impossibility. Combined with the fact that I wasn't working, and that Mandy had been battling cancer for a number of years, we had no insurance. To be considered for a bone-marrow transplant, we had to come up with $250,000. That's a tremendous amount of money for most people, and what's more, that would only be the deposit. The total cost, we were told, would be at least double that, with no guarantees the transplant would be successful. I was stunned. When I asked the doctor what we could do if I couldn't come up with the money, he said Mandy couldn't be put on the list until we did. I asked, *"So you're telling me that money is more important than my wife's health?"* He disagreed, but I forged ahead and asked, *"So if I can't come up with the money, Mandy won't even be considered? You can say whatever you want, but you won't convince me that the money is more important than her life."*

Since we didn't have $250,000 available, we began to look for other alternatives. We had heard of a physician in Greece from a couple who owned a restaurant in Concord, North Carolina, where we lived at the time. They had heard about our plight and contacted us. The doctor was reported to have been experiencing quite a bit of success with some non-conventional treatments. The couple told us they had family in Greece and that they would make us as comfortable as possible.. Not only that, but the couple helped us raise money for flight. When the life of someone you love is on the line, nothing is too farfetched to try, so we traveled to Greece for three weeks of treatment.

Mandy and I met some wonderful people at the clinic who had experienced great success through Dr. Hariton-Tzannis Alivizatos' efforts. They came back for follow-up visits years after there were no signs of their disease. But we weren't to be as fortunate. Mandy's illness had progressed so far that there would be no miracle for us. Dr. Alivizatos' treatments helped Mandy some, but we both knew it was too late to do much good. Nothing short of a miracle could change things for us and save Mandy's life, and as we would soon learn, there would be no miracle.

When we arrived back in the United States, Mandy asked if she could go to Alabama for a while to be with her family. After being there for only a day or two, she began getting weaker, and they immediately admitted her to the intensive care unit at the local hospital. When Mandy called to give me the news, I headed to Huntsville on Amtrak. I had been traveling a lot by Amtrak during that time, going back and forth to the Carolinas in an effort to make some money by doing special appearances. For the next six weeks, Mandy lay in bed and fought the cancer that was slowly taking her life. I spent most nights sleeping next to her bed on an egg crate on the floor so I would be near

Nikita and Mandy

her if she woke up and needed anything. I remember thinking about how far I had come, from hearing my name chanted by tens of thousands of fans to sleeping on the floor of a hospital room in Huntsville Alabama. I also realized something far more important. The life I led in the ring wasn't really what life was all about. It wasn't real. My life with Mandy was.

Mandy continued to get weaker as each day dragged into the next. I would be at her side most of the time, being spelled for short periods of time by some of Mandy's family or close friends, but only long enough to take a shower or to get something to eat.

About five weeks after Mandy was admitted to the ICU, Victoria Turner, Mandy's best friend, called to see if she could come see her. She was living in Florida, but was in the process of moving to North Carolina. She wanted to reroute her trip through Alabama so she could see Mandy and, perhaps, lend a hand for a short time. Victoria was a single mother with two small girls, but she wanted to take the time and drive a considerable distance out of her way to see her friend. I was impressed with the fact that Victoria had such a love and friendship for Mandy that she would do such a thing for her. I wasted no time in telling her that I knew Mandy would love to see her and that she would be most welcome.

Victoria and her girls arrived on June 12 and spent a couple of days visiting with us. I had never really talked with Victoria prior to that first night, or to any of Mandy's acquaintances, for that matter, whether they were Mandy's friends or not. I lived my life in the mode of protecting my character at whatever the cost.

Mandy's family took the girls home with them while Victoria and I stayed with Mandy. Victoria and I talked into the early hours of the morning and I learned that Victoria had promised Mandy that she would do her makeup when she died. I thought to myself that Victoria was certainly a true friend.

After a couple of days, Victoria decided to head on to North Carolina with her daughters, but decided to stay a while longer because she believed Mandy was not far away from death. Mandy was getting weaker by the day and her communication with us was now limited to writing in a notebook, and as her health waned, her writing became more and more illegible.

On the evening of June 13, Mandy's family decided they wouldn't come to the hospital the next morning. They would catch up on some much-needed rest and come stay with her after lunch. Knowing Mandy was resting and that Victoria was with her, I decided to go to a nearby gym and spend an hour or so working out. When I pulled back into the hospital parking lot around ten o'clock, I saw Mandy's family walking into the lobby. At first, it just struck me as odd that they would be there at that time, knowing they had planned not to come, but almost as soon as that thought entered my mind, a sense of eeriness flowed through my body. I parked my car and ran to the intensive care unit.

Just as I reached the door, Victoria walked out and told us we needed to get to Mandy's bedside immediately. She told us Mandy didn't have much time left, perhaps only a few hours. We gathered at her bedside, all taking turns telling her how much we loved her and thanking her for all she meant to us. Words came easily from our hearts, but not from our lips. It was very hard to speak and we stood there helplessly as her life ebbed away. All of our love couldn't make her well. She was in God's hands, which I would later come to realize was where she had been all along. I watched as her heart monitor dropped digit by digit, until there was nothing left but a flat line. I stood unable to speak, or move. I was no longer the Russian Nightmare. I was just a helpless bystander. Mandy passed away at one o'clock in the afternoon on June 14, 1989. She was only 26 years old.

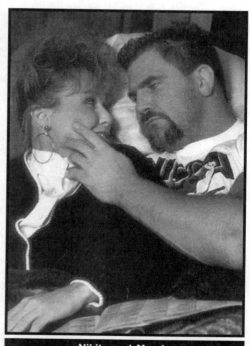

As she had promised, Victoria stayed to do her makeup, and my two closest friends, Tim Peltier and Joe Laurinaitis, flew down for the funeral. As it had for the previous months, their love and friendship brought a measure of solace and comfort to me during the time when I was left alone to face the road ahead.

Nikita and Mandy

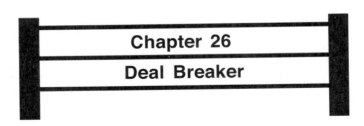

Chapter 26

Deal Breaker

After Mandy passed away, I wasn't sure what I wanted to do, or for that matter, what I should do. The WCW people had stayed in touch with me during my absence, calling to see how Mandy was doing and how I was holding up. Inevitably, every conversation led to the subject of when I would be coming back. I kept them at arm's length, repeating that I was not considering a return to the ring at that time. Mandy was my only concern, and I would let them know if and when I was ready to come back.

With Mandy gone, I didn't know which path to take. Fellow wrestler Gene Ligon and I owned a gym in Concord, just outside of Charlotte, called Nikita's Fortress of Fitness. It was doing well and I was happy running it and staying close to home, but I did miss the camaraderie with the boys and performing in the ring. I knew my career was far from over and I had a lot of good years in the ring ahead of me if I so chose. I just didn't know what to do.

During my hiatus, a lot of things changed in WCW. While I was gone, a whole new crew of wrestlers was being featured, including Rick and Scott Steiner, Barry Windham, Sid Vicious, Doom [Ron Simmons and Butch Reed], Stan Hansen, Michael Hayes, and Jimmy Garvin. Dusty had turned over the booking chores to the Nature Boy. Not only was he the world heavyweight champion, but Ric now was pretty much in charge of the entire company. He was one of the people who decided who was to beat whom, who carried the titles, and for how long. He had a good stable of wrestlers, but he wanted me back as well.

Ric called me one day and asked me to come to his home for lunch. He said he had an offer for me, one he believed I would be interested in hearing. I had known Ric for a long time and knew he had something up his sleeve, but I liked Ric and trusted him, so I figured I had nothing to lose. I agreed to meet him for lunch.

We sat by his pool and, as we ate, I kept thinking about what the fans would make of our meeting if they knew these two bitter rivals were eating together poolside and discussing business. After some small talk, Ric got to the point. *"Nik, you know they want you to come back. The fans want it and everyone in the company wants it, too. What do you say?"* I told him I was considering it, but I didn't know if I wanted to come back. My life had changed since I left and I wasn't sure if coming back was the right thing for me to do at the time.

Then Ric put an offer on the table that nearly knocked me off of my chair. *"Nik,"* he said, *"if you agree to come back, I will give you the title."*

"The title," I thought. *"He's offering me the title."* I knew he wasn't talking about the U.S. belt or any one of the regional titles. He was talking about *his* title, the NWA world heavyweight title. He was willing to hand over the most prestigious title in our sport ... the same title held by Frank Gotch, Joe Stecher, Strangler Lewis, Lou Thesz, Buddy Rogers, Gene Kiniski, Dory and Terry Funk, Jack Brisco, Harley Race, and Dusty Rhodes. Anyone in their right mind would have jumped at the chance. Anyone, that is, but me.

He told me that he had discussed it at length with the people who ran WCW and they had the utmost confidence and trust in my ability to carry the belt. Just the offer was a great honor, and at one time, I would have jumped at the chance. A lot of fans have asked why, with all the buildup, Ric didn't put me over and give me the title on the night of our first meeting in Charlotte. I had found myself wondering that, as well, but after I had spent some time in the business, I realized why they didn't make me the world heavyweight champion; I would have made a terrible champion at the time. I wasn't close to being ready to carry the belt. The Crockett's knew this and so did the bookers. Knowing what I know now, I'm glad they didn't give me the title, but this time, the circumstances were different. And so was I.

I'm not sure that even the most ardent wrestling fan truly understands the tremendous responsibility that goes with the belt. There is no greater honor than to be chosen to be the world heavyweight wrestling champion. It not only means you are the best, it means the NWA puts its trust in you. They trust you to carry the banner of the NWA wherever you appear and to draw well. Drawing well not only benefits the champion and NWA, but also the boys on the undercard, who make more money when the houses are larger. If the champion draws well at the box office, everyone prospers. The more money comes into the box office, the better the payoffs will be for everyone. Well, that was true until WCW began providing contracts to the wrestlers which stated they would get paid if they wrestled or not. That one change had almost as much to do with the downfall of the NWA and WCW as Vince McMahon's coming onslaught. But I'm getting ahead of myself.

It's also the champion's job to make the challenger look like he could beat the champion at any given moment. Every time the champion steps into the ring, he has to make his opponent look better than he is. That's the nature of the business. It's also the nature of the title. The bottom line is, the world heavyweight title belt might be around the champion's waist, but the weight of the National Wrestling Alliance sets squarely in his shoulders. Not only is it physically taxing to travel the country and defend the title, but it wears on you mentally, as well. Just ask anyone who has held the belt for a long period of time. Many will tell you the greatest day of their career was winning the title and the second greatest day would be the day they lost it.

I thought about Ric's offer and knew I had to decline. Physically, I was ready to meet the challenge, and I was far more mature in the business than I had been in 1987. But emotionally and mentally, I just wasn't ready, especially considering what I had been through the previous year. My problem was I just couldn't say "no" to Ric. He was the type of guy who thinks the word "no" is a figure of speech. You don't have the career Nature Boy had by taking no for an answer, and I knew how persuasive he could be, so I countered his offer with one I knew the NWA would never agree to accept.

"Okay, Ric." I said. *"I will take the title, but only on one condition. I know you want me to resume my old schedule, and I will have to put in even more time as the champion. I'll take the title if I can work Monday through Thursday with Friday, Saturday, and Sunday off."*

Ric told me they would never go for it and asked me to take a few days to think about it. I held fast and told him that was a deal breaker. So, that was that. I thanked Ric for his time, hospitality, and told him I would stay in touch. With that, I got back into my car and headed for home.

I realized one of the reasons I was offered the title was that business was beginning to sag a bit. Wrestling is no different than any other sport or form of entertainment. It is cyclical and it has highs and lows. Usually, when the ratings begin to sag, a major title change takes place and ratings head north again. They thought having me make a run with the world belt would help spike the ratings. It would have been fun, but the time just wasn't right.

From time to time, the question arises: *"In retrospect, do you think you made a mistake by not taking the belt when Ric offered it?"* With hindsight being what it is, I can honestly say no. It was a business, as well as a personal decision. It was a great honor to be offered the belt, but believe it or not, belts aren't everything. If you have a good character and are getting over, you really don't necessarily need a title. Take some of the biggest stars of the past few decades as examples. Roddy Piper didn't hold many titles for an extended period of time, and neither did Jesse Ventura, and they are two of the most well-known and successful wrestlers of our era. That isn't to say those who held major titles for a long time were not of the highest caliber. Just the opposite is true. But my point is that belt or no belt, the key to success in the ring is to know how to keep yourself over no matter what the particular pecking order is.

During my time away from the NWA, I made a few appearances in the AWA for Verne Gagne. We had worked with Verne a few years before when he and Jim Crockett combined efforts in an attempt to fend off McMahon by touting the NWA and AWA rosters and spotlighting their champions, calling their hybrid company, Pro Wrestling USA. Verne would fly me to Minneapolis for television tapings and an occasional house show, working mainly against Larry Zbyszko, who was Verne's son-in-law. Larry is a polished worker who knows his way around the ring and we had some good matches. I also worked some independent shows to pick up some cash while I contemplated my future. I would work only a handful of times a month and easily covered my expenses.

Please remember that professional wrestling is a business; a work. When you get a championship, it's not as if you have actually won anything. The promoters own the titles and the boys just borrow them for a while. I remember hearing a couple of the boys talking in the dressing room at one of the AWA shows, saying, *"I don't care if Verne Gagne pays me or not. If he'd let me have one of the belts, I would work for free."* They obviously weren't one of the headliners, and with that limited knowledge of the business, they probably never made it very far. As many of my contemporaries would agree, I would rather have the main-event payoff and give the fans more than the price of their ticket, than a belt, any day. And if you can do both, it's all the better.

After Mandy's death, I kept in touch with Victoria. We would call each other now and then, just to see how things were going. Vic and her two daughters had moved back to North Carolina, and when I was in town, she and I, along with another friend of mine, would go out and play miniature golf, or my friend and I would watch her play softball for the law firm where she worked. We would just kind of hang around together, like the three amigos. After we did that for about a year, Animal asked me, *"When are you going to ask her out?"* I had never really thought about it, but now I was. It took me awhile to work up the courage, but when I did, she accepted and we began going out. We hit it off right away and would spend a lot of our time together talking about all sorts of things: children, friends, family, past relationships, the ravages of divorce, our careers, what the future might hold for us, and almost anything else you could think about. Before I knew it, I had fallen in love.

Victoria's move back to the Carolinas had been a fresh start for them. She and the girls had not had it easy. Victoria had a short-lived second marriage and the girls had been moved around the country quite a bit. When we met, she was driving a Ford Escort that eventually was repossessed. Her first husband, in my opinion, was a poor excuse of a man. He gave her no financial support until I encouraged her to go after it, and even then, he still wasn't mature enough to fulfill his obligations. He never did. It's crystal clear to me why God hates divorce. Not only does it destroy men, women, and children, but it destroys the moral fabric of society. No one involved in a divorce escapes unscathed.

After a time, I asked her to move in with me. I owned a small house in Concord where Mandy and I had lived for a short time. Victoria had been renting an apartment with her two girls, Teryn, who was seven at the time, and Tawni, age four. I thought it would be a good move to get them out of the apartment and into a house.

Victoria moved in one weekend when the girls were with their father on a rare weekend visit. When they returned, it was a moment I will always remember. We told them we had a surprise for them, which usually generates excitement in any child. Little did they know that the surprise was a change of address. When we got to the new house, Tawni, the younger of the two, bounced around the house in sheer enjoyment. Teryn, the older, on the other hand, set off in a fit of rage, which was not exactly the reaction I had been hoping for or was expecting. But after a short while, things calmed down and we began to settle down into a regular routine.

It wasn't long, however, that Victoria and I began to feel uneasy about our relationship. We both realized that it wasn't healthy for the girls to see us living together. We agreed that we either needed to live separately or we needed to get married. Separation was not an option for me. I loved Victoria and was determined to marry her, so I planned a trip to Hawaii. While we were there, we went on a dinner cruise, which is where I asked Victoria to marry me. She accepted and we returned home to tell the girls. We had a repeat of what happened when we told the girls about the house. Teryn wasn't happy, but Tawni was overjoyed.

Teryn had a bond with her father that Tawni didn't have and that connection made thoughts of her mother in another relationship a lot harder on her. She, like a lot of children of divorce, held out hope that her mom and dad might get back together. Of course, that wasn't going to happen, so Victoria and I continued with our plans for our wedding. We decided to get married in Minnesota at Joe Laurinaitis' house, especially since he was the one who made me realize how my feelings for Victoria had grown.

We were married on August 17, 1990. It was a small, personal wedding as I was still doing everything I could to protect my character. In fact, I protected the character so much that I spoke with an accent whenever I was around Victoria's family, including Teryn and Tawni, for more than a year. I believed I needed to do that around the girls because children are so honest, and if someone asked them about me, they would easily give me up. I'll never forget the day when I finally spoke around them without the accident. Tawni asked Victoria, *"What's wrong with daddy's voice?"* Everyone erupted in laughter. I was enjoying my new family life.

Joe Laurinaitis and Nikita

After my discussion with Ric, more than a year went by before I decided to return to the ring. In 1991, I began talking with the people at WCW and, after a few weeks of negotiating, we came to an agreement. Again, Dusty Rhodes played a big part in my return. I had nothing against Ric or his offer, but a big part of my decision was based on my friendship with Dusty, and he was the one who finally persuaded me to return to wrestling.

Things were going to be different, though. The promotion wanted me to return as a "heel." I hadn't worked heel for several years, and when I left wrestling, it was as a good guy. That change, much to my surprise, had gone over well with the fans, especially after I stepped up to take Magnum's place with Dusty. That turn had touched the hearts of the fans. It had such an emotional impact with the fans at the time that my friend, Bill Apter, who was the senior editor of *Pro Wrestling Illustrated*, did a cover story titled, *"I Cry a Tear for Magnum T.A."* That storyline, coupled with all the magazine coverage on my life with Mandy, convinced me it wouldn't work. With all the fan support I had received up to that point, turning heel didn't make any sense, but I had been away for more than two years and things had changed since my departure, so I didn't have any positioning power with the company. And with that, Nikita Koloff became a heel, once again.

Chapter 27
Return to the Dark Side

My return to the "dark side" took place on a live show broadcast from the Veterans Memorial Coliseum in Phoenix, Arizona on February 24, 1991. I was there to honor the reigning U.S. heavyweight champion, Lex Luger, and present him with a new title belt. We had been friends when I had left, so it would be only natural that I would return to the public eye by showing up at the live WrestleWar '91 event.

I came out at the beginning of the show with Jason Hervey of *The Wonder Years* television show. He and I were scheduled to do some commentary on the early matches before I made the presentation to Lex. When I walked through the curtain and the fans saw me heading to the commentators' table, they went crazy. After being gone as long as I was, I'm sure the last thing they expected to see was Nikita Koloff back at ringside.

After several preliminary matches, Lex entered the ring to a standing ovation. I made my way over to a platform with the announcer and motioned for Lex to come join us. He walked towards me as I waited with the new belt, ready to hand it over to him. I took the microphone and told Lex what a great athlete and exceptional wrestler he was, and how he brought honor to the U.S. title. I told him how proud I was of the way he defended the title and how it was a great pleasure for me to present him with the new belt. As he thanked me and reached for the belt, I moved it out of his reach and slammed it against his head, knocking him down. When he fell to the platform, I began putting the boots to him and pushed him off the platform. He took a six-foot drop on the concrete

While that was taking place, I witnessed one of the strangest things that had ever happened to me during my career. As I was stomping on Lex, the fans began to boo me, as expected, but there were many others who were cheering! I had to work to hide my surprise. I had the backing of the people as a babyface before, but I had never had their support as a heel. What can I say? This is professional wrestling.

Of course, that angle set off an instant rivalry between the two of us. We wrestled around the country for the next few months and what we saw in Phoenix remained the same during our program together. The fans seemed to be split 50-50 between Lex and me, but we made the most of it. I did everything a good heel was supposed to do and Lex was the perfect good guy, but a large number of the fans kept cheering for me. In fact, the more villainous I became, the more they cheered.

Even the booking team couldn't believe what was going on with the fans. Lex was over strong as a babyface. In fact, the only one stronger in the company as a "face" was Sting. One night before a match with Lex, I told someone from the promotion, *"I told you I was too strong as a babyface. No matter what I do to Lex in the ring, they cheer me. This is crazy; I think I should turn back."*

What we didn't realize at the time was, it wasn't what we were doing in the ring that was causing the fans reactions as much as it was the change of the mindset of the fans. Cheering for the heel seemed to be the popular thing to do. We saw the same thing happen in the late '90s when "Stone Cold" Steve Austin wrestled Bret Hart. The more dastardly Steve became, the more the fans cheered him on to take the Hitman's title. Likewise, I was getting over as an anti-hero, not as a Russian heel. We were on the cutting edge and we should have pushed it to the limit, but the problem was, we didn't know it.. The conventional thinking of the booking office didn't realize what we had. They stayed true to the course that had been tried and true since the 1950s.

When the company admitted that our program wasn't working, we had to make a quick course correction in order to make the storyline continue without interruption. Momentum is everything in wrestling. To lose it can set your character, and possibly the promotion, back months. As an angle begins to lose steam, the fans lose interest in a hurry. To keep the fans' attention from waning, one chapter of a story must be right on the heels of the one they've been watching. That keeps the business moving ahead and the fans lining up at the box office, but the transition has to be seamless. If there is any lapse at all, the fans will move on to something else, and we might as well close up shop and go home. We had to do something fast to keep the energy in our program, so we went to the guy who was getting over like no one else in WCW at the time: Steve Borden, who the wrestling world knows better as "Sting."

As part of a group of bodybuilders called Power Team USA, Sting's wrestling career began in 1985 with promoter Rick Bassman in Venice Beach, California. Steve teamed up with Jim Hellwig , who later became the WWF champion known as the Ultimate Warrior, and together, they trained under Red Bastien. They eventually moved to Memphis, where they wrestled as the Freedom Fighters, and then joined Bill Watts' UWF as the Blade Runners. Less than six months later, Hellwig left for somewhat greener pastures in the WWF, where he had a good run, reaching the pinnacle of the wrestling world with a win over then-WWF-champion Hulk Hogan for the title in the Toronto SkyDome on April 1, 1990 at *Wrestlemania VI.*

Sting heard another call and remained with the UWF. He came to national prominence when Jim Crockett promotions began their expansion and ran joint cards with the UWF. When Crockett bought Watts' promotion, Sting fell right in step with what he was doing in the UWF and became a top man on the talent roster. A natural to challenge Flair for the world title, Sting shot into the number-one contender slot on the nationally-televised *Clash of Champions* in March 1988 by catching the Nature Boy in his finishing maneuver, the "scorpion death-lock," as the bell rang to end the 45-minute time limit match.

In the months that followed, the fans came out in legions to cheer their new hero. Sting's feud with Flair lit up WCW and he finally took the title when Ric put him over at the *Great American Bash* in Baltimore on July 7, 1990. Sting held the title for six months before dropping the belt back to Ric in New Jersey the following January. Sting didn't lose a step and captured the world championship again on five different occasions. With his expansive resume and top-card drawing ability, Sting was the perfect man to breathe life into my program with Lex.

We kicked off the new program at the *SuperBrawl* pay-per-view at the Bayfront Arena in St. Petersburg, Florida on May 19, 1991.

Sting and Lex were wrestling a babyface match against their friends and WCW world tag team champions, Rick and Scott Steiner. As the match grew more and more furious, Sting caught Scott in his Scorpion Deathlock and it appeared as if the title was going to change hands. I walked to the ring and, wrapping my chain around my hand and arm, I tried to nail Lex with my Russian Sickle. Lex had his back turned towards me and, even though the fans begged Lex to turn around, he remained focused on the action in the ring. As I swung at Lex from behind with the chain, Sting released the deathlock and pushed Lex out of the way, taking the full brunt of the clothesline himself.

With Sting laying flat on the mat, Scott Steiner made the most of it and pinned him to take the match and retain the title. When a bloody Sting finally made it to his feet, he ran to the dressing room with the camera crew in tow. He found me and proceeded to extract his revenge as we brawled through the dressing room and out into the parking lot. And there we had it … an instant feud.

The program with Sting went over much better than the one with Luger. For the next three weeks, I finished up my program with Lex, and in the months after that, Sting and I had a series of Texas death, steel cage, and Russian chain matches across the country. Chain matches are definitely one of the most dangerous matches in the sport. There are variations of the match, such as the Indian strap match, where the contestants are tethered together by a six-foot strap that can cut you like a razor if it hits you just right. The Indian strap version was normally used by wrestlers like Wahoo McDaniel and other Native American wrestlers, while the Russian chain match was reserved for … well, the Russians.

Like the Indian strap match, whoever was lucky enough to be chosen for the Russian chain match had to actually be chained together by a six to eight-foot length of chain which could be used as a weapon in any fashion during the match. No matter how careful you or your opponent are, it's almost certain that one, or both of you, are going to leave the ring with some sort of injury, be it a broken or chipped tooth, black eye, or a good old-fashioned knot on the head.

The rules for a chain match are somewhat different than those found in regular matches. As I said, the chain can be used as a weapon, so there is no disqualification. Pinfalls and submissions don't decide the outcome of the match. The winner is declared when one wrestler drags the other around the ring and touches each of the four corners of the ring in succession. As tough as the matches were, they also could be a lot of fun. The fans really get into it. You can keep them on their feet by touching three of the four corners and, just when it looks like the fourth one is about to be slapped, the other wrestler mounts a comeback and stops his opponent just short of victory. You can do this all night and keep the fans involved in the match from the opening bell until the fourth turnbuckle is touched.

Sting was a great opponent and a close friend. He was an erstwhile champion whose match with Ric Flair, the last match under the WCW banner, brought the WCW/NWA reign to a close. During that show, Vince McMahon appeared on a segment taped in Cleveland, Ohio, where he announced he had bought WCW. I can't think of any better way to end an era than to have Sting and Flair wrestle each other in such a grand style. There could not have been a greater honor for our sport.

As my program with Sting came to a close, I began negotiating with WCW for a new contract. I had decided to negotiate a short-term contract when I first returned because I still wasn't sure if going back to the ring was the right thing for me to do. I had been gone for more than two years and I didn't know if I would like being back on the road or if I would feel comfortable in the ring.

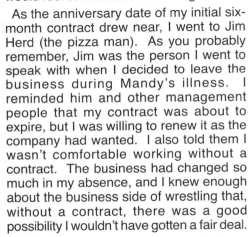

As the anniversary date of my initial six-month contract drew near, I went to Jim Herd (the pizza man). As you probably remember, Jim was the person I went to speak with when I decided to leave the business during Mandy's illness. I reminded him and other management people that my contract was about to expire, but I was willing to renew it as the company had wanted. I also told them I wasn't comfortable working without a contract. The business had changed so much in my absence, and I knew enough about the business side of wrestling that, without a contract, there was a good possibility I wouldn't have gotten a fair deal.

Management kept telling me, *"We know, Nik, we know. It will be taken care of."* But it never was. For more than a month, I kept asking them to put together a contract. When they did produce one, we couldn't agree on terms, and they dragged their feet during negotiations.

I suppose they thought I would continue to work without a contract, which would pretty much mean I would work under their terms. I had seen a number of the boys taken advantage of and knew I would be no different. Even Flair had enough of the games they were playing with him and his contract. When it expired, he left for the WWF with the world championship belt in tow. I decided that if we couldn't come to terms by the time my contract expired, I would leave.

We wrestled in St. Petersburg on August 23 and stayed in Tampa that night, with plans to work in Jacksonville the following night. I had made up my mind that I was going home in the morning. I went to Arn Anderson and told him, *"Arn, I'm leaving in the morning. I'm flying home."*

Now as you remember me saying, Arn and I were never close. In fact, we really didn't get along all that well personally. He wasn't a bad guy. It was just that our personalities didn't mesh. I have to say that Arn has one of the sharpest and quickest wits of anyone I have ever known. He is a master of words second to none. He has a comeback for everything and can cut you to ribbons in the blink of an eye. He has the ability to undress someone with his words and leave them standing humiliated and emotionally naked. To his credit, Arn could get away with it because he was so funny.

Having said that, I trusted Arn, and he was the one I went to when I decided to leave. He was less than happy with what I told him. *"Oh, man. Don't do this. If you go, I'll be the first person Grizzly Smith comes to and asks where you are. Then he'll make me wrestle twice."* I had to laugh, but I told him I was heading for home in the morning.

And that's exactly what I did. I do have to say, in retrospect, that I'm not proud of how I handled the negotiations. I still believe that what I was wanting was fair, but I don't think I handled the situation in a professional manner. Thinking back, I could have let them know of my plans to leave and given them one last chance to make a deal. I do regret not being more professional about it.

I had only been home for a day when Arn called and told me what had happened the night after I left. He told me Griz had approached him and asked where I was.

Grizzly Smith was a road agent, the person who took care of the backstage business. He made sure the ring was up and talent was ready and in place. He evaluated matches and levied fines if we didn't toe the line. Griz knew wrestling inside out. He had gained a measure of fame teaming with Luke Brown as the Kentuckians, holding the WWA world tag team title in Los Angeles in 1965 and winning various single and tag titles throughout the '60s and early '70s. He also had three children follow him into the family business: Jake "The Snake" Roberts, Sam Houston, and "Rockin" Robin.

When Grizzly asked Arn where I was, Arn told him he hadn't seen me. That was true at the time, I guess, because at the time of their conversation, I was hundreds of miles away at home in Charlotte. But Arn was right about one thing, though. With me being nowhere to be found, Arn did have to wrestle twice that night.

I knew I needed some time off to sort some things out. I still loved wrestling, but I was becoming more aware that I liked some of the aspects of the business less and less. Each time I went on the road, it was becoming more difficult to leave my new family. The business was changing rapidly and it was becoming increasingly difficult to recognize it as the business it had been when I first entered the ring, or even the business I had known only a few years earlier. As with most businesses, things evolve and change with the times. Sometimes, it's for the benefit of the industry, while at others, to its detriment, and sometimes it's neither. It's just different. Internal politics were becoming more evident and WCW seemed to be a ship without a rudder, first heading in one direction, and then another, with no real rhyme or reason to what they were doing. When coupled with Vince McMahon single-handedly changing the face of wrestling, the landscape of professional wrestling was shifting and would never be the same again.

Chapter 28

The Little Stinger

I had been out for about six months, enjoying my new life, when I agreed to go back. The office began calling me almost as soon as I had left. Vic and I discussed the issue together and I finally agreed to return. Even though I had left six months before due to not having a contract, I returned the same way … with no written contract.

This time was different, though. WCW and I verbally agreed on all points of our contract and I would come back as a babyface appearing first on the television show taped in the Atlanta studio. Once again, as far as the fans were concerned, my comeback came from out of the blue. Not only was my unannounced appearance a shock to them, but so was my appearance. I had trimmed down and I was sporting a crewcut. I took the look from my old buddy, Dolph Lundgren, who got the part I had auditioned for in *Rocky III*. I remember the announcers saying in their best surprised-sounding voice, *"Is that Nikita Koloff? What is he doing here?"*

Since my last angle had been with Sting, I came back in an appeal to him. As I entered the ring to the cheers of the fans, I called out to Sting for him to come to ringside. To heighten my sincerity and get over with the fans, I brought a little "Stinger" with me, my daughter Teryn. She was dressed like Sting, face paint and all. As I approached Sting, I explained that it had been an accident when I nailed him during his match with Luger, and I asked him for his forgiveness. I pointed out that my little girl was his biggest fan and that she had insisted on coming with me to see her hero. As Sting looked on and listened, I held my "little Stinger" and poured out my heart, and explained again how the blow had been meant for Luger. Sting entered the ring and we embraced … and the fans cheered. All was well in the wrestling world.

One major change that occurred during my absence was a change at the helm. Jim Herd had gone the way of so many others in WCW and had been replaced by the one man I had claimed I would never work for: Cowboy Bill Watts. Bill came to run the show at WCW in May 1992, and he brought with him that same old bravado that had "endeared" him to all the boys back in the Mid-South days.

I did get along pretty well with Bill, partly because we kept our relationship on a business level and I wasn't afraid of him or his authority. I respected his position in the company and the fact that he was in charge, but I never hesitated to speak to him directly or address him when I believed something was wrong or unfair. I do believe Bill respected me for being straightforward while still showing him respect. Getting to know Bill as time went on, I did realize that as rough as he was with the wrestlers who worked for him, a good portion of it was that he expected a lot from his boys and set the bar high.

I had been working for him for awhile when he pulled me aside one night and said, *"Nik, the accounting office called and told me they owe you quite a lot of money. In fact, they haven't issued you a check since you came back. You haven't been paid all this time. Why haven't you said anything?"*

I was well aware that WCW owed me a lot of money, but I really hadn't given it much thought. Even with all the craziness going on, I trusted those with whom I was working. *"Bill,"* I said, *"I know what I'm owed and it's okay. Besides, I think Ted Turner is good for it, don't you? We have an agreement and I trust him."*

Watts shook his head and looked at me like I was out of my mind. *"Yeah, I guess he is. Where were you when I had Mid-South? I've never met anyone with your kind of attitude towards the business."* He then promised me he would make sure my contract was completed and he would get me a copy to sign.

If that was the end of the story of my contract, we could just stop here and all join in on a chorus of "We Are the World," but this is the world of professional wrestling I'm talking about, and in that world, the dollar is king.

As Bill was working on the contract, he began talking to me about making some changes in our agreement before the final contact was drafted for me to sign. This time, I pulled Bill aside and very politely explained to him that WCW and I had an agreement before he arrived, and I thoroughly expected them to be as good as their word. As businessmen, I anticipated them complying with our verbal terms and fulfilling them with no changes. I went on to explain that I originally came back to WCW as a favor to Dusty, and with all due respect to him and WCW, they needed to understand that I did come back as a favor and that I didn't need to be there. Unlike many of the boys, there were other things I could do. I had a college degree and I owned a number of health clubs. I also had a business manager who helped me invest my wrestling earnings so I didn't have to take a lesser deal than what was agreed. I told him, *"If the games continue with my contract, you can consider this my notice and I'll be leaving, and this time, I won't consider coming back."* In no way was my statement meant to be an ultimatum or a threat. It was just business and I wasn't going to accept any less than what we had agreed upon. I would expect WCW to do the same. I think Watts understood, and I believe I gained a new measure of respect from him that night.

Bill, I'm sure, had dealt with a lot of wrestlers who lived from paycheck to paycheck. Many of them didn't plan for their future. It's because of that fact that many of them yielded the upper hand to the promoters who were less than fair with them. I always felt badly for the wrestlers who would come to me and say, *"But, Nikita. I don't know how to do anything else."*

Had I known then what I know from experience now, I would have told them to look out for their future because no one else was going to, and not to let anyone's perception of them define who they are. Had the boys been smart enough and had the right guidance and enough forethought, they could have had a future for themselves and their families outside of the ring, but unfortunately, a great number of them didn't. I have seen too many of them spend more in one night of partying than a lot of people make in a week or even a month. Many of them could have retired several times over with the money they made, but they threw it all away.

We finally got the contract squared away, but I was beginning to think it was time for me to hang up my boots for good. Things were changing so much with the new company that I knew I had to give some serious consideration to retiring.

A lot of people have asked me through the years for my thoughts on what led to the decline and eventual demise of WCW. I don't believe there is one answer. A lot of things contributed to it: the vision of Vince McMahon, the growth of the World Wrestling Federation from a regional promotion to a national power, the end of the old territory system, a loss of focus in what made professional wrestling successful, and large corporations taking it over as one of their divisions. There were many reasons over a long period of time to bring about the end of an era, but as an eyewitness to the beginning of the end, I believe one of the things that kick-started the decline of WCW was the institution of the new contracts. There certainly is nothing wrong with contracts in wrestling. It has taken the position of the wrestlers from independent contractors to a more professional status, but that is when the contract benefits both the company and the wrestlers. When the agreements favor one over the other, problems arise, and that's just what happened in WCW.

Since the early days of professional wrestling, the wrestlers made a living by doing one thing … and that was wrestling. We wrestled whether we felt like it or not. We wrestled when we were sick, when we were hurt, when we were injured, and we wrestled when we were so exhausted from our nonstop schedule that we could hardly walk. We did it for the love of the sport, and for the fans who braved all kinds of weather and spent their hard earned dollars to watch us perform. If we didn't, we didn't get paid. If we didn't show for a match for whatever reason, we lost a payday, and very well could have lost our spot in the lineup. And, as I said before, there were plenty of guys waiting to step into our place. Night after night, town after town, and match after match, that was the way it was and the way it had been since the days of the great William Muldoon. That was the way it was until the new era of wrestling began, when the boys began to sign contracts with a company that knew little about the business of professional wrestling. That was the way it was until the inmates were given the keys to the asylum.

One night in St. Louis, as I was getting ready to head to the ring, I asked someone where a particular wrestler was. One of the boys heard my question and said, *"Oh, he went home."*

"Went home?" I asked. *"What do you mean, he went home?"*

"He had a stomach ache, so he flew home."

That's a true story. I had heard and seen a lot of bizarre things in wrestling, but I would have to say that was one of the strangest. Going home for a stomach ache, when so many that went before him, and some of whom were still in the ring to that day, had times when they literally crawled to the ring to wrestle … and that guy took the first plane to wherever it was because of an upset stomach. An even crazier part of the story is that nobody seemed to care. The guy kept his job, kept his spot, and still got paid for the night. As

Archie Bunker once said, *"Someone should hang a sign out on the world saying, 'Closed, owner gone nuts.'"*

Another thing that began happening was the bookers would change the card at the drop of the hat for no reason at all. The main event advertised might have been Arn Anderson versus Vader, and even though both guys were in the building, before they got to the ring, the main event would change to Vader versus Bobby Eaton and Arn Anderson versus Sam Houston. When asked for a reason for the change, no one could give an answer. More than likely, it was because there was no answer to give.

When Jim Crockett held the reins of the NWA, everything was based in Charlotte, where the Crocketts lived, but now that Turner owned the company, everything was run out of CNN Center in Atlanta. That being the case, WCW announced that all flights wrestlers were to take to the towns in which they were wrestling were to originate from Atlanta. I think this was part of their plan to relocate the center of wrestling from North Carolina to Georgia, ushering in the new era of World Championship Wrestling and cutting ties with the old National Wrestling Alliance. To do this, it made sense to have everyone living in Atlanta where they would be close to the home office. We were forbidden to fly from anywhere else. We had to find our way to Atlanta and fly from Hartsfield Airport to wherever we were wrestling.

In my case, I would have to drive or fly from Charlotte to Atlanta and change planes. In most cases, I could fly cheaper out of Charlotte to most cities than I could from Atlanta. I tried to explain that to the office, but they wouldn't listen. Again, I couldn't believe it. I was telling my employer how they could save money and they turned a deaf ear. For example, I could fly from Charlotte-Douglas Airport to Cincinnati for $180. The price of a ticket from Atlanta was $300. The company was overspending $120 on just one ticket for one night.

That may not seem like a lot of money in the scheme of things, but multiply that by six or seven nights a week and the number of the boys traveling, and you can begin to see the extravagance of the madness. I kept trying to tell them, but they didn't seem to care. I thought it was a strange way to do business, but it was their money, at least for the time being.

Since WCW didn't seem to be concerned about the air travel, I came up with my own travel plan, and so, "Koloff Airlines" was born. The home office would send me, in advance, my airline tickets to each town from Atlanta and expected nothing more of me than to be in the right town on the right night. They didn't care if I flew from Atlanta, Charlotte, or the planet Krypton, so I would trade in my ticket from Atlanta to one from Charlotte and pocket the change. I was averaging about $1,000 a week from "Koloff Airlines." WCW didn't mind and neither did the rest of the people at the asylum.

Chapter 29

Trust and Responsibility

There were a lot of changes in wrestlers in the 1980s from those in the past, just as athletes of all sports changed, but the biggest change had to do with their size. It seemed like they became bigger almost overnight. In the 1970s, the average wrestler probably weighed about 225 to 240 pounds. Some may take issue with that when they recall, *"I remember so-and so weighed 265, and then there was what's-his-name, who was always announced at 280."* That may be the case with some wrestlers, but they were few and far between. It was not any more unusual for promoters to stack (add weight or height) a wrestler than it was to take a guy from Minnesota and make him a Russian.

The 1980s were the dawn of the musclemen in wrestling, and the one thing that ushered that in was the wholesale use of steroids. I have been asked in various forums if I had ever taken steroids, and I have to answer truthfully … yes. I used them sparingly while in college. The story back then was if you wanted to make it in the NFL, you had to do what the big boys did. Since I dreamed from childhood about playing in the NFL, I did what I thought I needed to do to have an optimal chance of making it in the big leagues. I'm not saying this to minimize my participation with them. It was as stupid as it was wrong. I am very thankful that I didn't get sucked into the steroid culture and use them to enhance my performance. More times than not, use quickly becomes abuse, and the thought prevails that if two makes me look like this, then four will make me twice as big. The sport went from finesse to power, and many of the boys took steroids to look the part and try to move ahead in the business.

One of the most-recognized names and greatest stars of the 1980s was a close friend of mine, Wayne Coleman, better known to the world as "Superstar" Billy Graham. Billy began his wrestling career in California after training in Calgary down in Stu Hart's dungeon and then was brought into Los Angeles to team with Dr. Jerry Graham. Almost from the beginning, Billy was given a push. With his unbelievable interviewing skills, larger-than-life personality, and mythic physique, he wrestled top card everywhere and reaching the zenith of his career by defeating the WWWF world heavyweight champion, Bruno Sammartino, on April 30, 1977 in Baltimore.

Of course, there is another Billy Graham, one who is well known throughout the world, and that's the highly-regarded evangelist from Black Mountain, North Carolina. I don't know if their paths ever crossed, but I do remember a funny conversation regarding the two famous Billy Grahams that happened a few years ago in Asheville, North Carolina, during the Outback Night of the Legends auction. The auction is part of the Brad Johnson Celebrity Golf Classic played to benefit the Eblen Charities. Brad, of course, was the quarterback of the Super Bowl XXXVII champion Tampa Bay Buccaneers, and is also a native of Black Mountain (as is Cleveland Cavalier and NBA great Brad Daugherty).

On the night of the auction, the Reverend Graham was watching the local news. When he heard Brad was in town, he wanted to send him his regards. He also saw that Governor Jesse Ventura was appearing at the event and wanted to send him regards, as well. He told long-time aide, Maury Scobee, and Maury drove across town to the event to greet Brad and the governor.

A friend of both Ventura and Maury introduced them and told the governor that Maury worked for Billy Graham. *"Really,"* said Ventura. *"Billy is one of my closest friends. I had no idea that he had an assistant. In fact, I've known him for more than twenty years and I am surprised that I've never met you. I saw him two weeks ago in New York when we both were inducted into the WWE Hall of Fame."*

Maury looked a bit puzzled and said, *"Yes, sir. I've worked for him for 25 years or so. I travel with him nearly everywhere."*

The mutual friend spoke up and said, *"Gentlemen, I think you two are talking about two different Billy Grahams. Governor, Maury works for the Reverend Billy Graham. Maury, the governor is talking about "Superstar" Billy Graham, the wrestler."*

Governor Ventura and Maury both laughed and the governor said, *"Well. that makes sense. I was talking about the bigger Billy Graham,"* referring to his size. *"That's funny,"* Maury responded, *"so was I."* They shook hands and had their picture taken together, both grinning from ear to ear.

"Superstar" was one of the first "big" men in wrestling and part of the reason for that was his use of steroids. He now readily admits his abuse and uses his celebrity status to warn athletes of the dangers of the drugs. Superstar paid a tremendous price for his steroid abuse. In 2002, Billy received a liver transplant to replace his damaged liver caused by his many years of using steroids. God truly blessed him with a number of willing donors, including a number of wrestlers who were disqualified for one reason or another. A liver was made available from a 26-year-old woman who died tragically in a car accident.

Superstar has made the most of his "new life" and spends his time in service to others, advocating for organ donors and speaking passionately against the use of steroids. I am proud to number him as one of my dear friends and is someone whom I admire greatly.

Big men like the Road Warriors, Hulk Hogan, Lex Luger, and Yokozuna all became superstars and power moves replaced the finesse the fans had witnessed in the ring prior to this new era. But as the wrestlers became more muscular and massive, injuries began to appear more frequently.

Fans flocked to the matches to see these larger-than-life characters do battle. One who ruled the roost in WCW was a giant from Denver, Colorado. Born Leon White, he carved a path through his competition and left a lot of wrestlers in his wake. In Japan, he was known as Super Vader. In the States, he was known simply as Vader. He was promoted successfully as one of the premier "super heavyweights" of the late '80s and '90s. Standing 6-foot-5 and weighing close to 450 pounds, Vader was a behemoth. Before turning to wrestling, he played football at the University of Colorado and, for two years, was on the roster of the Los Angeles Rams. Trained by the great Olympian and Lou Thesz/George Tragos Professional Wrestling Hall of Fame member, Brad Rheingans, Leon began his career in 1985 wrestling for Verne Gagne as "Baby Bull" Leon White.

As big as he was, Leon was not getting over in Minnesota, so he began looking for greener pastures. He went to Germany and signed with Otto Wanz's Catch Wrestling Alliance. Wrestling as "Bull Power," he defeated Wanz for the CWA "world" title. He then headed for Japan, where he wrestled as Super Vader, and took the IWGP title from Shinya Hashimoto. He also upset El Canek in Mexico for the UWA title. He is the only man I am aware of to hold three versions of the world heavyweight title simultaneously.

In Japan as Super Vader, Leon would come to the ring wearing a huge black-horned headgear, shaped like some sort of Minotaur, from which smoke billowed out. In a profession that thrives on hype and hyperbole, this one took the cake. He was a cross between mythology and mayhem, a heavy-handed monster in the ring.

On July 12, 1992, at the Great American Bash in Albany, Georgia, Vader defeated Sting for the WCW world heavyweight title, but lost it to Ron Simmons less than a month later. He took the WCW title for a second time on December 30 in Baltimore. It was between his first and second title reigns that we met in the ring for the final time.

I suppose it's just natural that wrestlers remember their first match and their last. We all remember the significant matches of our careers and the major angles and titles won, but the matches that always stand out are the two at each end: the one that begins your mat career and the one that sends you off to another way of life.

My last match was memorable in a number of ways. First, it wasn't planned to be my last match, and secondly, I received two of the most serious injuries of my career.

The Thanksgiving and Christmas holidays were just around the corner and my outlook towards the upcoming celebrations had changed quite a bit. In the past, I had been alone and really didn't give a lot of thought to the holidays. It wasn't because I didn't hold them in high regard, but not having any family, they didn't seem all that much different than any other day. Besides, I spent both Thanksgiving and Christmas working. There always was an evening show on Thanksgiving and an afternoon and evening show on Christmas Day. But my situation in 1992 gave me a new perspective.

When Vic and I got married, my priorities quickly began to change. I not only had a wife, but an instant family: Teryn and Tawni, Vic's two daughters from her first marriage. In June 1992, our first child, Kendra, was born. I laugh when I think back to when Kendra was a baby. I was afraid to pick her up and hold her. The "Russian Nightmare," fearless in the ring, trembled at the thought of picking up that tiny little girl and holding her in his arms. It did get easier as I became more used to being a father, but it happened all over again when our daughter Kolby was born in 1996. Even though I began my marriage with two daughters, I had to learn to be a father from scratch. Not having had a father in my life while I was growing up, I didn't have a model I could follow, so I know I made my fair share of mistakes. Okay, I probably made more than my fair share, but fortunately for me, I had Victoria, whose infinite love and patience helped me through those early, tenuous days of fatherhood. If anything, Vic's example of the way she treated Teryn and Tawny showed me how to love and care for our four daughters. If it hadn't been for Victoria, I can't imagine being the parent I am now. She and the girls have made me a complete person, more than I ever could have envisioned.

With a family at home, the allure of the road began to wane. There was something about being home in the evening and tucking my daughters into bed after reading them a story that appealed to me more than nailing an opponent with a chain. As my girls grew up, it became harder and harder for me to leave for the matches. I still loved wrestling, but I loved my family more.

By the latter part of the year, I didn't have any particular opponent. Most of the year had been spent in a program with Rick Rude or against a variety of opponents with Ricky Steamboat as my partner. I was just being matched with whomever the bookers and promoters thought might be a good idea for that particular night and town. No angle or program, just meaningless match after match. Meaningless, that is, in regards to a lack of storyline or buildup to anything I was doing. Each night was just a different show in a different town. There was no reason why Vader and I should be wrestling each other and I'm not even sure how that particular match came about. As far as I know, they just pulled our names out of a hat.

The fans seemed to enjoy it, but a match is supposed to tell a story, like a chapter in a book that leads to a bigger story, and climax with a final match in a large venue or pay-per-view where we set up the beginning of another story. Those days in WCW were long gone, and gone were the days of great minds like George Scott, and along with that, a lot of the fun.

I was booked to wrestle Vader on Sunday, November 8, 1992 in Winston-Salem, North Carolina and I knew I was in for a hard night and an extremely physical match. Seeing his matches, I knew that there would not be a lot of wrestling; just a lot of power moves like body slams, clothes-lines, and heavy-handed forearms and elbow-drops.

When you are in the ring, you have a dual responsibility. One is to protect yourself and the other is to protect your opponent. Trust is the key. If you don't trust your opponent and he doesn't trust you, the fans will likely be in store for a terrible match. If you are always on guard because you're worried about being injured, you can't pay attention to the things you should, like psychology and fan reaction.

Vader was someone I didn't trust in the ring. He was rough and much too reckless, which is why I refused to let him pick me up over his back and "power-bomb" me. Putting on a good match with him was difficult at best.

There were others I didn't trust in the ring, as well. Jake "The Snake" Roberts was one, albeit to a lesser degree. It was, unfortunately, well documented in the film *Beyond the Mat* that Jake has been dealing with a drug dependency for some time. This is in no way is meant to be a judgment on Jake. I only say this to highlight the fact that when you enter the ring, you have to be at your best. At times, that might not be possible physically, but the mental acumen of a wrestler has to be at its utmost.

When we wrestled Jake, we could never be sure what condition he would be in, so high spots were held to a minimum. He, like Vader, was not ring conscious and was careless when he worked with you. I'm sure I wasn't the only wrestler who limited his maneuvers in the ring with those two, but even if I was, it was for self-preservation, to make sure I would be able to walk out of the ring at the end of the match.

Joe Laurinaitis (Animal) was another story altogether. Joe took care of his opponents and we had never had to be cautious when we were in the ring with him. That is, other than one night when Ivan and I were wrestling Joe and his partner, Hawk. Joe and I always had good matches together and we would test each other from time to time for fun. Sometime during the match, Joe caught me off guard and pressed me over his head. He caught me when I wasn't paying attention to him, and the next thing I knew, I was suspended over his head. It must have been an amazing sight to the fans because a collective gasp came from the crowd. I couldn't believe Joe had pulled it on me. His strength was unbelievable, and he certainly had the skill to pull it off. I know he saw it as a big joke, so, suspended in air, I decided to play a joke of my own. When you are in the position to take a press slam, you are supposed to assist your opponent by putting your hands on his shoulders to help disperse the weight. *"Well,"* I thought, *"if Joe thinks this is so funny, then I'll let him do all the work."* I extended my arms like George Reeves in *The Adventures of Superman* and let Joe carry the entire load.

As strong as Joe was, holding 275 pounds of dead weight over his head was no easy task, but he held me aloft for at least fifteen seconds before he slammed me to the mat. He stood over me and gave me that "gotcha" kind of a grin. I shook my head, smiled, and said to him, *"Never again, Joe."* After that, I was a lot more cautious in the ring with my old friend.

Working with Joe was like a walk in the park compared to wrestling Vader. His size and strength were unbelievable. Combine those attributes with his total abandon in the ring and Leon White became a very dangerous man in the ring, as I would learn that night in Winston-Salem.

Vader and I were scheduled as the semi-final match on the card. We had the customary Vader match: a lot of power moves, clubbing forearms, kicks, and a great deal of pushing. It wasn't difficult to sell Vader's onslaught because, on that particular night, he seemed rougher than usual. He threw me through the ropes and followed me out to the floor. As we fought outside of the ring, I knocked him down and was walking back to get into the ring.

Unbeknownst to me, Vader took about a ten-yard charge and clotheslined me from behind, smashing me in the back of my head. I dropped to the floor with my head spinning. As I struggled to stand up, I realized I didn't have any feeling in my left arm. It was limp and just hanging at my side. After he nailed me, he rolled back into the ring to beat referee Tommy Young's twenty count. I wasn't sure what to do, but instinctively, I rolled into the ring after Vader to finish the match.

When Tommy approached me, I told him I couldn't use my left arm. He began to panic and asked me what I thought he should do. I was still into the match and, with the adrenaline flowing, told him not to do anything and that I would be fine. I wanted the match to continue. I'm not sure what it was, stupidity, or just my crazy attitude, but to me, any wrestler worth his salt wouldn't leave a match unless it was absolutely necessary. Men have died in the ring holding onto this credo; Men like "Iron" Mike DiBiase, Luther Lindsay, and Chick Garibaldi, to name a few.

I fought off Vader the best I could for the next several minutes with one arm, selling everything he was doing to me and trading punches and kicks. Somewhere around the four-minute mark of us being back in the ring, the feeling returned. I don't know what brought the feeling back, but I assume one of Vader's kick or punches knocked whatever it was that caused the loss of feeling back into place. We fought on for another ten minutes or so, at which point I did the job for Vader in the center of the ring. It would be the last time I would be in the ring when the bell rang.

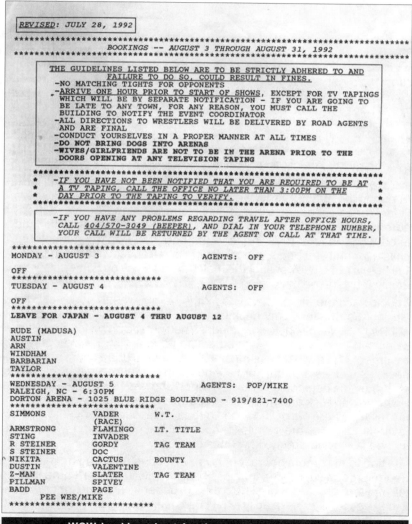

WCW booking sheet for the month of August 1992

Chapter 30
Maalox and Rolaids

After the match, I reported my injury to Grizzly Smith, the agent in charge of the matches that night. He told me to have it checked out in the morning when I got back to Charlotte. Vic was there that night with our five-month-old daughter, Kendra. I told her about the problem with my arm, but I assured her I didn't think it was any big deal since the feeling had come back into my arm. However, I told her I had promised Griz that I would go to the doctor when I got home. At five o'clock the next morning, I awoke with a pain shooting through my lower right side. I hadn't felt such pain since I injured my back with Flair. I thought it was awfully strange that my side would be hurting while my arm felt normal. Later in the morning, I called my physician and went to his office.

After the examination, he told me I had suffered a hernia when I had picked up Vader during the match. Vader weighed a legitimate 450 pounds at the time. I didn't feel the injury during the match, which wasn't all that unusual. With all the adrenaline pumping through your body during the heat of battle, and your focus on what needed to be done in the ring, you don't feel much until the match is over and you begin to cool down. In retrospect, I'm surprised I didn't feel the hernia in the shower after the match or while driving home. Nonetheless, I certainly felt it the next morning.

My doctor told me the only way to fix the hernia was to operate. While he was telling me the news, my neck began to ache. I thought that while I was there, I would have my neck examined, so he sent me down for an MRI. When it was all said and done, I had seen seven doctors, from a chiropractor to a neurosurgeon. The MRI revealed that I had several bone spurs at the base of my neck, as well as arthritis from all the bumps I I had taken over the years. That was just the beginning. The MRI report showed I also had a deteriorated disc in my lower neck and more bone spurring in the middle in my back. Due to that, my hips were out of line. I had already noticed that when I would get up in the morning, it took me a while to move without hurting, and when I walked, it sounded like a symphony of walnuts cracking.

In addition to my hernia operation, I would need to do rehab on my neck and the neurosurgeon suggested the possibility of having my vertebrae fused. He did tell me, though, the longer I held off, the better it would be for me. None of what they had to say was exactly what I had been hoping to hear when I left the house that day. I had more than my share of decisions to make, so I decided to take some time off during Thanksgiving and Christmas to be with my family and make some decisions about what my future might hold.

The physician also recommended that I consider another line of work. He explained that the longer I remained active in the ring, the greater the possibility for permanent injury and possible paralysis. That was what finally hit home. I wasn't fearful of what might happen in the ring, or the fact that I might have to live with some kind of injury, but what did frighten me was the potential of me not being able to pick up, hold, or play with my children.

I have a pretty high tolerance for pain. If you make your living in the ring, you better have the ability to stand pain and to work when you are hurt or injured. I recall one instance in 1991 when I was experiencing a great deal of abdominal pain. I was combating it by drinking gallons of Maalox and eating handfuls of Rolaids like they were M&M's. Vic kept pressuring me to see a doctor, but I told her I probably had eaten some bad chicken. Instead of seeing the doctor as Vic suggested, I went and played in a charity golf tournament and worked out as usual, until I finally relented and took her advice.

Two days later, we learned that I had appendicitis. As usual, I should have listened to my wife. The most bizarre thing about the appendicitis was that my appendix had ruptured three days before I went to see the doctor. As I said, I played in a golf tournament on a Friday and Saturday and then worked out on Sunday. I really felt okay and did everything without a lot of discomfort, but by late Monday night, the pain was almost unbearable. Vic and I went to the emergency room and the physician explained how serious the situation was. If I didn't undergo emergency surgery immediately, I could die. What she didn't know at the time was that it had already ruptured, and it wasn't until she opened me up that she realized it. She was astounded and later told Vic that I should have died. We attributed my life to my good health and the fact that I took care of myself.

The same sort of thing happened to Harry Houdini in 1926. When a college student heard that the athletic magician and escape artist could withstand forceful blows to his stomach, he asked Houdini if it was true and if he could test the Appleton, Wisconsin native. Houdini, who was distracted by reading his mail, agreed, but before he could brace himself, the student struck him in the area of his appendix. Houdini stubbornly refused to seek any medical attention since "the show must go on," and he died a short time later. I know what he meant by continuing on with the show, but I didn't want to end up like Houdini. There would be other days, but not if I followed his courageous, albeit unwise, path.

The attending physician explained to me that after the appendix operation, I would be sidelined for at least six weeks. That meant no working out and certainly no wrestling. She told me I should have died before reaching the hospital. I had the operation and, against her advice, was back in the ring by the end of the month. It was time to get back to work.

In 1992, though, my condition was a bit more serious. I was seeing seven doctors, a chiropractor, an orthopedist, and a neurologist. The one thing they all had in common was they all gave me similar advice: start thinking about another line of work.

I had a lot to think about and to discuss with Victoria.

Whatever I was to decide, I was in no particular hurry. I knew I had to have the hernia operation and would have to take some time away from the ring to recuperate and sort out what I wanted to do, so I called the WCW office and talked to Bill Watts. I told him what was going on and he told me to call when I was ready to come back.

That was it! No concern. No inquiries on how I was. Just matter-of-factly (in so many words), *"Call me when you can be of some use to me."* As callous as that was, I wasn't surprised or offended. It was just the direction and attitude of WCW at the time, which was all the more reason for me to reevaluate my career and my future.

I planned to take my time with the decision on whether to give up wrestling and pursue another career. I was enjoying my time at home with Vic and the girls. I had been very careful with my ring earnings and had been very fortunate in taking my business manager's advice in another area. Tim Peltier, my best friend growing up, became my business manager early in my wrestling career. I had all my checks, bills, bank statements, and other financial information sent to Tim and he would send me expense money each week, so I was in pretty good financial shape. Besides that, I was receiving a disability check from Lloyd's of London.

I was among the first of the boys to hire a business manager to handle his financial affairs. I knew I had enough to do with learning the wrestling business, the travel, and focusing on developing my character. It just made good sense. Today, a lot of the boys have agents and business managers, but back in the 1980s, it was unheard of.

It was Tim who brought my attention to Lloyd's of London and their penchant for unusual insurance policies. It was through an insurance agent from North Dakota that Tim heard about it and passed the information on to me. The way the policy worked was if I was out of the ring due to an injury, the policy would pay me a sum of money each month for up to two years. At the end of two years, if doctors verified that I was still unable to go back to wrestle, I would receive a lump-sum payment. The monthly premiums were pretty stiff, but they turned out to be more than worth it.

I wasn't the only one of the boys who signed up with Lloyd's. After I purchased my policy, Rick Rude, Curt Hennig, Barry Darsow, and both of the Road Warriors bought policies. In fact, we were reported to have damaged the insurance company for a time as a number of the guys had all been injured around the same time and were drawing on their policies, causing Lloyd's to pay out a massive amount of cash. It got so bad that they stopped insuring wrestlers altogether.

With my checks coming in and plenty of time to heal, I was in no hurry to go back to the ring, or even make a decision on what I was going to do. I was injured in November, had my hernia surgery, and was enjoying being home for the Thanksgiving holidays. I had always been on the road and in the ring on Thanksgiving, Christmas, New Years, and most other, if not all, holidays. As Thanksgiving turned to Christmas and Christmas turned to New Year's, I began thinking, *"You know, this isn't so bad."* And the longer I was out of the ring and with my family, the less I began to miss it.

I have always heard that the word "decision" came from a Greek origin meaning "to cut off." In other words, when you make a decision, you "cut off" all other decisions or paths. You set your mind on one thing and there are no longer any other thoughts to entertain. You have made up your mind and do not have to seek other options. That is what I knew I had to do. Continue in the ring, with the sport I have grown to love, or to leave wrestling and begin another chapter in my life. The choice was mine to make … and I was torn as to what to do. It was a difficult choice at best, especially for one to make alone. Fortunately, I had help in making the resolution.

When I was on my own, I didn't give a lot of thought to many things. The chances I took in the ring, the long days away from home, and other eccentricities of the road didn't matter much. I figured no matter what happened at the time, I could handle it. I had no one to be concerned about but me. But now I was no longer alone. I had a family that filled my thoughts in the place where wrestling had been not that long ago. If I returned to wrestling now, I had to leave Vic and the girls. When it was just me, it didn't matter to me whether I slept in my apartment or in a hotel room, but now it would matter a great deal. Returning to the ring at that time would mean leaving my wife, my baby, my two daughters, and our home. Besides that, I had to consider my injuries, and in the back of my mind was the goal I had set when I broke into the business. I had promised myself that I would leave the sport by the time I was 35. I was 33, soon to be 34. Traveling became more and more of a chore. Just the thought of getting on a plane and heading to a different town, night after night, gave me more than a moment's pause. Not only that, but the days of the territories were all but gone and wrestling had become part of the corporate world. The very essence of the business I loved had changed to the point where, even without a family at home, I would have had to seriously evaluate whether or not I wanted to go back. It slowly began to dawn on me that the curtain was coming down on my career.

In the movie *North Dallas Forty*, Nick Nolte and Mac Davis were two aging pro football players who were trying to puzzle out the changing of the sport they had given so much of their lives playing. In one scene, Nolte, who was knee-deep in frustration, confronted his Maalox-swigging coach: *"Every time we call football a game, you call it a business, and every time we call it a business, you call it a game. Get your story straight!"*

It was the same with the boys. When we would try to have some fun and break the tension of the road, management would come in and slap a fine on us, but when we became serious and treated it as a robber baron would treat his bank, the management would say, *"Hey, guys. Loosen up. Have some fun."* We might have been able to have "some fun" if it wasn't for the politics. When Turner took over, everything became far too political for me. Dusty once told me he couldn't even carry on a conversation with the guy in the office next door to his. He had to send the guy a memo because everything had to be documented. As the craziness of the airline travel situation showed what the business had become, they played the game as it was a business and played business as if it were a game.

That all contributed to my decision to forgo a return to the ring. Sure the injuries played a part. My chiropractor told me that, at the age of 33, I had the neck of a 55-year-old man, thanks to the suplexes, clotheslines, piledrivers, and body slams. I had deterioration and bone spurs which caused a great deal of discomfort. But not once did a doctor tell me not to go back in the ring. What they did tell me, however, was the longer I stayed in the ring, the higher the chances would be that I could incur more serious injuries, and they might be career-ending.

Every wrestler knows he or she is just one bodyslam or hard bump away from serious injury. Just ask Steve Austin, Mick Foley, or Darren Drozdov. Even though the thought is there, it stays buried somewhere in the dark corridors of our subconscious, as if to think about it may hasten a disaster. We might ignore it from our own minds, but to hear the warning audibly from a physician brings it to a reality that hits you like a left hook from Lennox Lewis. That was all it took for me to decide and "cut off" all other thoughts.

Once again, all I could think about was Victoria and the girls. I honestly thought I probably could have wrestled for another five or ten years, but what if I did get injured and ended up a quadriplegic or paraplegic? What if I became so incapacitated due to aggregate ring injuries that I couldn't do anything with my children at the age of 40? That wasn't the life I had envisioned for my family or myself. It was time to walk away. I still had two years left on my contract, but I was sure of my decision. A friend of mine told me his grandfather used to tell him, *"Many people will tell you that it is hard to do the right thing. It may be hard to figure out what the right thing to do is, but once you figure it out, the right thing is easy to do."* He was right. I struggled with it in my mind for such a long time, but now I knew without any doubt what the right thing was. And now that I did, it was easy to do. I became the Barry Sanders of wrestling. The ring days of the Russian Nightmare had come to a close.

It's somewhat ironic that my career would end in such a quiet way, especially seeing how it began with such fanfare. Nobody from the WCW office ever called to check on me to see when I was coming back. I guess they were standing by their comment for me to let them know when I was ready to return, and since I didn't call, they probably figured I wasn't coming back.

I wasn't on bad terms with the company when my career ended. My career wasn't over because I was injured to a point where I couldn't walk. It didn't end with a big loser-leave-wrestling match, or a farewell tour. It just ended. It was sort of like switching channels, or finishing one chapter of a book and going on to the next. I was ready to start my new chapter with Vic and the girls.

Not much was said in WCW about my absence, although six months after I wrestled him for the last time, Vader bragged on television about how he was "the man who ended Nikita Koloff's career." It served him well for a short while, I suppose, and if it did well for him; that's just the nature of the business. But, of course, the reality of it was … the only man who ended Nikita Koloff's career was me. And I couldn't have been more satisfied.

Chapter 31

A Stroke of the Pen

I still owned my gym, Nikita's Fitness Center, and it was doing well, so it wasn't as if I was going to be bored. I had invested my money, thanks to my business manager, and combined with my Lloyd's of London policy, the gym, and a few other interests, I could leave the ring without any major concerns.

I had opened Nikita's Fortress of Fitness in 1988 as a place where I could work out, create some revenue, and help others train. Early in 1993, as membership continued to grow, I changed the name of the gym to Nikita's Fitness Center. I can't tell you how much I was enjoying being at home with Vic and the girls and training and coaching the members at the gym.

Like any small business, I was finding that Vic and I were spending an inordinate amount of time in the gym. It was not unusual for one of us, if not both, to be there eight to ten hours a day, and that quickly turned into twelve to fourteen hours a day. When I realized I was spending more time at the gym than I had spent on the road just a year or so before, I began thinking about selling the gym and finding something that would give me a little more freedom and still provide a challenge.

Things had actually begun to unfold in that direction for me in December 1992 when Vic and I took the girls back to Minnesota for Christmas. We were staying at Animal's house, as we usually did, and he and I headed out to the Mall of America to do some Christmas shopping. While we were there, we ran into an old college buddy of mine that we both knew. As we were catching up, he told us about his new multi-level marketing business, Quorum, which sold and distributed personal-alarm systems and other personal safety devices. I had never given much thought to multi-level marketing, but since our friend seemed so excited about the potential for big income, Animal and I agreed to go to one of his meetings to hear more about it. So Animal and I, along with our wives, drove through a snowstorm to the informational meeting, and by the end of the evening, the two of us signed up as distributors.

Within a couple of years, we moved our business into a media company, The People's Network, which was a dedicated satellite station that produced and broadcasted motivational and positive family programming. They later partnered with PrimeStar, a direct satellite broadcasting company. The company was in operation from 1994 to 1998 and got off to a good start, but I guess there wasn't enough of a market to sell enough of the satellite systems to keep the programs going, even if it was, by my estimation, the absolute best programming money could buy. It really is a shame that it didn't go. It was a great concept and the speakers were great. Besides, I had spent the better part of those four years selling and installing satellite systems across the Southeast. I put them in hundreds of backyards and rooftops and calibrated the angle to receive the best signals. In more cases than not, I did so with a small audience as the subscribers would call their friends and tell them, *"You won't believe who's setting up my satellite system. You need to get over here right away."*

I not only worked as a distributor, but I had invested in the company, getting in on the ground floor. TPN was resilient, and even though the concept didn't take off as hoped, it attracted the interest of another company. Prepaid Legal was created to provide legal services to individuals, companies, and their employees as an addition to their benefit package. They purchased the People's Network in September 1998, bringing TPN to a close, but opening up a world of new opportunities.

Even though none of those concepts actually scaled the heights of the corporate world, they provided invaluable training for me and what the future held. If nothing else, I do owe the industry a huge debt of gratitude for the skills it taught me. What I learned from them was how to speak in front of large crowds with a message that would keep their interest. You would think that, after all the years I spent in the ring and was on television, I would be comfortable speaking in front of large crowds. It's not that I was totally uncomfortable in that situation, but there was a world of difference between selling a match as the Russian Nightmare and keeping the interest of a large crowd for an hour or so. However, thanks to the training I received and the opportunity I had to work with speakers like Og Mandino, Jim Rohn, Zig Zigler, Geoffrey Gitomer, Ty Boyd, and Brian Tracy, I was getting the education of a lifetime, preparing me for what would be the vocation of a lifetime.

As 1995 rolled around, I was confronted with two more major decisions. The gym, as I said, was consuming a disproportional amount of our time, as well as taking us away from our other business interests. It didn't take long to realize that the gym we owned now owned us, so without too much hesitation, we sold the gym and happily took back our time and lives.

My second year of payments from Lloyd's also ended that year, which left me with a monumental decision. I had to decide if I was going to take one last lump-sum payment from the policy and turn my back on ever returning to active work in the ring, or refuse the payment and leave the door open to a possible return somewhere in the future. I was now 35 and it was still possible to have ten or more years in the ring.

Vic and I spent hour upon hour discussing the options. What would be best for our family? What did I really want to do? I called Lloyd's and told them I believed the injuries I had sustained may not keep me from the ring entirely, but the possibility of being permanently injured was too great and that was a risk no amount of money or recognition could possibly be worth.

Lloyd's required me to be seen by a team of doctors in Charlotte to see if, indeed, my ring days were over, and that my career as an active wrestler was a thing of the past. I went through a battery of tests and the physicians concluded that it would be in my best interest to retire from wrestling. If I chose to do so, I could still be involved in the sport as an announcer, manager, or referee, but to actively wrestle was out of the question. I agreed and signed the necessary papers to receive the final lump-sum payment and retire.

So, in reality, Vader didn't end the career of the Russian Nightmare. A stroke of the pen did. Little did I know at the time that the most important chapter of my story was still to be written.

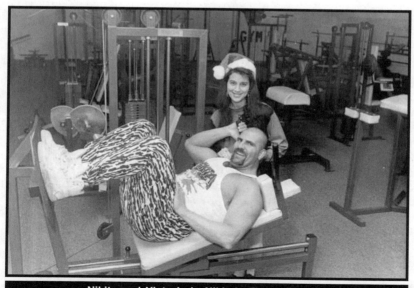

Nikita and Victoria in Nikita's Fitness Center

Chapter 32

Nikita Meets Nikita

Vic and I were content and never had the first moment of regret about our decision to leave wrestling behind. Our other interests and investments kept us busy and we were anxious about new opportunities that might come our way.

The biggest challenge I encountered during my first year out of the ring came from a most unexpected place. I have to be honest and say I did miss the ring some, and at times, I still do. I certainly don't miss the politics, both inside the corporate offices and the dressing room, but I do miss the ring. By that, I mean I miss the time from the opening bell until the sound of the bell signaling the end of the match. It was just a lot of fun to be able to entertain so many wonderful fans and have them play such a big part of the Russian Nightmare's story. Please don't get me wrong. I don't pine away for the old days, spend hours waxing nostalgic, or lay awake at night wishing I could relive those days. My time has come and gone, but when I do think about being in the ring, I have to smile.

Many of the boys, when they retire, have a difficult time assimilating into a world that is not confined to a 20-by-20-foot "squared circle." I was ready to leave and had set a path, so when the time came, I could move on without any consternation. For me, the difficulty didn't stem from what was going on in my mind and heart, but from all that was going on around me. As much as Nikita Koloff brought me recognition and all the good things that came with it, now it became my biggest obstacle.

The persona of the Russian Nightmare had became an imposing force in my life. I melded into the character 24 hours a day, seven days a week, and now I had to find a way out, at least in regards to how I spoke. Since the day Nikita was born in Jim Crockett's office, I made sure that everyone I came into contact with believed they were seeing an authentic Russian athlete. I never for a minute believed I was the character I played, but unfortunately, I have seen so many wrestlers who began to believe they were the character they portrayed in the ring. That is essential when you are on camera, in the ring, or being seen by the fans, but not to a point where you lose who you are to yourself. I knew who I was, but my job was to make sure the fans didn't.

One of the best examples I can recall about keeping that balance was something my dear friend, the late Curt Hennig, told me. He was at the height of his WWE career as "Mr. Perfect" and was spending a rare few days back at home with his wife and family. His youngest son, Hank, who was about five or so at the time, walked up to him in the kitchen one day and asked, *"Daddy, are you Mr. Perfect?"*

Now Curt always kept his business and home life separate. On the road he was Mr. Perfect, Intercontinental heavyweight champion and former heavyweight champion of the world. At home, he was dad. After giving a few seconds thought to Hank's question, he kneeled down, looked at his son, smiled, and said, *"Sometimes."* Hank was satisfied with the answer and said, *"Okay."* He walked away to continue doing whatever he had been doing before his question came to mind. Curt knew and practiced what all the boys would do good to remember.

Even though I knew I was Nelson Scott Simpson, very few others did. Well, I better explain that a bit. As my career began to take off, I decided to change my name legally. I wanted to make sure I did everything possible to swerve any doubters about my ring persona. I flew back to Minneapolis and asked a judge to officially change my name to Nikita Koloff. I chose Minnesota to do so primarily because not that many people knew about Nikita Koloff, the wrestler. Cable had not hit its zenith, and what little the fans knew about me came from the magazines and whatever matches they might have seen.

As I stood in front of the judge, she was somewhat incredulous about what I wanted to do. When I explained my reasoning to her, she had a puzzled look on her face. She did her best to enlighten me about how I didn't have to go to those lengths to be known by another name, citing the example of how John Wayne never actually changed his name from Marion Morrison. He simply used his screen name, and in legal matters, just wrote AKA, or "also known as." I guess she thought that if it was good enough for the "Duke," it should be good enough for me. I told her I appreciated her council, but I wanted to change my name legally to the one by which I was known more readily. She agreed, and for all legal purposes, I became Nikita Koloff.

Recently, while going through some legal papers at home, I came across our daughter Kendra's birth certificate. I was so protective of the sport and my character that I actually wrote "Lithuania" as the birthplace of her father. I couldn't believe I did that. I thought, *"Oh, my gosh."* Maybe I did take it a little too far.

I knew I had to make a transformation from my perceived public persona to my actual personality. There wasn't really any difference from who people saw me as and who I really was … except for one thing. My accent.

No matter where I was, I continued to speak broken English. I spent twelve hours a day working with club members in my gym, developing workout routines and nutrition plans, and working out side by side with clients, and doing it all in character. I kept wondering, *"How am I going to transition out of this?"* At the time, I just couldn't see myself just walking in and speaking in my normal voice. Today, it wouldn't be a big deal to break character, but back then, I thought it was still important to protect the business.

It was a slow process and it took a little more than a year to do it, but it worked. I just phased out the accent over a period of months. I guess everyone just accepted it over time, or perhaps they got used to it. It was like having braces on your teeth for years, and when you finally get them off, no one notices. No one ever came up to me and said, *"Hey, what happened to your accent?"*

However, now and then, I still meet fans that I jokingly refer to as "one of those." That comes from the fans who come up to me and say, *"You know, I'm one of those who believed all those years that you were from Russia."* Some time back, I was at a wrestling reunion show in New Jersey, and while I was sitting at a table talking to fans and signing autographs, I noticed that one of the security guards kept walking back and forth and stopping at the table. After an hour or so, he walked up and introduced himself. When I told him I had noticed him walking by the table quite a bit, he said he couldn't help himself. He explained that the reason he kept coming around the table was that he couldn't believe I was speaking English.

It always has been nice to have the fans' support. Even as a heel. I knew the fans were following me by the jeers and hate mail I received. I was the guy they loved to hate. In those days, the more I was reviled, the more pleasure I had. It was good to know I was doing my job well. As a babyface, I got to see the other side of the fans and the loyalty they gave to their heroes, which they now shared with me.

I've met so many wonderful people who have followed my career and have honored me in so many ways. I've talked to fans who have told me they had named their pets, guitars, and even their children, after me. It's extremely sobering and humbling to have a child named after you. I met two children that were named after me. The first one lived not too far from my home.

One night, I was in Rocky Mount, North Carolina, having dinner at a local steakhouse. As I was going through the line with my tray, a very polite young lady asked me what I wanted to drink. I looked up and noticed her name-tag. It read *"Nikita."* I smiled at her, commented on her unusual name, and asked what her real name was. She told me Nikita was her actual name. She explained that her mother was the biggest wrestling fan on the planet and she loved this guy named Nikita Koloff.. I said *"Really? That's funny. My name is Nikita Koloff."* She didn't believe me, but when I showed her my driver's license, she started jumping up and down and screaming, and then ran to the back to call her mother.

I don't have any idea what it was like for that young lady to grow up being named after the Russian Nightmare, but I was impressed with her outgoing personality, politeness, and kindness. I hope her parents are proud of her. They have reason to be.

Chapter 33

The Conversation

There is a God, and I know him personally through my Savior, the Lord Jesus. As I was reviewing the last two chapters of this book, I was sitting in Uganda, Africa, finishing a two-week ministering trip; speaking in schools and prisons, at crusades, and to groups of athletes. I have witnessed the hand of God move in mighty ways, but none more so than in my own life.

I was raised a Lutheran, albeit marginally. I would attend church at Park Avenue Lutheran from time to time with my mother on Christmas, Easter, and the usual church holidays when I couldn't find a way to get out of it. As I grew up and set my sights on other goals, and moved out to the suburbs, church moved steadily down my list of priorities until it dropped off the list altogether.

As far back as my childhood takes me, I believed in God. I don't think I ever rebelled against Him. I just never gave Him much thought. That was until I left the ring and had a family. I'm not trying to convert anyone here. All I'm doing is telling what has happened to me since I left the ring. I believe that faith and a relationship with God is just that; a relationship between God and an individual. He touches one heart at a time, in His time. If reading this strikes a chord somewhere, don't stop reading. If it doesn't, that's okay, too.

My turn towards Christianity was far from what Paul experienced on the road to Damascus. It was more of a process that ended up changing my life and that of my family. And it started, as you might guess, in the gym.

Mark Beebe and his wife Barbara were members of our gym. Vic and I got to know them, as we did most of our members, since they visited the "Fortress of Fitness" several times a week to work out. As we were becoming acquainted, we learned that Mark was the pastor of our local Lutheran church, and like any pastor worth his salt, he and Barbara kept inviting us to attend church with them. At first, we kept making excuses on why we couldn't come; we had to pick up the girls from a sleepover, we needed to open the gym, one or both of us were going to be out of town.

It was amazing how many excuses we could come up with week after week … until we had run the course of all our excuses and agreed to go with them one Sunday. I wasn't totally against it as I thought that since they were paying members of the gym, it would probably be good for business and it never hurts to keep a customer happy. Vic also reasoned that it would be good for the girls because any and all positive influences on them would be most welcome.

I had grown pretty jaded as far as religion was concerned. I thought, whether right or wrong, ministers and churches were more interested in the size of your bank account than in the state of your soul, so I wasn't expecting much as we began to attend church with Mark and Barbara. I must say, we were both pleasantly surprised by the service. The sermons were not only topical and current, but also resonate in our thoughts as we found ourselves discussing the sermon on the way home, and sometimes throughout the week. We found ourselves attending services more and more as time went on. I began to realize that my thoughts towards Christians and religion had been somewhat skewed.

One Sunday, Vic and I were in total disagreement on Mark's message. She drew one thing from his sermon and I another. We just couldn't find common ground on what we thought was the key message. We didn't know enough to analyze the message, but we did know enough to know who to call who might offer the insight each of us sought.

Another friend, who we met through a business contact, attended the First Assembly Church of Concord. He was extremely knowledgeable in theology and Biblical history, so Vic and I asked him and his wife over to our house to have coffee and give us his thoughts on the sermon. Their names are Dick and Charlotte Elston.

We talked for what seemed a short time, but what was actually hours. As we talked, I kept questioning him on various points and the many hard questions that popped into my head. I was sure I'd had conversations as deep and thoughtful as that one, but I really can't remember when. With each question, his kind and thoughtful answers seemed to reach into my heart.

As the conversation deepened, he said, *"I want you to know that what I am going to tell you will be the most important information you may ever receive in your life. But, as many times as I have shared this story, I have never done it without being interrupted."* I thought that was a bit strange, but I kept listening. He then pointed out the fact that even though we had been talking for hours, we hadn't been interrupted by the girls, the phone, or anything else. The story Dick told me was about the life of Jesus, about how God sent his Son to earth to save mankind and willingly die a horrifying death in my place. It was a story I had heard before, but he told it in a *way* I had never heard before. I sat in awe. Sure enough, while he told the story, the phone rang, the girls were hungry, the phone rang again, the girls needed something else, again the phone rang, and when it was all said and done, we had been interrupted a dozen times. I couldn't believe it; it was absolutely amazing. Even with the interruptions and the phone ringing incessantly for the first time in hours, I still heard what my friend was saying.

He finished by saying a prayer for us and then they headed home. As I walked back into the house, it dawned on me that it was 3:05 in the morning. We had been talking for twelve hours. It was as if time stood still. When Vic and I headed off to bed, Dick's story was still running through my mind.

In the fall 1993, Teryn began her freshman year in high school. Like so many of her friends, she attended public school, but after about a month, we thought it would be better for her to go to the school that was run by First Assembly Church. Teryn had some difficulty adjusting to the change, so Vic and I thought if we went to church there, perhaps she would make new friends who would help with her transition. We called Dick to let him know we would be coming to church on Sunday.

One Sunday, we were running late. When we got to the church, we found it nearly full, so the only seats we could find were in the balcony. We climbed the stairs as unobtrusively as a former professional wrestler, his wife, and three daughters could. At this particular service, there was no message given by the pastor. Instead, he led the congregation in praise and worship. He led us in prayer for each other, other churches, and our nation. As he prayed, I began to feel as if someone was whispering in a singular voice, one I had never heard before. As the service went on, something deep inside me was beating. It was as if someone was pounding on the door. With my eyes closed and my face buried in my hands, I felt a battle between my head and my heart that would rival any physical battle I had with any opponent in the ring.

When they passed the offering plate, I reached into my wallet, pulled out $100 bill, and placed it in the plate as it passed by me. I didn't give it any thought and I certainly wasn't trying to make a statement. I just put the bill in the plate. Vic looked at me like I had just grown a second head. It wasn't that she minded my contribution. It just surprised her that her husband, who my sister called "Mr. Frugal," would part with that much money at one time. It was a running joke with my wrestling buddies that I had the first dollar I had ever earned. I would tell them, *"I don't have the first dollar I earned, but I think I still have the third."* Anyway, Vic knew something was afoot.

Towards the end of the service, the pastor gave an altar call. He said if anyone God had spoken to during the service wanted to give their lives to Jesus and make a new start, to come down to the altar. II Corinthians 5:17 reads: *"Therefore if anyone is in Christ, he is a new creation: old things have passed away; behold, all things have become new."* And that's exactly how I felt inside. There is no way I can ever fully explain what happened to me that Sunday, but I do know there is, indeed, a peace that passes all understanding, and for the first time in my life, I felt a calmness inside my heart.

In retrospect, I still find it a bit bizarre that for so many years, I wrestled before hundreds of thousands of people and never gave any quarter to any man I faced, but on a Sunday morning in a church in a town that most people had probably never heard of, I bowed for the first time to someone I couldn't see. And nothing has been the same since.

At the end of the service, as Vic and I were leaving with the girls, an elderly man approached us and asked if he could speak to me for a moment. I said, *"Of course,"* and he began to relate a story that began five years earlier. He told me he knew who I was, even though he had never been a wrestling fan. One Saturday, he had been watching television and had been changing the channels when he came upon a wrestling program with me being interviewed. As he paused to hear what the guy was screaming about, he wondered why he was so angry. He went on to tell me that he felt God speaking to his heart to pray for me and for my salvation because He had a call to ministry on my life, and that he had prayed for me every day since then.

I wasn't exactly sure what he was talking about, but I could tell he was speaking to me straight from his heart of heart. He also went on to tell me that he had been ill for some time and had not been able to attend church. He had hesitated about coming that particular Sunday, but felt prompted to come by the Holy Spirit. He had no idea that I would be there until he saw me get up during the altar call and walk downstairs from the balcony. He told me he couldn't believe his eyes. He thought, out of all the churches in the world, God sent me to this service and allowed me to witness Nikita Koloff, "The Russian Nightmare," bow a knee to the King of Kings and Lord of Lords. His eyes glistened with tears as he spoke. He said he would continue to pray for me and the plan God had for me, Vic, and the girls. He shook my hand and left.

From that morning on, my life changed. I know it sounds somewhat trite, but it's true all the same. My life didn't change by inches over a period of time. It changed as if someone had turned on a light in a darkened room. It was that quick. It wasn't just emotion, or an experience that would wane by lunchtime the next day. It took decades to get me to a point where I was ready for my life to take a different path — a road and life I never intended. Proverbs 16:9 says, *In his heart a man plans his course, but the Lord determines his steps.* My steps were directed to the cross of an itinerant Jewish teacher who never traveled more than 100 miles from where he was born; a man whose words and teachings have transformed all of human history; not with the force of weaponry, but with a more powerful one; the force of the heart and the love and sacrifice of God's own Son.

It was as if, on that Sunday morning in the balcony of the First Assembly Church, God had looked at me with eyes that reached into my heart, shone a light on all I had done, and exposed my life in a sea of madness. When faced with a choice, I chose a new life that would prove all the more challenging than the one I had lived up until now. But it was one I wouldn't have to travel alone.

After that, I made sure I attended church whenever I was in town. I didn't go out of obligation, but because I had a hunger for learning that I had never before experienced. I had a lot to learn and I didn't want to waste a minute. Not only was I growing and learning in my new faith, but with time on my hands, I was invited to travel on mission trips to Trinidad, Caracas, and Africa to help with the construction of schools and churches. I was eager to go and the pastors who led the trips would always say the same thing: *"I'm sure we can find something for you to do."* This usually meant there was something heavy for me to carry, usually in the form of cinder blocks.

It wasn't long before I was ready to expand my construction skills and began learning how to lay the blocks to form foundations, but there was more behind my interest in masonry than the actual block-laying skills. I realized that if I was laying them, I wouldn't have to carry them.

Christianity wasn't the only thing I was learning about in my travels. I would be doing those wonderful people a disservice if I were merely to say life in those countries was different. I learned that what we experience in America is like being on a different planet compared to the places I was visiting.

On one particular day in Caracas, Venezuela, where I helped build a Bible school with my daughter Teryn and a mission group, we realized we hadn't seen a woman whom we had seen every day since we arrived. She was living on the property and was obviously late in her pregnancy. She came out of her hut, went to the church office, and did the best she could to explain that she needed to get to the hospital. Thinking she was about to give birth, we began marshalling our folks to get her medical attention before her baby arrived. When we went into her hut, we discovered that her child had already been born. She had delivered it herself. She only wanted to take the child to the hospital to be sure everything was okay. I was astounded. I had been around the world and spent time in many countries when I was in the ring, but it was nothing more than cursory. I never had a chance to touch peoples' lives for more than an hour, or for them to touch mine. This woman also had three other children, the oldest being about ten. That little boy helped his mother by making sure his younger brother and sister were fed and taken care of. I couldn't help but think, *"How blessed I am to actually have a part in all this."*

In 1995, while I was building a church with a group in Angola, I saw another side of the world and realized how volatile world politics can be. Angola had a strong military presence with armed guards patrolling the streets with AK-47s. There were craters in the roads as a reminder of the civil war that had ravaged their country just four years earlier. When the Portuguese abandoned Angola some thirty years before, the progress of the country seemed to leave with them. Buildings on which construction had begun in the late 1960s were left in their unfinished, rotting state. With no skilled labor or ability for upkeep, the world in Angola stood still. I was given new eyes to see an old world that had been forgotten by so many, and whose existence was unknown by so many more.

To get into Angola, we had to fly in a small airplane up to the Zaire border. Of all things, we flew in a Russian cargo plane which was manufactured at the beginning of the cold war in the 1950s. Once there, we were enclosed in a government compound and were given strict orders not to venture out of our quarters after dark. Even with no water, we couldn't complain. We were so much better off than those we were there to serve.

Food was another story altogether. There weren't any McDonald's or Arby's on that side of the world, but our hosts were kind enough to share their local fare with us. The mainstay of their diet was a mixture of onions and termites. Yes, termites. They weren't the kind you see on an Orkin commercial, but the type you see in photos in *National Geographic* magazine that are a half-inch in length and live in eight-foot mounds. They are mixed in with the chopped onions and served in a large bowl. I politely declined when offered, but most of our group decided to partake, whether by hunger or curiosity. Whenever I asked them how the meal was, they always replied that the crunching wasn't so bad, but the feel of the legs on their lips and in their mouth was another thing altogether.

When we arrived in Angola, the military confiscated all of the video and camera equipment we had brought to make a record of our project. I'm sure there were a number of reasons why security was so tight, but I do know a great part of it was that Angola is one of the diamond capitals of the world.

The mayor of the town we were in, who actually was more like a governor, asked us to have lunch with him in his palatial home. All during the meal, we were questioned: *"What are you doing in our country?"* *"How long are you planning to stay?"* *"Why did you want to come to our country?"* We were honest in our answers, but very careful so we wouldn't upset him in any way. He had the power over life and death, and spending time in an Angolan prison was not something we looked forward to.

I suppose our answers satisfied him because he let us work undisturbed for our three-week stay, but there was no doubt they were not going to let us leave without a final exclamation point on who was in charge. At seven o'clock in the morning on the day we were supposed to leave the country, we arrived at the airport, carrying our luggage and equipment, and went right to the tarmac where we expected to board our plane. We sat on the hot tarmac, with not a tree in sight, baking, until one-thirty that afternoon. The missionary we were working with found the authorities to talk with and returned to tell us they were not going to let us leave because we had not filled out the correct government papers. We had filled out the papers days before we were scheduled to leave, but somehow, they were never processed, so we all had to leave the tarmac and go into the small terminal to fill out the papers once again.

The papers we were handed to fill out were nearly illegible. They were like copies of a fax of a fax of a fax. The forms on the pages were crooked and nearly impossible to fill out. We did the best we could to fill out the forms and turned them in with a hope and a prayer that this time they would not be "lost."

We were escorted back to the runway where the cargo plane had been parked all morning. After another 30 minutes or so, we were escorted back to the terminal for a reason we never knew. We then walked back to the tarmac, only to once again be sent back to the terminal. We made that trek six times by the end of the afternoon. It was like the Keystone Cops running back and forth. At four o'clock, we were told to return to the tarmac, where we would be allowed to board. We had been there for nine hours with nothing to eat and we were still no closer to taking off than we had been that morning. As we approached the plane for (what we thought was) the last time, it began to taxi and took off … with all of us standing and watching in disbelief as what we thought might be our last chance of freedom faded into the distant sky. An Angolan official informed us that there would be no more planes that day.

So instead of heading to Lawanda and on to the United States, we were driven back to the government compound where we had lived for the previous three weeks. This time, we had a different kind of surprise. When we got back to our quarters, much to our surprise, the water was miraculously working again. Apparently, they had turned off the water shortly before we arrived and kept it off during our stay. I suppose they thought we were gone and it was safe to turn it back on again.

The next morning, we returned to the airport and, after a thorough inspection of our luggage, we were allowed to board a commercial jet that was used to fly animals, both caged and uncaged, throughout the continent. It was all we could do not to retch as we boarded. We made it to Lawanda, but not without a few stops to pick up other passengers, which caused us to arrive late in the evening … and late in the evening is not a good time be off grounds of a secured base.

When our luggage was unloaded, we saw it had been mixed in with raw meat. When I say raw meat, I mean sides of beef, halves, and quarters of cows that had probably been enjoying their cud a day or so earlier. The meat was not wrapped or refrigerated. It had just been thrown in and then unloaded with our gear.

Of course, with no tags to identify the owners of the beef, it was a free-for-all at the baggage claim as everyone fought over the meat. Every surface of our luggage was covered in cow's blood. And I thought professional wrestling was crazy.

We couldn't get a taxi from the airport to the compound due to the late hour and the ever-present threat of terrorist attacks, but to our rescue came a most unlikely hero, or heroine, actually. A wonderful 73-year-old English woman, who had been a missionary in Angola for 43 years, braved the darkness and the threats to pick us up for the night and get us back to the airport the next morning. It still strikes me as somewhat funny that there was no man anywhere around who had the courage of that woman. The next morning, she fixed us a traditional English breakfast, checked her two-way radio to make sure the roads were safe, and got us back to the compound on time.

As much as I was enjoying working with various church outreaches, I was still not sure what I should do or what plan God had for me. That would change in spring 1995 when I met Terence Rose.

Terence was born in England and moved to South Africa as a young man. In Johannesburg in the 1970s, he flourished due to a vibrant economy and his brilliant business mind. Terrance created a clothing line, owned restaurants, imported Lamborghini automobiles, and delved into various business ventures. Somewhere in the midst of his affluence, God touched him and called him into another line of work ... the ministry. He gave his life to Christ at the Johannesburg Rhema Bible Church.

He moved to Atlanta and, in March 1995, I met him after hearing him speak at a church in North Carolina. I was impressed with him from the start and, with some time on my hands, decided to take the next three weeks to work with him at an upcoming crusade. From the first night, I could see the power of God's word and the effect it has on those whose lives are broken, and whose hearts are seeking more than this life can give. The more I witnessed it, the more I believed that was what God wanted me to do, as well. I wasn't sure why, but I felt a serenity about it that I hadn't experienced before.

In September 1995, in Monroe, Louisiana, Terence spoke to me about entering the ministry full-time. I continued to ask God for guidance and agreed to accompany Terence to South Africa for a dedication of a church he had helped build. There were lines of people ten deep waiting to attend their new church for the first time, with some of them walking twenty to thirty miles to get there. As we were getting ready for the dedication, the pastor, Bill Riley, asked me to speak. I was petrified. I had no idea what to say. I was more nervous than during my first match in Raleigh against Barry Horowitz. There certainly was a lot more at stake. I reluctantly agreed and began scribbling down notes. Fortunately for me, I was to speak towards the end of the dedication and I would have two interpreters to translate for me, for there were two dialects spoken there. I knew then that this is what I am called to do, no matter how apprehensive I was that day.

So with that, Koloff for Christ Ministries was born. Since then, I have traveled to South America, Moldavia (my former "motherland"), Singapore, across the continent of Africa, all over the United States, and numerous other countries. I have been fortunate to have been a part of touching so many lives by helping build churches, schools, hospitals, and orphanages, and speaking in churches, sports camps, schools, and businesses.

Traveling across the country and around the world has opened my eyes to many opportunities to expand Koloff for Christ Ministries. So many, in fact, that I knew if we were to continue to meet the needs we were seeing, another arm of our ministries would have to be formed to focus on medical, education, and building projects the world over, without neglecting our speaking and other opportunities for ministry. In 2002, along with Pastor Jeff Black, Community World Outreach was formed to touch communities in tangible ways to meet both physical and spiritual needs. It does no one any good to tell folks about Jesus' love and leave them hungry, cold, and sick.

I believe in my heart that this is what I was meant to do and the reason my life has traveled in the path it has. It has been worth each dusty mile.

Chapter 34
Changing Times

I'm frequently asked what I think of wrestling today. I don't watch it often, if at all. My answer, however, is this: Professional wrestling used to be wrestling with a flavor of entertainment, and now it's entertainment with a flavor of wrestling. It used to be classic "good versus evil" and you could tell the difference between the two. It wasn't difficult to discern on which side Magnum T.A., Ricky Steamboat, the Rock 'n' Roll Express, Sting, and others like them were. Now it seems that the good guy appears to be evil, and the evil guy appears to be good. You have the good guy guzzling beer, cursing, and giving people "the finger." It's hard to imagine that as a role model for the youth of today. I do see a glimmer of hope as the storylines seem to be leaving the bedroom and returning to the ring. I'm hopeful it continues in that direction.

I don't mean this as a knock on the business. I just don't agree with it, probably because I was trained by Ivan in the "old school" tradition and I have a heart for the purity of the business. I was educated in the business to think the story outside the ring should have something to do with the story inside the ring. Wrestling has always been a sport with great entertainment value, but during the last fifteen years, it seems to have become all entertainment. If you're lucky, you might catch glimpses of something that remotely resembles wrestling as it was in the past, but times and tastes do change and professional wrestling is a business first and foremost. As with any business, the bottom line is the dollar. To sum up my feelings for the record, I don't like or advocate it, but it is what it is. I did well during my time and I would be hypocritical not to wish the boys well and hope they all have a safe and profitable career.

The history of wrestling is as rich and colorful as that of any other professional sport. From the days of William Muldoon during the late 19th century to the men who paved the way for us to follow — Frank Gotch, Joe Stecher, Earl Caddock, Strangler Lewis, Lou Thesz, Buddy Rogers, Pat O'Connor, Gene Kiniski, Dory and Terry Funk, and Jack and Jerry Brisco — they all weaved a tapestry of fascinating stories that are worth repeating time after time.

The only thing lacking in wrestling history are the number of people who are aware of it. Wrestling historians of the caliber of Bill Murdock, Greg Oliver, J Michael Kenyon, Mike Chapman, Scott Teal, Steve Johnson, and Steve Yohe, are few and far between. Vince McMahon has established the World Wrestling Entertainment Hall of Fame to recognize and honor those who have gone before. The George Tragos/Lou Thesz Professional Wrestling Hall of Fame at the Dan

Gable International Wrestling Institute in Waterloo, Iowa brings attention to our sport from as far back as the days of Greeks and the Romans. The Professional Wrestling Hall of Fame in Amsterdam, New York, acquires and maintains records, memorabilia, and artifacts related to professional wrestling's past. It's good to remember and pay tribute to the legends who paved the way for the wrestlers of today. Canton, Ohio has done it with pro football and Cooperstown, New York has done the same with baseball.

When I left the ring, however, as with many who left their careers unexpectedly, it was as if we never had existed. Nothing was mentioned when Jack Brisco walked away, or when Ricky Steamboat retired due to injuries. No tributes, no retirement matches, and no final interviews. All that was done was to find someone to fill the vacant spot, and believe me, that was not hard to do. In wrestling, there is always someone waiting in the wings to move up the card. I'm not saying this to imply that we deserved special treatment, or that a big deal should have been made about us hanging up our boots, but it was certainly an opportunity lost. Closing a career and passing the torch can make for a great story and give the fans more to talk about than *"Whatever happened to ...?"*

When I retired, I still had a few years on my contract and, if I had been cautious, I could have wrestled a while longer, but my mind was made up and I had no doubt that retirement was the way for me to go. A few years ago, while I was doing a radio interview, a fan called in and asked, *"What happened to you? You just disappeared."*

"Yeah," I replied. *"I'm sure it seemed that way."*

Shortly after my retirement, WCW contacted me by phone to see if I would return to the ring for them. True to form, they called me on a Friday night and asked if I could be in Baltimore on Sunday morning. No talk of money, contracts, or anything in the business realm. I had seen that movie before, so I thanked them, wished them well, and said goodbye.

I think another reason WCW went out of business was the total disrespect they held for the titles, especially the world heavyweight title. They took one of the most important championships in all of sports, and certainly the most valuable commodity the wrestling industry had, and turned the gold into so much dross. The world heavyweight title was, and is, the pinnacle of our sport. In the territory days of wrestling, the man who held it was revered, and rightfully so. It has been that way in boxing from the days of John L. Sullivan, Jack Dempsey, and Gene Tunney, and thanks to men like Lou Thesz, the heavyweight wrestling title of the world set apart the champion from the contenders. It signified that the man who held it was the singular best wrestler, and perhaps athlete, on the planet. The belt he wore was emblematic of sports supremacy. Throughout the decades, it was the one thing that set us apart from other athletes. Great athletes held the title for years on end. When they lost it, it may have taken them years to regain it, but it all added to the lore of the sport.

Strangler Lewis held the title on five different occasions between 1920-1931, holding the title five out of the eleven years and making him the world champion with the most world title reigns for 30 years. At least, that record held until Lou Thesz broke his record. Thesz held it six times, winning it at the age of 21 in 1936 and losing it for the last time in 1966. At one point, he held it for almost eight years at one stretch. No one tired of him having it, except for the lines of contenders who wanted to wear the crown. Gene Kiniski held the title for almost four years and his successor, Dory Funk Jr., held it for nearly five years. Harley Race held the belt eight times, while Oklahoma great, Jack Brisco, held the title twice during a nearly three-year run. Ric Flair, the perennial champion of the 1980s, held the title 16 times (or 21 depending on who does the counting). What did all these athletes have in common? They held the title with great dignity and made sure the world title was held above the fray of the politics of the wrestling industry. And the fans turned out in droves every time the world champion came to their town to defend their laurels.

When the NWA became WCW, the dignity and prestige of the world title, and all other titles for that matter, meant nothing; nothing to the fans and, probably sadder still, nothing to the boys. The long run of the world champion turned into weekend or overnight title holders. The U.S. title fared no better. "Nature Boy" Buddy Rogers held the United States heavyweight title for 15 years before taking the world title from Pat O'Connor at Comiskey Park in Chicago in 1961. But with the WCW brass at the helm, a champion barely had time to strap the belt around their waist before they did the honors and passed the belt on to a new champion.

To me, without a doubt, the lowest point in the history of the world heavyweight title was when WCW awarded the title to actor David Arquette. I don't know if the man had been an athlete at one time, but he certainly was not a wrestler. That decision, made through the infinite wisdom of WCW executives, tarnished the title held by the lineage of Brisco, Thesz, Lewis, Kiniski, and Funk. As a friend of mine used to say, *"A blind man in Australia looking the other way could see it coming."* This may have been true, but the men who proclaimed themselves the future of wrestling not only destroyed the future of the WCW, but tarnished its past beyond recognition.

When George Scott took over the book for Jim Crockett during the 1970s and again in the 1980s, he did what very few had done before him; he retired from the ring. Many bookers would still be active in the ring and would be compelled to keep the championship on themselves, or put themselves at the center of the angles and programs. George knew the danger in this and removed himself from the ring so he could devote all of his time to building other stars. He could make an unbiased opinion about who was getting over and what direction the company should take. But in the waning days of WCW, not only the bookers, but the writers were now writing themselves into the story and taking the world title. And to think some people still wonder why WCW folded and Vince McMahon won the wrestling wars. Napoleon Bonaparte once said, *"Never interrupt your enemy when he is making a mistake."* McMahon stayed focused and waited for WCW to implode. It did, and with its demise, a new era of wrestling was born.

It's difficult to compare the wrestling industry today with that of the past. I may not like what wrestling has become, but I do have to say what Vince McMahon has done with the sport is nothing less than phenomenal. Some fans think it's better than ever, others think true professional wrestling no longer exists. Times change, and if you look through the history of wrestling, it has changed with the times better than most industries. Whether that's true or not is up to the individual, I suppose. The one thing we can all agree on is that it's different than it was in the past. And there is one other thing that is certain:

wrestling will continue to change as the times demand, and as long as Vince McMahon is leading the WWE, wrestling will be at the forefront of sports.

I'm grateful to have had the opportunity to have been a part of the wonderful sport of wrestling and to everyone who has touched my life: my mom and dad; Victoria, my wife of 16 years; my four beautiful daughters, Tawni, Teryn, Kendra, and Kolby; my family and friends; the fans who made Nikita Koloff who he was and who I am today; and most importantly, my Lord Jesus Christ. I thank you all.

For we must all appear before the judgment seat of Christ, that each one may receive the things done in the body, according to what he has done, whether good or bad.
2 Corinthians 5:10

Photo Gallery

Ivan and Nikita Koloff

Krusher Khrushchev and Nikita

Ivan Koloff, Nikita Koloff and Don Kernodle

Nikita Koloff

Ivan Koloff, Nikita's uncle, brought this young man from Russia to help the Soviet Union dominate yet another world sport. He later broke the ties with his family and country and adopted a lifestyle of his own. There is no doubt that he has always been one of the most respected men in the world of professional wrestling.

He is known for his physical shape, his power, and strength in the ring. The most awesome move he employs is the "Russian Sickle" which has left many opponents lying on the mat. Considered to be one of the top professional athletes of all time, he is one of the main contenders to the N.W.A. World Heavyweight Championship.

Nikita with Ronnie Garvin

Nikita with Sting

Nikita with Hawk, Lex Luger, Animal and Sting

A Study in Contrasts

**Nikita Koloff and Magnum TA
Bitter enemies**

**Nikita Koloff and Magnum TA
Best of friends**

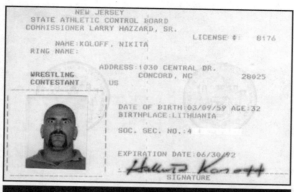

**1992 New Jersey wrestling license
(note birthplace)**

TALENT	DATE	CITY	BUILDING	ADDRESS	PHONE NUMBER	ARRIVAL TIME	AGENT
NIKITA KOLOFF	11/01/92	KNOXVILLE, TN	CIVIC AUDITORIUM/COLISEUM	500 CHURCH AVE	615/544-5399	2:00PM	POP/MIKE
	11/03/92	ANDERSON, SC - TV	CIVIC CENTER	3027 MALL ROAD	803/260-4800	4:00PM	ALL STAFF IN
	11/05/92	FT. BRAGG, NC	RITZ-EPPS PHYSICAL FITNESS CENTER	18 AIRBORNE CORP	919/396-3502	6:30PM	POP
	11/06/92	ROANOKE, VA	CIVIC CENTER	710 WILLIAMSON ROAD	703/981-2241	7:00PM	POP
	11/07/92	CHARLESTON, WV	CIVIC CENTER	200 CIVIC CENTER DRIVE	304/345-1500	7:00PM	POP
	11/08/92	WINSTON-SALEM, NC	LAWRENCE JOEL MEMORIAL ANNEX		919/727-2900	6:30PM	POP/MIKE
	11/09/92	RALEIGH, NC	DORTON ARENA	1025 BLUE RIDGE BOULEVARD	919/821-7400	6:30PM	POP/MIKE
NIKITA KOLOFF - CHECK WITH OFFICE	11/07/92	ATLANTA, GA - TV	CENTER STAGE	1374 W. PEACHTREE	404/874-1511	4:00PM	ALL STAFF IN
	11/10/92	GAINESVILLE, GA - TV	GEORGIA MOUNTAINS CENTER	301 MAIN STREET	404/536-8420	4:00PM	ALL STAFF IN
	11/13/92	ATLANTA, GA - TV	CENTER STAGE	1374 W. PEACHTREE	404/874-1511	4:00PM	ALL STAFF IN
	11/16/92	ATLANTA, GA - TV	CENTER STAGE	1374 W. PEACHTREE	404/874-1511	4:00PM	ALL STAFF IN

WCW booking sheet · November 1-16, 1992

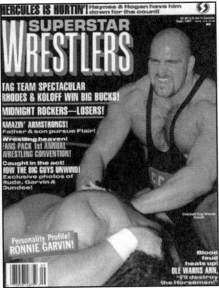

AEROSERVICES CHARLOTTE

THURSDAY, JULY 21, 1988

DEPART: CHARLOTTE(BUTLER AVIATION) TO CINCINNATI, CONTINUE ONTO ST LOUIS
AFTER MATCHES IN CINCINNATI, OVERNIGHT IN ST LOUIS, JULY 22
CONTINUE ONTO PHILADELPHIA AFTER MATCHES IN ST LOUIS FOR OVERNIGHT
IN PHILADELPHIA, JULY 23 AFTER MATCHES IN PHILLY CONTINUE ONTO
ROANOKE FOR OVERNIGHT THERE, CONTINUE ONTO JOHNSON CITY, RETURN
TO CHARLOTTE AFTER MATCHES IHN JOHNSON CITY.
****

GULFSTREAM
DEPARTURE TIME 4:15pm-

CHARLOTTE TO CINCINNATI TO ST LOUIS	ST LOUIS TO PHILADELPHIA
MIKE ROTUNDA	MIKE ROTUNDA
KEVIN SULLIVAN Stay	LARRY ZBYSZKO 2 nights
DR DEATH Thurs Fri. 2 nights	DR DEATH
BOBBY FULTON	BOBBY FULTON
TOMMY ROGERS	TOMMY ROGERS
BOBBY EATON	BOBBY EATON
STAN LANE	STAN LANE
JIM CORNETTE	JIM CORNETTE
NIKITA KOLOFF	NIKITA KOLOFF
IVAN KOLOFF	IVAN KOLOFF
PAUL JONES	PAUL JONES
AL PEREZ	AL PEREZ
GARY HART	GAPY HART
DICK MURDOCH	DICK MURDOCH
RICK MORTON	RICK MORTON
ROBERT GIBSON	ROBERT GIBSON

NUMBER ON PLANE 16   NUMBER ON PLANE 16

PHILADELPHIA TO ROANOKE	ROANOKE TO JOHNSON CITY TO CHARLOTTE
MIKE ROTUNDA Sun. morning	MIKE ROTUNDA
KEVIN SULLIVAN	KEVIN SULLIVAN
DR DEATH	DR DEATH
BOBBY FULTON	BOBBY FULTON
TOMMY ROGERS	TOMMY ROGERS
BOBBY EATON	BOBBY EATON
STAN LANE	STAN LANE
JIM CORNETTE	JIM CORNETTE
NIKITA KOLOFF	NIKITA KOLOFF
IVAN KOLOFF	AL PEREZ
PAUL JONES	GARY HART
LARRY ZBYSZXKO	LARRY ZBYSZKO
RICK MORTON	RICK MORTON
ROBERT GIBSON	ROBERT GIBSON
~~IVAN KOLOFF~~ A Perez	
~~PAUL JONES~~ G Hart	

NUMBER ON PLANE 16   NUMBER ONPLANE 14

Aeroservices Charlotte air schedule · July 21, 1988

U.S. Air flight receipt · May 11, 1992

Nikita dances with Tawni

Grandpa, Nikita and Kendra

Teryn, Tawni, Kendra, Kolby

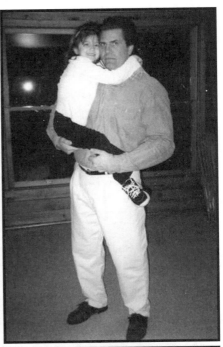

Nikita and Kendra (Sweetpea)

(l to r) Morgan McCurdy, Kendra, Lauren Bowman, Kolby (front), Nikita

(l to r) Teryn, Kendra, Victoria, Tawni, Nikita, Kolby (on lap)

Dan Gable Wrestling Museum · July 13-14, 2006

(top l.) Baron von Raschke and Nikita; (top r.) Bob Roop and Nikita; (center) Danny Hodge, Tom Drake, Nikita and Harley Race; (bottom l.) Nikita with BJ and Harley Race; (bottom r.) Nikita and Larry Hennig

Brad Johnson Celebrity Golf Classic · Asheville, North Carolina

Nikita with (top l.) Ken O'Connor [2011]; (top r.) Charlie Lunsford [2010]; (center) Tampa Bay QB Brad Johnson, New York Yankee Darren Holmes, Sinclair Broadcasting Jack Connors [2010]; (bottom l.) volunteers [2009]; (bottom r.) unknown

First Place

1988 James Larkin Pearson Poetry Contest — Free Verse
The Poetry Council of North Carolina

AND NOW PRESENTING NIKITA KOLOFF

The glasnost gladiator, premier ambassador of destruction,
Muscovy's pride, the New Russian bearing an old soul
Steps from the pooled shadows of the colisieum's murky deeps
With quiet grace, gliding like a silent snow tiger
Picking a deliberate path along the rocky Uralian icy steeps.
He studies the screaming throngs with a quick raking sideglance,
Face emotionless, a frozen death mask borrowed from Ivan the Dread,
Except for the fierce smoldering eyes which mirror the Baltic's stormy breakers
And spell the pitched heat and enormity of a life force so huge so vast
Ages dissolve like rain polishing fragrant firs and gleaming conifers
Near the banks of the Volga where wild poppies upraise their flaming throats
To the honeybee's practiced sensors and dark forests hold close
The scattered bones of lost travelers and restless wolves
Serenade the silver sickle of a hunter's moon with mournful liturgies:

> On a golden porch there sat a tsar, his son; a king, his son;
> A shoemaker, a woodsman — Answer now, which are you?

He tests the turnbuckle's tension, sheds his scarlet sateen jacket
With practiced ease like a cobra sloughing off dead skin
And lifts his arms for the referee's preliminary examination.
Here now is the first of patriarchial mysteries, the oldest martial ritual:
The warrior's public self-display, garbed in black and blood-red,
Death's traditional colors, ready for a man's final measuring,
Where power is pitted against its possessor and fire tests the bearer.

Cloaked in a shimmering aura of radiance raining from the hot strobes,
He waits poised in a half-crouch, hands braced above his knees,
Glorious as any renegade Cossack or newly incarnated virility god,
Another soldier of light, born to cosmic combat, prepared to give up his life
For those he has sworn to serve, whether as victor or sacrifice.

He hushes the giant arena with a toss of his head as the opening bell shrills
And every heart stops when his first lightning strikes, official proclamation
Of another battle joined joyously, today's war ready to be won.

—Virginia Love Long

(clockwise from top l.) Nikita's publicity photo; Tony Atlas and Nikita at the Hampton Coliseum, Hampton, VA; Nikita reads the Frank Gotch biography; Guys goofing off; Nikita and a young friend; Kitty Kat and Nikita take a much-needed nap

INDEX

Is That Wrestling Fake?
The Bear Facts

by Ivan Koloff
with Scott Teal

ISBN: 978-0-9745545-4-9
6 x 9 Perfect Bound
208 pages, 205 B&W photographs

For decades, professional wrestling fans have asked the question — "Is that wrestling fake?"

However, they wouldn't have dared ask that question directly to Ivan Koloff, whose work in the ring made believers out of the most cynical viewers.

Growing up on a farm in Ontario, Ivan learned the meaning of hard work and discipline. Unfortunately, he made wrong choices and wound up in prison for cattle rustling. Upon his release, he enrolled in a wrestling school and began a career in pro wrestling as Red McNulty, the Irish Rogue.

Five years later, on January 18, 1971, he appeared in Madison Square Garden under the name Ivan Koloff and did what had never been done before. He pinned Bruno Sammartino's shoulders to the mat and won the WWWF heavyweight title. When the referee called for the bell, you could have heard a pin drop as the more than 21,000 screaming fans were instantly moved to a stunned, disbelieving silence.

That accomplishment made Ivan Koloff one of wrestling's biggest superstars until his retirement from the ring in the mid-1990s. Competing in virtually every major promotion throughout the world, he feuded with every top name in the wrestling business, including Andre the Giant, Ric Flair, Dick the Bruiser, Bob Backlund, Billy Robinson, Dusty Rhodes, and Ivan Putski.

Here for the first time, Ivan tells the story of his life: the highs and the lows; his admission of alcohol and drug abuse; reflections of a life spent on the road and the toll it took on his body and soul; and the event that took place in a small church in Kannapolis, North Carolina, that changed his life forever.

This is a revealing memoir that will take you into the mind of the Russian Bear, both in and out of the ring.

One extra bonus is the inclusion of over 205 photographs, most of which are from Ivan's personal collection.

A second bonus is a section called "Christian Facts Guidance," which is written by Blackjack Mulligan and shared here in print form for the first time.

Crowbar Press, 106 Tattnall Court, Gallatin TN 37066, crowbarpress.com